D0949951

MAKING SCIENTISTS

MAKING

SIX PRINCIPLES FOR EFFECTIVE COLLEGE TEACHING

SCIENTISTS

Gregory Light

Marina Micari

HARVARD UNIVERSITY PRESS

Cambridge, Massachusetts, and London, England

2013

Library of Congress Cataloging-in-Publication Data

Light, Greg, 1951–

   Making scientists : six principles for effective college teaching / Gregory Light, Marina Micari.

      pages   cm

   Includes bibliographical references and index.

   ISBN 978-0-674-05292-5 (alk. paper)

  1. Science—Study and teaching (Higher)   2. Effective teaching.

3. College teaching.   I. Micari, Marina.   II. Title.

   Q181.L67   2013

   507.1'1—dc23   2012033307

To our families, colleagues, and friends
who have supported us in this project.

Contents

MAKING SCIENTISTS

Introduction

LIKE SCIENCE ITSELF, this book is the result of the cumulative work and research of many people over many years. From its early beginnings until the present day, the ongoing Gateway Science Workshop (GSW) and the Science Research Workshop (SRW) programs,[1] which this book describes and draws upon, have involved thousands of students, hundreds of student mentors, many dozens of science faculty, and over twenty-five program directors, coordinators, and educational researchers. And every year that number increases. Except for a number of students who became our colleagues through their dedication and work over several years, we are unable to mention by name the thousands of student participants. Nevertheless, these students constitute the very heart of this book. Their ideas, thoughts, insights, and comments resonate in its pages. They are the book.

We do at the very outset want to mention a number of people by name. They are our "coauthors." Their published and unpublished work contributes to the substance of this book, and their intellectual influence is apparent in every chapter. Without the day-to-day conversations and research collaborations we shared with them at the Searle Center, this book could not have been written. We will inevitably leave out many critical contributions for which we apologize in advance. We are focusing here on those who provided seminal ideas and sustained long-term contributions to the project.

In the first instance we must mention the work of Larry Pinto, whose concerns and questions as a biology professor reflecting on important issues of student learning in the classroom provided the initial impetus for this program. Not only was Larry instrumental in starting and championing the program in its first years, but he has remained with the program every year—advising, advocating, and critiquing—as it expanded well beyond his own discipline. We also are indebted to Wendy Born, Ken Bain, and Dan Linzer, who worked with Larry in the early years. Wendy's doctoral work first carefully examined the program and its impact on students. In this capacity she was the first coordinator and evaluator of the program. Ken's leadership was instrumental in moving the program forward early on, and Dan has been an ever-present source of support as chair, dean, and provost.

At the risk of leaving out many colleagues who should clearly be named here, we want to acknowledge a number of key faculty who have made substantial contributions to the program over the years, both as formal and informal advisers. In addition to Ron Braeutigam, Eugene Lowe, and Steve Fisher, who have chaired our Advisory Board for more years than they want to remember, they include Martina Bode and Mike Stein in math; Debbie Brown, David Buchholz, and David Taylor in physics; Rick Gaber and John Mordacq in biology; Franz Geiger, SonBinh Nguyen, and Mark Ratner in chemistry; Steve Carr and Joe Holtgreive in engineering; and Bruce Sherin in education. Particular thanks are due to Penny Hirsch, Rick Gaber, and SonBinh Nguyen for their support in the development and implementation of the SRW program. We would especially like to thank our three external advisers on this project: Richard Light (Harvard), Uri Treisman (Texas-Austin), and Claude Steele (Stanford). Their advice, ideas, and gentle guidance provided us with a constant source of inspiration and support.

Over the last decade the program has profited from a series of exceptional program coordinators and assistants, young professionals with a deep passion for science, education, and young people. In smooth succession, Su Swarat, Bettina Chow, Annette Munkeby, Cynthia Pederson, Carol Smith, Amy Gould, Louie Lainez, Sara Woods, and Casey Prouty have been the backbone of the program. They not only performed as the program's mission control, ensuring the day-to-day quality of nearly a hundred workshops per week, they were also at the center of the ongoing cycles of innovation and expansion for which the program became known.

Working closely with the coordinators over the years, three colleagues deserve special mention for their sustained contributions to the study of the program. Bernhard Streitwieser, Su Swarat, and Pilar Pazos have all served as leaders and lead researchers on the GSW and SRW programs. All three have spent many years at the Searle Center contributing to the development, writing, and implementation of the major projects, research grants, and research publications that underpin this book. Their work with SRW has also sparked several other innovative science education programs.

In addition we want to mention our Searle Center colleague Susanna Calkins. Her research has also contributed to this book, and her editorial input helped bring life to the decade of GSW stories. We also wish to thank Stanley Lo for his editorial suggestions and his support in the planned expansion of the program into introductory lab sections.

Finally, we cannot overstate the exceptional contributions to the content and nature of this book by our colleague Denise Drane. Denise has been a central member of our study of the program since she was first lured into conducting "a couple of statistical analyses" during the winter holidays of 2000. As a lead researcher on the project for over ten years, she has contributed in thought, word, and deed to almost all of the innovations and studies reported in the book and has been the major force behind the assessment of the program's impact on student achievement, persistence, and experience. Her influence has been immense.

This book would not be what it is without their input.

OVERVIEW OF THE BOOK

This book presents six learning principles that have been critical to the success of the GSW program:

1. Learning Deeply
2. Engaging Problems
3. Connecting Peers
4. Mentoring Learning
5. Creating Community
6. Doing Research

These principles characterize the environments in which the best science is conducted. The book offers discussion and guidance in two related areas: (1) how to use these principles to design courses to help students learn well in STEM fields (science, technology, engineering, and mathematics) and (2) how to develop educational STEM innovations, large or small. The book begins with an overview of the GSW program, focusing on its rationale, structure, and goals as well as its growth and resilience over the past dozen years. In this first chapter we also look at the program's extensive evaluation and the strong positive outcomes found for both grades and retention of participants. Each principle is then addressed in a single chapter, drawn from GSW program experience and supported by educational research and theory.

Chapter 2 addresses the nature of meaningful learning. We contrast "deep" with "surface" learning approaches and the ways in which students can be encouraged to move toward deep approaches. We also share GSW research project findings to shed light on the motivations and anxieties that STEM students bring to their work, and how these influence their studying. In that study students fell into one of three categories of learning, which we termed *reliance, engagement,* and *independence.* Together these categories describe a kind of journey toward thinking scientifically, from rote memorization to wanting to make sense of new ideas and concepts to a desire to map them out within the wider scientific landscape.

In Chapter 3 we focus on using problems effectively in teaching. We contrast problem-oriented approaches to teaching with more traditional approaches, with a particular focus on the structure of the problems. We share our own students' evaluation of the problems used in the GSW—and the insights those evaluations gave us into the nature of a good group problem. In their evaluations students tended to address one of three characteristics of the problem: how well it promoted their knowledge of key science concepts; how well it fostered conceptual understanding; or how well it facilitated discussion. For each of these three characteristics, we enumerate more specific qualities that promote learning. We also highlight the importance of designing problems that challenge students to work beyond their current understanding. We end with guidelines for constructing problems.

Chapter 4 focuses on peer learning. Just as scientists work and learn collaboratively, students, we argue, should be working and learning together. We outline the characteristics of a productive learning group, and we review our own research into group dynamics in the GSW, which shows that groups with greater levels of collaboration and deeper engagement with concepts had better learning outcomes. We discuss the key features of effective learning groups, including clear goals, appropriate material, adequate support, and solid leadership. We end with a set of strategies about how to establish a group-learning program.

We focus on mentoring in Chapter 5. We review the nature of the mentoring relationship within a peer-led program, and we share a mentoring model we developed based on our research with GSW students and their peer facilitators, paying particular attention to the cognitive, behavioral, and interpersonal components of mentoring. We then describe our approach to training mentors, which takes the form of a year-long education course required of all peer facilitators in which they gain knowledge of key issues in STEM education and engage in their own group educational research project. We also present what we have learned about how peer mentors develop through the experience of mentoring, with benefits to their academic abilities, leadership skills, and career preparedness.

Chapter 6 addresses learning communities. We introduce a model of participation in which learners are considered active members of a professional community, albeit on the periphery. Using this model, we describe the ways in which the GSW allows students to engage in science in parallel to their professors and to feel they are genuine members of their academic departments. We describe the benefits that accrue for students as members of these communities: a better sense of the "big picture" of the material they are studying; increased comfort with faculty; access to the informal wisdom of the department; tacit knowledge about how to be a good student; and a better understanding of how to navigate the path to a science-related career. We address who gets to join communities of science, particularly how women and underrepresented minority students can be more fully included within such communities.

In Chapter 7 we discuss the role of research in undergraduate student learning and introduce the SRW program. SRW students also meet in small groups with a peer leader, but rather than working on course problems they are developing their own original research proposals to obtain funding for summer research. Drawing from qualitative evaluations of the program, we describe the impact of this SRW experience on participating students: gaining firsthand knowledge of what happens in a lab; developing a sense of belonging in that environment; and gaining a scientific mind-set. Finally, we offer suggestions on developing high-quality research experiences for undergraduates, including developing meaningful content and providing a structure that allows students to be active participants in the research.

Chapter 8 applies to the classroom each of the *six learning principles* presented in Chapters 2–7. We provide concrete examples of how faculty can create, and how they have created, change in their classrooms without a large outlay of resources. In the second half of the chapter, we describe a model for sustainability of educational innovations, large or small. We explore five stages of development: generating the idea, piloting it, implementing it, expanding it, and consolidating it. We also provide guidelines for program evaluation and for using evaluation as a tool for sustainability.

Throughout the book we tell the story of a program devoted to developing scientific minds—illustrated by a wealth of student and faculty voices (with names changed to preserve anonymity), real-life examples, and concrete suggestions—and dedicated to assisting anyone interested in creating lasting change in STEM education.

ONE

The Gateway Science Workshop Program

The important thing in science is not so much to obtain new facts as to discover new ways of thinking about them.
—Sir William Bragg

ON A CRISP November evening five freshmen make their way across campus to an empty classroom in Northwestern's sprawling Technological Institute. The two young men and three young women are going to a workshop where they will spend two hours discussing and working on a set of advanced conceptual problems related to the introductory chemistry course they have been taking since they started their university life a few months earlier. They will not be working with a faculty member or even a graduate student. They will be led in this meeting by a peer, a fellow student who is only a year ahead of them in their undergraduate studies. The goal of the meeting is not necessarily to solve the problems that their professors have created especially for them but to think about these problems, to consider them deeply, to identify the key concepts that characterize them, to analyze the relationships among those concepts, and to suggest possible approaches to solving the problems. The solution is optional; the critical thinking at the heart of the solution is not.

The students' attendance at this meeting is not academically essential or mandatory, nor does participation add anything to the students' course grades. The workshop is entirely voluntary and must vigorously contend for time in each student's hectic life, competing with the demands of required studies, personal obligations, jobs, clubs, and diverse social activities. The peer student who facilitates the group discussion is likewise a volunteer. While she is offered an education credit for the training she receives, she earns no additional science course credit or payment of any kind. Indeed, in addition to giving two hours to the five students gathered together with her in the classroom, the peer facilitator also attends a meeting with the course professor to go over the problems. And the workshop with the students is not a once-only meeting. These same five students and their peer facilitator will venture out together nine times—once a week throughout the quarter.

Perhaps more extraordinary is the fact that there is nothing especially distinctive about these five students. For the most part they are representative of their peers studying in the university. They are not the best students academically, nor are they necessarily the most driven. Nor are they alone. Every week throughout the term, five or six hundred fellow students in twelve different courses in chemistry, biology, physics, math, and engineering join them in their own small groups. All these students meet across the university, in some one hundred scheduled workshops a week, on weekends, on weekdays, in the morning, afternoon, and evening. They meet in classrooms, residential halls, or meeting rooms, whenever it is convenient for the facilitator and the five or six students he leads. They meet to learn and share new ideas, concepts, and approaches to interesting, real problems in the subject they are studying in class. They meet to exchange experiences, good and bad. And they all do this with no guarantee of extra credit, improved grades, or teacher favor. And the following year large numbers of these students volunteer to be group facilitators and pass on their experience to others. For over ten years this phenomenon has been experienced, shared, and repeated. The members of these small academic communities have developed such commitment and enthusiasm that the experience has become a permanent feature of the undergraduate curricula in science, engineering, and mathematics at the university. It is called the Gateway Science Workshop (GSW) program.

COLLEGE SCIENCE LEARNING AT ITS BEST

In a moment we will talk about the genesis and history of the phenomenon described earlier. And we will talk about the program's overall success: how it has improved student outcomes and helped students successfully complete the course sequences in which they are enrolled, particularly with respect to student groups traditionally underrepresented[1] in the sciences and engineering. We will present data to show that it worked across a range of important indicators assessing student accomplishment in college science, including student academic performance, student persistence, student satisfaction, and student engagement.

We will describe the program and how it was designed and developed, and we will identify the key features and learning principles that underpin its success. We will also show how assisting students to participate in legitimate communities of science—bringing students together in small groups with trained mentors to work on challenging problems—can make a substantial difference in their experience and learning of science. The book explores this difference and what teachers can do to facilitate it. It is the story of college science told by the students in the program: a story of learning as meaningful conceptual change and deeper understanding, not simply in getting right answers. This book, then, is the story of the best college science learning.

The best science learning happens all the time and everywhere that meaningful scientific practice is conducted. Indeed, the essence of science is learning. That learning is not limited to universities and colleges but occurs in a diverse range of public, private, and nonprofit businesses, industries, and countless other local, national, and international organizations. In higher education science professionals engage in science learning every day: science professors work on their latest research projects, postdocs and grad students engage in science research in their labs, and engineering and medical faculty and clinicians explore the implications of science in their professions. It is one of those telling eccentricities of higher education, however, that these kinds of learning—the best ones—are often not even regarded as learning.

In a study we conducted of science, engineering, and medical faculty, we asked faculty members to talk about their research and professional practices, and also about what made them who they are as professionals in their specific disciplines and fields.[2] The faculty spoke about their work enthusiastically and with passion, describing in moving detail the nature of their research, the experiments they were conducting, the projects they were supervising, and the colleagues and graduate students with whom they were working.

When they finished their descriptions, we asked them a simple question: Is your work a learning experience? They all responded in a very similar way. In the first instance they all replied that they had never really thought about their work in terms of learning. It had not really crossed their minds to think of their work in quite that way. Then, after a slight pause, they would continue: yes, absolutely, it was a learning experience—a very meaningful learning experience. When we asked them to talk about what that learning consisted of, they spoke of experiences that were as varied and distinct as the different questions, literature, methods, and communities that characterized their research and professional practices. But they all spoke of these experiences in ways that portrayed their own learning as a deep process aimed at asking questions, understanding, problem solving, making connections, working with peers, and doing experiments. As a computer scientist commented: "It's hard to differentiate research and learning, because to do research you have to solve the problem, and at the same time you need to know what other people are doing. Then you go back and think about that and come up with some solutions."

When formulated in terms of what professors, scientists, and research scientists experience in their own research, the best science learning is frequently referred to as "cutting edge." Indeed, the use of the term "cutting edge" is ubiquitous in academic science communities for such experiences, the learning outcomes, and the knowledge resulting from it. On the other hand, this same term is rarely (if ever) used with respect to undergraduate student learning. And yet it has essentially the same meaning: the construction and discovery of ideas that are new, exciting, and meaningful. The scientist's research peer group is national and international in scope, and new often means the original discovery and/or construction of knowledge and skills *never* before encountered. The student peer group, on the other hand, is local, and the learning is rarely original—but the learning and personal construction of knowledge are nevertheless new, exciting, and deeply original for the student and his or her peer group.

The best science learning, then, is vastly different from what has too often come to be synonymous with learning in college: the simple acquisition of science facts and concepts through rote memorization, with little critical reflection on meaning or connection to other facts and concepts. It is, rather, the same thing for students as it is for their science professors and other practicing scientists. It engages students with science material through cutting-edge learning approaches within legitimate science communities. And it takes place in environments with practices[3] where the main outcomes of both the undergraduates and their professors are essentially one and the same: deeper learning and understanding.[4]

In the moments where this is achieved, the purest form of the university's mission is realized. Research and teaching are simply names for practices in higher education, practices whose goals are the same, in this case the advancement of scientific learning and knowledge.

THE GATEWAY SCIENCE WORKSHOP PROGRAM

Innovative educational ideas for promoting learning abound. Colleges and universities are awash with excellent educational innovations, usually more than resources permit to be funded.[5] And many of them are realized. Even so, too many of these innovations fail to deliver on their promises beyond the initial situation in which they are implemented, or beyond the contribution of one or two dedicated faculty, students, and/or administrators.[6] Once in a while, however, educational innovations take on lives beyond their own initial goals and achieve large-scale transformative impact.

In the mid-1990s Larry Pinto, a biology professor at Northwestern, felt compelled to help improve the way his students learned. He saw some of his undergraduate students struggling to get through his introductory course, and he felt that somehow the traditional learning environments and teaching methods used in these large lecture courses were failing them. He was particularly concerned about the learning progress of the African American and Hispanic students in his class. He observed that despite their elevated academic achievements on standardized tests such as the SAT and ACT, and their acceptance at Northwestern, a highly selective and prestigious school, by the junior year these underrepresented students were not represented in science courses at all. The department, the university, and the nation were losing talented and creative scientific minds. To remedy the situation, Pinto teamed up with Northwestern's Searle Center for Teaching Excellence and with a graduate student in the psychology department to try an innovative approach that would engage his students in a more productive learning environment.

This team researched the problem and found that many universities approached the challenge of high attrition in the sciences by focusing on an apparent deficit in the student, offering extra tutoring, remedial instruction, special preparatory programs, or introductory programs, especially for students deemed "at risk." While the effects of remedial education at the college level are not well understood, there are potential problems with this approach, including student perceptions that the institution does not expect a lot of them and the stigma often associated with being enrolled in such programs. The issue of remediation can be particularly acute for students from traditionally underrepresented groups in a discipline in which certain groups have been stereotyped as less likely to succeed, as remedial programs can send the message that participants are less talented than their peers. The widespread stereotypes of women not being good at mathematics and of African Americans not excelling in science are such examples. Claude Steele and his colleagues have found that even the performance of otherwise quite brilliant students can be undermined by what he calls stereotype threat.[7] In addition, such remedial programs have been challenged by a national agenda critical of initiatives regarded as employing affirmative action–like policies.[8] Research has found, however, that other kinds of programs had been successful in addressing similar challenges by using a peer-facilitated, small-group learning approach.[9] Rather than seeing the problem as simply a student deficit to be fixed, these approaches focused on remedying shortfalls or deficits in traditional learning environments, deficits that often hindered the development of student learning. While having the desired impact on underrepresented groups, these approaches had the added value of improving the learning outcomes and retention of all students.

As with many ideas, the program started modestly. In 1997 Professor Pinto described the idea of the workshops to the students in his biology course and invited volunteers to take part. A group of thirty students participated in five workshop groups, and five additional students, who had taken the course and excelled in it the previous year, were recruited and trained as peer facilitators by the Searle Center. The facilitators met weekly with Pinto to discuss the problems he had constructed, focusing on the concepts central to their solution and how to best facilitate the students' engagement with those concepts. The peer facilitators then met with their workshop students for two hours during the same week.

Initial program evaluation results were positive, and the program began to thrive. And as it flourished, it stimulated interest in other disciplines and grew. Perhaps more important, as the program expanded something very interesting happened: It began to feel normal, no longer, as a skeptical colleague once commented, "that strange little experiment in biology." It had become a natural feature of the academic landscape, offering every student studying science an opportunity to experience a unique learning environment with peers engaging with the same kinds of intellectual, social, and personal challenges in their studies. Within five years the GSW program was fully assimilated into the university science terrain, growing from a single program of just thirty students and five facilitators to one comprising over five hundred students and more than one hundred facilitators each quarter, across gateway course sequences in five disciplines. It had arrived.

In 2007, the tenth year of the GSW's initial inception, the program spun off a further initiative—the Science Research Workshop (SRW) program. With a few small but substantive changes, the SRW program extended the goal of providing students with learning experiences that mirrored the learning experiences of their science professors. The alteration was to simply substitute the advanced conceptual science problems with actual research problems related to individual scientists' labs.

The rest of the structure essentially remains the same. The SRW program is focused on freshmen and sophomores. The students meet in workshops of five to seven students. The workshops are led by peer facilitators who have previous undergraduate research experience. Once again, faculty provide guidance on the research problems and approaches to their solution. One change is that instead of working with peers to look at the key concepts and possible approaches involved in solving the problems, students in the SRW work with peers to develop an original scientific research proposal— complete with question, literature review, methods, and lab—for submission to a panel of scientists with the goal of funding and conducting the research.[10] What the best science students do is become the best student scientists.

THE PROGRAM'S IMPACT

So does it work?

That is the question—we heard it from funders wondering whether they had invested well, from our advisory board wondering whether we were headed in the right direction, from faculty wondering whether they should take the time to help us, and from students wondering whether they should give up two of their precious study hours a week to attend a workshop.

To assess whether the program worked, we began with three goals—three ways of defining success: to improve course grades; to increase student retention over the three-quarter course sequences (courses that build on one another and often are required to complete a major); and to ensure that students enjoyed their experience in the program.

At the outset, the most nagging question we faced—and one often raised by science faculty—was the "selection bias" question. Even if the program students did better on exams, could this not simply be due to the fact that the students who chose to enroll were already the more motivated and gifted students, and would that not in itself account for any grade improvement?

To address this question the original team designed a randomized study to see whether students in the program would fare better than those not in the program, even when both groups of students had expressed interest in the program and could both thus be considered "motivated" students. They put students who were interested in the program either into the program or into a control group that did not participate in the program. They also adjusted for student GPA in the analysis so that the effect of any difference in prior academic performance would be reduced. Exam scores of students enrolled in the program were significantly higher than those of students in the control group, with the advantage seen across all three quarters during the academic year. And similar results were seen for traditionally underrepresented students.[11]

Following that initial pilot study, we built in a mechanism for assessing the impact of the program on a regular basis. After consulting with different stakeholders about the kind of evidence that might persuade them of the program's value, we came up with three key questions related to our program goals: Are the students who participate earning higher grades in their classes than those who do not participate? Are they staying in the course sequences at rates higher than those who do not participate? What is the participants' experience like?

For the first question—regarding student grades—each academic quarter, within each course, we compared the grades of students who did and did not participate in the GSW. We adjusted for any prior differences in academic achievement by including in our statistical model the student's incoming SAT math score or previous quarter GPA. For the second question—regarding retention in the course sequences—we simply looked to see whether students who had taken part in the GSW were more likely to remain in the three-quarter course sequence than their peers who did not participate. Finally, for the third question—the students' experience—we developed a survey that asked students to rate various facets of the program at the end of each quarter. Although the answers we obtained to these three questions are primarily given here in terms of numbers, as we will see later, they were supplemented by rich veins of qualitative data gathered through studies that employed interviews, focus groups, and observations.

Student Grades

While, here and there, results for an individual course in a particular academic term did not come out as expected, the general picture and certainly the long view were encouraging. For instance, in a comprehensive study in 2004 looking at the data over the four academic years following the pilot study, we found that GSW participants earned, on average, a half-letter grade better than students who did not participate, and these differences were statistically significant.[12] Moreover, when we looked more closely at the data, we often found that for students from underrepresented minority groups—in this case, African American and Hispanic students—the differences were even greater. In biology and chemistry, for exam-

ple, the positive effect of minority workshop participation ran between one-third and more than twice the positive effect found for
majority student participation in the workshops. In the other
disciplines—physics, engineering, and math—we saw similar patterns of student achievement, all with grade differences that were
statistically significant.

After five more years we merged the data once again, this time
for ten years. Again we found that workshop students on average
earned significantly better grades than did those students who did
not participate in the program.[13] Similar patterns appeared in most
disciplines, with participants earning the best grades in greater
numbers than students not participating in the program. Across
the ten years, in the chemistry workshops, for example, on average,
40 percent of participating students earned grades of a B+ or better
versus only 33 percent of the students who did not participate. And
in biology, 48 percent of participating students earned B+ or better
against only 38 percent of those students who did not take the workshops. During this same time period, in the challenging calculus-
based physics course the difference in the achievement of the best
grades was also as dramatic, with 50 percent of workshop students
earning grades of B+ or better, while only 41 percent of those not
participating earned similar grades. This difference was particularly pronounced for minority students. While only 13 percent of
minority students who did not take the workshops earned a B+ or
better, 28 percent of minority students who took the workshops
earned a B+ or higher.

In addition, we often found a "dose effect" of the workshop. For
instance, students who participated in the program in all three
quarters were more likely to earn a grade of B+ or better than were

students who participated during fewer than three quarters—and again, these differences were statistically significant. Perhaps even more important, though, the differences in course grades were significant in very real ways: for individual students, they frequently meant "doing okay" instead of "struggling"—and often made the difference between moving on in the discipline and giving up on it entirely.

A final note on selection bias: while all of these findings were encouraging, and despite controlling for previous grade and/or incoming SAT math scores, we still wondered whether it was not just that the "best" students were signing up for the program. We had the data from the original randomized study, but we had for some time wondered if there might be differences in personal characteristics—for instance, in motivation—between students who did and did not choose to join the program, and whether such differences might account for the effects we were seeing on grades and retention. So in the fall of 2003 we decided to test this hypothesis. We first measured students' motivation—anxiety levels, interest in the material, and desire to master the material—using established, validated questionnaires. And we did find some differences: students who participated had slightly higher scores on all of these measures. So was this the reason they were doing better than the nonparticipating students? To find out we compared the grades of participants and nonparticipants while statistically adjusting for the differences in these personal characteristics. The grade difference still held: even accounting for these preexisting differences in motivation, students who participated in the program did better in their courses than students who did not participate.

Student Retention

One of the most critical measures of student success in science is not simply whether students do well in a subject but whether they stick with the course. In the GSW program, this means completing a three-quarter course sequence spread over the entire academic year. And, indeed, when we compared students who participated in the program with those who did not, we clearly saw that the former were more likely to complete the full required sequence of courses in which they enrolled. For example, in the four-year study mentioned earlier, we found that students participating in the biology workshops were two and a half times as likely to stay in the course sequences than were their classmates who did not participate. And, again, this effect holds even when prior differences in GPA are taken into account. Here too we often saw an even greater impact on minority students.[14]

The trends for chemistry and engineering, the two other disciplines in which the completion of the course sequence is required, were much the same. In chemistry, for example, students in both the majority and minority populations who engaged in the workshop experience were over twice as likely to successfully complete the course sequence as were non-GSW students.

In our follow-up study looking at the ten years of merged data, we found that these patterns persisted (Figure 1.1).[15] In those large introductory courses in which most students were required to complete a full-year sequence, students participating in the program were much more likely to complete the sequence. In biology, for example, approximately 81 percent of the students who participated in workshops completed the three quarters of the biology sequence,

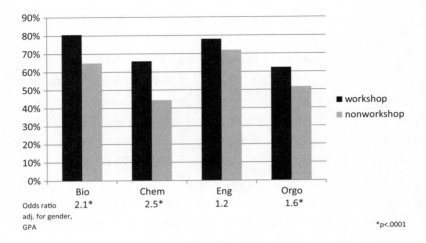

Figure 1.1   Course Retention by Workshop Participation and Discipline
(2001–2002 through 2010–2011 academic years)

versus 65 percent of those students who did not participate. And in the first-year chemistry and second-year organic chemistry sequences, 66 percent and 62 percent of the GSW workshop participants completed the three quarter sequences versus only 44 percent and 52 percent, respectively, of the non-GSW students. In addition, over this ten-year period, biology and chemistry students who participated in the program were over two times more likely to complete the course sequence than those who did not participate in it.

Once again, this increased retention outcome was strongly reflected in the minority student population. Indeed, when we broke out the numbers by minority and majority status, the historical gap[16] between minority and majority students completely disappeared (Figures 1.2 and 1.3). A higher proportion of minority students in

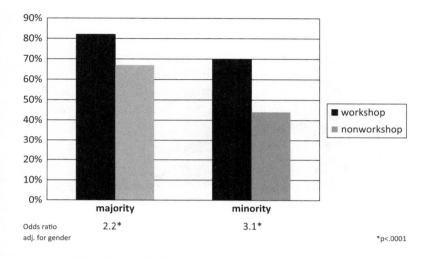

Figure 1.2   Biology Retention by Workshop Participation
(2001–2002 through 2010–2011 academic years)

the program completed the full sequence than did majority students not engaged in the program. In biology, 70 percent of minority students engaged in the workshop program completed the full
course sequence compared to 67 percent of majority students who
did not engage in the program and only 44 percent of minority students who did not engage in the workshop. In chemistry the pat-
tern was similar: 53 percent of minority students engaged in the
workshop program completed the full course sequence compared
to 48 percent of majority students who did not engage in the workshop and only 30 percent of minority students who did not engage
in the workshop.

Most important perhaps, insofar as completing the main introductory course is a critical prerequisite for completing a major in

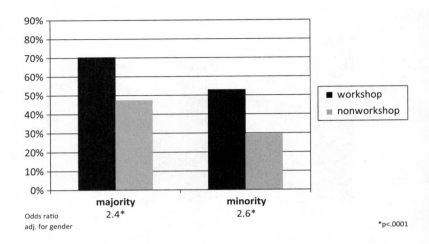

Figure 1.3   Chemistry Retention by Workshop Participation
(2001–2002 through 2010–2011 academic years)

the discipline, these results suggest that engaging in the workshops substantially improved the odds of a student continuing on in science by two to three times.

Student Experience

Of all of our measures of the program's success, the students' attachment to the program has been the most constant. Year after year they gave high ratings to the overall experience, with survey items consistently averaging 4 on a 1-to-5 scale. On surveys that polled them on their perceptions of the key aspects of the program, participants repeatedly told us they would recommend the program to other students, that their facilitators encouraged them to work through problems, that the workshop helped their grades, that they enjoyed interacting with peers, that the problems enhanced their understanding of the course concepts, and that the problems helped them on exams.

In separate surveys about their experience of working with peer mentors, the students' feedback was even more positive and unswerving. Across all the categories on which we asked students to provide feedback—from feeling comfortable with the facilitator, facilitator preparedness, and interactions with facilitators—their ratings were consistently in the 4.5 to 5 (out of 5) range. It did not seem to matter which discipline, which term, or in which year. Exceptions were always only with individual facilitators. We came to think about these results as reflecting a kind of immutable law of the program.

In our conversations with students in focus groups and interviews, we looked deeper into what they felt they gained through the program. While we asked them about these gains in terms of an academic program, what they spoke to us about was by and large phrased around the same kinds of things we all generally value and feel good about as people: a sense of accomplishment, meaningful conversation with others, and enjoyment. In the following chapters of this book we will explore these benefits much more fully and richly. For now, benefits included

- gaining a deeper understanding of the concepts;
- being "forced" to spend more time studying;
- being exposed to other people's thinking;
- working with capable and caring people;
- feeling more engaged in the course; and, finally,
- simply having a good time.

On the other side of the equation, surveys of the facilitators' experience were equally positive, again with consistently high ratings in the 4 to 4.5 range (out of 5). Indeed, the high satisfaction ratings that the facilitators gave for their experience became a critical element of the program's existence. Their participation and engagement in the program was a critical feature of its success. In the early years of the program we paid the facilitators but quickly realized that if we were to considerably expand the program, especially once the initial external funding ended, this was not going to be possible. We decided to offer participants academic credit for the substantial training they received to participate. It turned out that the vast majority of them were not particularly motivated by the academic credit, nor were they bothered by not being paid. They wanted to do it because of how much they enjoyed the experience as student participants in the previous year. "I like having people that are a year older than me and being able to go up to them and ask them what should I or should I not do," one facilitator told us, adding, "and I like to be in that position for someone else too." As a result, applications to become a facilitator have been oversubscribed for every year of the program. It is a persuasive measure of the positive experience they enjoyed in the program.

In one sense these experiential responses are the most powerful findings. Certainly the quantitative data on grades and retention provide solid evidence of the program's impact. But hearing from the students themselves that the program is personally worthwhile— and hearing specifically how they believe it is worthwhile—lets those numbers come alive. The students were doing better, but they were also *feeling* better, and this told us that the program really was making an impact on people's lives.

SIX LEARNING PRINCIPLES

So to answer our question, *yes, the program works.* It works well. Not just for the students we designed it to help but also for the peer leaders and the faculty who support the program. In fact it works better than most of these people ever expected. The next logical question is: *How?* What is the nature of the pedagogical principles that make it work? What lessons can we draw from the program for the improvement of teaching science, for assisting our students to become the best college science students they can be?

These questions are addressed throughout the rest of this book. During our decade-long evaluation of the GSW program, we studied the essential features of the program that promote the learning of science in higher education. We also engaged students, peer facilitators, faculty, and administrators in many of the studies and evaluation. We attended conferences where we talked with people involved in similar programs around the country, wrote and presented about what we felt had worked well and not as well, heard feedback, and often revised our understanding as a result.

Based on this evolving analysis, we identified six learning principles that have been critical to the program's success—and that we believe are critical to the success of the learning and teaching initiatives that share our fundamental goal of deeply engaging students in learning and persisting in science. In the next six chapters of this book we will share our encounters and studies with respect to each of these principles, illustrating them in terms of the experiences and voices of the students, teachers, and scientists who engaged with them and looking at how they might be applied in a variety of different contexts by readers. In the final chapter, we will look at how these principles can be used in educational innovations of any size, from cross-institutional programs to specific courses and even to individual sessions in the classroom. We also present a model describing the key practices and activities for implementing and sustaining such innovations. But first, an overview of the learning principles follows.

Deep Conceptual Learning

The first learning principle is, appropriately, about learning, about developing real scientific thinking and knowledge. This principle focuses on deeper conceptual change or what we earlier called the best science learning. It is concerned with students' understanding of science content in terms of a critical and creative examination of the conceptual relationships within the content and their application in solving problems.

We contrast this with surface learning, which is focused on the simple remembering and recall of science content with little reflection on the conceptual relationships within it and their use in solving problems. Very often the importance of deeper learning in a science course is not recognized by students and is not felt to be as helpful for achieving the best grades. Through their encounter with the GSW program, students became aware of the role of deeper learning. And student facilitators recognized the importance of facilitating this kind of learning. Describing the goal of his workshop to students after their first midterm, a biology peer facilitator told them, "This isn't about grades; it's about knowledge, and that is something that is greater and more important."

Conceptually Rich Problems

In Chapter 3 we look at the importance of engaging students with meaningful, conceptually rich problems and questions. Programs and courses that wish to facilitate the best college science learning experiences focus on providing students with opportunities to encounter rich problems that engage their abilities to think scientifically. This is where science and learning begin. The problems should not be so trivial as to require no effort, nor so difficult as to evoke the kind of frustration that shuts down thought. The challenge is finding that balance. We also found that to engage students the problems need to be meaningful in terms of the multiple contexts in which students live. One of the chemistry students on the program, for example, explained to us that she found everyday world problems to be the most valuable "because they are a combination of many different science things occurring." Such problems not only make learning science relevant to understanding real-life phenomena, but they also bring together multiple concepts.

Working with Peers

Working together with peers in groups is increasingly being recognized as an essential principle of the college student experience.[17] Groups of student peers have always, of course, engaged in academic student exchange in multiple ways. Seminars, study groups, and lab groups, for example, have a long history. However, the idea of groups being entirely peer organized, managed, and facilitated week after week is less common. And yet the interplay involved in this principle performs a major role in advancing student learning. As a young physics student put it, "If there is a certain topic that I don't understand, then to hear how others reason it out makes sense. My peers are on the same level as I am, but they have the process worked out better. And the same is true in reverse, where if they don't know something, I have the opportunity to give them a hint of how I figure it out." Drawing on the lessons divulged from the program, Chapter 4 examines the nature and promise of working with peers.

Mentoring and Being Mentored

The fourth learning principle focuses on the impact of a peer guide on student learning. Drawing on studies of the facilitators' mentoring and facilitation styles, Chapter 5 examines the experience of mentoring and being mentored. The studies indicate a relationship between the different ways in which mentoring is implemented and differences in how students engage learning. Not only did students consistently rank being mentored as one of their top experiences in the program, but many facilitators talked about how it was their experience of being mentored that led to the desire to become a mentor. As one engineering student explained, "I really like being able to watch someone literally grow, to be able to see them not understanding it at first and then progress to the point where they feel like they've mastered the material," particularly, she continued, "when I remember the effect my facilitator had on me and how important that was in my success."

Working in a Science Community

While providing student peers an opportunity to meet in groups to exchange insights on solving problems is important, students, facilitators, and faculty all pointed to the nature of the workshop group as a micro-community within the wider science community as a rich aspect of the program. The fifth principle looks at the experience of a community and encompasses the more personal, social, and practical issues of learning science—issues that are critical to the development of science identities and persisting in science. The simple sharing of information on which courses to take next, what faculty members to speak to, what research is taking place, how to approach a lab—or, as one student described it, how to work one's way up the "diverse and hierarchical scientific community food-chain"—often provides the key to helping students make sense of, and consolidate, their learning.

Doing Research

The final principle highlights the importance of research. Students participating in the SRW program commented on the powerful experience that engaging in scientific research had on them and their learning of science. This experience took the students well beyond the traditional student experience of science in other courses to aspects of science that are often not addressed until graduate school—until, unfortunately, after many students have decided they do not want to continue in science. As a biology student explained, "I learned of the humility that comes along with scientific research" and "the attitudes and thought processes required by a successful researcher." This is the kind of experience that impels students more deeply into the wider community of science practice where deeper, cutting-edge learning is the order of the day.

A NOTE ON THE LEARNING PRINCIPLES

These six learning principles should not be unfamiliar to scientists and college science teachers. After all, they characterize the nature of the communities in which the best science is conducted. These are communities in which thinking deeply, critically, and creatively about important and exciting problems is prized; where working in multilevel research-focused teams with peers (mentoring and being mentored by one another) to advance science is essentially what it is all about. Over the years remarkable students with an intuitive understanding of the very best science learning have sought out environments that tacitly employ these principles. With sympathetic peers, graduate students, and faculty they have instinctively discovered and created their own extraordinary learning opportunities on and off campus.

In this respect these principles are inherent phenomena of learning. They emerge seamlessly from the natural enterprise of doing science. Indeed, they have been at the very heart of scientific thinking and practice for centuries. For the most part, however, they are not meaningfully reflected in science education. Despite growing calls for educational reform, and countless references to the efficacy of these and similar principles in the science education literature, change has been exceedingly slow.[18] In part, this is because these principles, and the educational transformation they call for, comprise a genuine paradigm change in the teaching and learning of science.[19] They herald a change in our thinking about science education similar in scope to the change in our thinking about the solar system launched by the Copernican Revolution.[20] They draw upon a model of learning that does not regard learning as simply the acquisition of a set of remarkable concepts and facts but also as consisting of participation in authentic scientific thinking and practice.[21]

The six learning principles are about the process of learning as well as the learning outcomes achieved. Chapter 2, for instance, is just as much about the practice of learning how to learn as it is about the goal of thinking scientifically. And Chapters 5 and 7, for example—on mentoring and research, respectively—are just as much about important outcomes of becoming a mentor and becoming a researcher as they are about the respective science practices they describe. Together these principles provide a practical framework for designing and implementing educational innovations consistent with the actual practice of science.

Engagement with these principles will challenge the traditional teaching environments that prevail in college science classrooms. They will also challenge the majority of students studying science, just as they did the five students making their way to their chemistry workshop one November evening. It challenged their experience of studying science and disturbed their expectations of what it is to be taught in college. And changing students' ideas of learning science is the key to the future of science itself.

TWO

Learning Deeply

What I cannot create, I do not understand.

—Richard Feynman

EARLY ONE SATURDAY MORNING we conducted an educational training workshop for about fifteen undergraduate physics and engineering facilitators. They were being prepared for their new role as peer mentors. The workshop focused on the development of their understanding and skills in the facilitation of learning. And although they did not know what to expect, they were surprisingly engaged in the new experience. As part of the activities, we shared with them research findings about the different ways in which students approach learning in higher education. We wanted to provide them with a conceptual framework that would help them understand the key goals of the program.

Most students regard learning as simply the outcome of their study or their experience in college, but they rarely reflect upon it much further. We told the facilitators that multiple studies of college students[1] have revealed important distinctions in the way in which students understand the idea of learning and, as a consequence, how they approach learning in a particular course. We explained that these approaches are not innate characteristics of a person; rather, they mainly relate to how students have previously experienced learning science and how they see learning in the new context. As such, the context, in large part, determines the sort of approach students will take. Indeed, students will often take different approaches to their learning in different contexts.

Broadly speaking, the distinction here is between regarding learning as a reproducing experience and seeing it as a transforming experience. Some students understand learning as simply acquiring and increasing their knowledge and storing methods for reproducing and applying that knowledge, often through memorization. These students take what is referred to as a *surface* approach to their learning.[2] Students taking a surface approach in a course are focused on coping with the basic requirements of the course. They treat the course uncritically, seeing the course content as unrelated bits of knowledge to be memorized and replicated on exams. And they are anxious about it all the time.

But some students see learning as a transformative experience, aimed at understanding a set of concepts or a topic through the construction of meaning and knowledge.[3] They take a *deep* approach to learning. They actively try to make sense of the concepts and ideas presented in the course in terms of their relationship to each other and to their previous knowledge and experience. They critically examine the evidence and logic behind the content presented, developing and consolidating their interest in the material. In short, they take an approach that actively seeks conceptual understanding. In Richard Feynman's terms, students create to understand.

The peer facilitators immediately understood what we were describing. They all talked about late-night sessions before midterms and finals when, for example, their approach was surface, when they were just trying to stuff in as many concepts and equations as they could, hoping they would be asked the next day on the exam. But they also remembered times when they took deep approaches, usually in smaller classes or when they participated in the workshops and could explore concepts and problems with their peers and the professor.

The students also said that the approach often depended on the nature of the class—a different course, a different approach. Consider Dee, a Gateway Science Workshop (GSW) program physics student. She contrasted her experiences as a participant in the workshops, which "are not aimed at just seeing if you can remember the topics but to see if you can understand the method behind them," with classroom experiences in which "you kind of see what the professor says and try to regurgitate it. Basically the lecture is just copying notes. You really don't understand what it is. It goes from the professor's voice to paper, and that's as far as it goes. It never really sinks in."

And then there is the third approach, the *strategic* approach to learning. Often working in conjunction with the other two approaches, it is aimed at getting the highest possible grade. Students taking this approach are very alert to the assessment criteria of a course and are focused on efficient studying, effort, and use of time to achieve their goal. They are not averse to deeper understanding, but if memorization and a surface understanding will get them the grade, thus memorization it is. This approach resonated with the students even more strongly than the other two. Indeed, they described elaborate organizational ploys involving the careful parceling out of work to individuals to complete assignments and problem sets. "We are a mini-corporation when it comes to achieving our course goals," one engineering student replied, and the others all laughed in agreement.

When we asked the facilitators what they wanted to achieve for the students in their workshops, however, they became more serious. They agreed that deeper learning was the aim. One of them then asked, "Does that mean that our professors are responsible for providing the content and we are responsible for the thinking part in the workshops? I mean, the professor is supposed to give us the facts in the lecture." A number of students nodded. The irony of the different roles of professor and student in the provision of learning was entirely absent for a moment. Finally, one young engineering student commented, "I think we really should be deep learners in our lectures too."

Does it seem right that a deeper encounter with the material is left to student peers, while their professors, many of them top scientists in the country, all master learners in their fields, are responsible for the students' surface learning in lectures?

ARE LECTURES REALLY THE PROBLEM?

Science education, particularly in the early college years, has been severely criticized for its overreliance on large lecture courses in which students sit passively before a science lecturer and receive a stream of facts and concepts. The traditional hour-long lecture is still the preferred method in science, despite this criticism and despite a substantial body of educational research that has demonstrated that the lecture is overused and generally ineffective for facilitating learning. Sadly, even innovative approaches to the lecture, strongly supported by research evidence, are ignored in favor of the traditional lecture.[4] The latter has a rigid hold on science pedagogy in higher education and will not let go. Innovations improve and gain ground on the periphery, but they have yet to substantially transform student educational experience.

The lecture is not the problem, certainly not in its rather simple formulation as merely any large-group teaching. And its complete disappearance is not the "cure." The real problem is the fragmented belief many scientists and science professors hold of the nature of human learning that the lecture generally perpetuates: that college science learning is a fundamentally different process for students of science than it is for those who practice science. This pervades the way science faculty think about students, the way they think about teaching, and the way they eventually go about teaching. Blaming the lecture is missing the point. Despite all the terrible lectures, there are also those exceptional instances of really excellent teachers who regularly engage in activities that look suspiciously like lectures, and yet connect with and inspire students to learn in amazing and transformative ways. Nevertheless, lectures are easily abused. They provide a shelter for all kinds of poor teaching habits, behaviors, and deeds.

It is not as if scientists do not use the lecture format to communicate to each other. Presentations at conferences and symposia furnish a common and widespread case in point. And the presentation of scientific conference papers is, of course, not without its share of deadly dull experiences. But, presumably, it is not the intention of scientists to present their findings in this manner: "Here are the results. I'm an expert. Take my word for it. Do not look at these with a critical eye. Take them on faith." We might continue "and be prepared to regurgitate them back to me on an exam exactly as I have presented them." The underlying assumption of scientists is that their colleagues have the ability to think about what is being presented at a conceptual and critical level. Indeed, poor presentations are those that do not contribute, engage, provoke, and stimulate thinking at this level.

So we are not talking so much about teaching here as we are about *learning*. When we ask students to accept ideas as fact, and later to reproduce those ideas on an exam, no real learning occurs. The chief educational challenge is the facilitation of a critical stance toward science in our students, to encourage an intention to understand, make sense of, figure out, piece together, and discover. Sometimes lectures can effect such conceptual change. When they do, they are often designed in ways that do not resemble the traditional lecture but incorporate many of the elements stressed in this book.[5] And when they do, they foster a deeper conceptual understanding.[6]

LEARNING SCIENCE: THE PATH TO DEEPER CONCEPTUAL UNDERSTANDING

The aforementioned contrast between the lecture and science learning is illustrated in a study we conducted of students' experiences of courses consisting mainly of traditional lectures to which the peer-led workshops in the GSW program were attached.[7] There were forty-five students in the study drawn from a range of backgrounds. Over half the subjects were women, for example, and over half came from ethnic groups—African American and Hispanic

American—historically underrepresented in mathematics, science, and engineering. All the students participated in both the traditional lecture classes and the small-group peer-led workshops. They were also drawn more or less evenly from courses in biology, chemistry, physics, math, and engineering. All of the students were interviewed at length about their experiences, including in-depth questions about their learning.

Other than the commonality of subject matter, the students reported very little that was similar in their experiences of the classroom lecture and the GSW sessions. The contrast between learning science in a workshop setting and learning science in a lecture class could not have been more dramatic.

Being in a large science lecture course was accompanied by powerful feelings of anonymity, information overload, fear and anxiety, and even intimidation. Students felt unable to participate or actively engage with the content. Learning was less a participant activity and more a boring ordeal to be silently borne. In stark contrast, positive feelings of belonging, support, intellectual contribution, and opportunities to take risks attended student accounts of their learning experience in the workshop. An engineering student studying calculus, for example, reported that any inclination to contribute in his lecture would be seen as an interruption at best: "It's like a hundred people in the class, so you don't want to interrupt," whereas, "you're not as shy or intimidated to speak when it's a small group." In a similar account a fellow engineering student, this time studying chemistry, recounted how his natural inclination to "learn from doing examples" was supported by the workshop activities and hindered by the lecture: "When it is just a straight lecture, I don't really learn that much," he admitted, describing the process as almost futile: "I can sit there and learn the concepts, but if you don't go over problems, I don't think it's going to help me too much." A second-year student in organic chemistry reinforces the importance of this distinction. "In that two-hour period in the workshop, I learn the material better than if someone just tells me 'this is how you do it.' "

Ironically, in a traditional lecture the professor's age and authority, which represent her or his experience and expertise, are often detriments to student learning rather than catalysts for it. "There's two hundred and fifty people in a lecture, and asking a question, I just feel very intimidated by all the people, plus the teacher who's a lot older," a first-year chemistry student commented. On the other hand, the workshop, she said, "is a lot more laid back," and the facilitator, "who took this class last year, and knows [the material]— it's much easier to ask him a question than it is to ask a professor."

To a large degree the differences described here are familiar—it would have been surprising if they had not been found. The same and similar findings have been known for many years and have been widely reported in countless studies.[8] A closer examination of them raises important lessons for science education, which we will discuss in more detail in later chapters. Moreover, as we saw in the previous chapter, the GSW program was designed and developed in large part to address these issues, as well as the negative impacts on student educational experience and learning associated with some of the distancing characteristics of lectures.

The main point of this study of student experience of the GSW program was not to identify the differences between traditional lectures and small-group sessions. It was to examine the nature of learning in more inclusive environments that can inform our teaching—including the design of lectures. That is, what can we discover about the nature of learning science from student experiences of learning science in environments designed to more closely reflect the problem-oriented, peer-run, participatory practices of scientists? This, it turns out, is a very revealing question—although it is rarely asked by college teachers. At this point we should mention that by student experience we do not mean how students feel about a course or course instructor or whether they like the course or not. Nor are we concerned with what the student thinks about the challenge of the readings, assignments, and projects or whether or not they like the course content, pedagogical activities, or even fellow students. What we were after was how the students actually thought about and approached their learning in the GSW science context.

In that respect it is worth remembering that the students' experience of learning is framed by their perceptions of the courses they are taking.[9] While they naturally bring certain elements of their personalities and past learning to their courses, the approaches students take to learning science, in large part, are *not* innate to the individual student. Rather, they are a response to the demands of the learning environment. If a course demands rapid note-taking and memorization, for instance, most students will try to deliver that.

Differing Experiences of Learning Science

In this study we identified three distinct ways in which students who participated in the workshops approached the learning of science: *reliance, engagement,* and *independence.* These terms describe how students view the workshop in relation to their goal of learning science, math, and engineering—what the workshops contribute, how they are used, and, ultimately, what they are (see Table 2.1). While the three ways differ in the sophistication of their approach, they are linked as if on a continuum. Succeeding approaches appear to pick up where the earlier approaches leave off. In this way, together, the approaches paint a rich picture of an intellectual expedition toward conceptual understanding.

The notion of an expedition comes directly from the students' depiction of their efforts in learning science. As the students described each approach, they made reference to a goal or an intention—a state they wanted to move toward—and an accompanying state from which they wanted to depart. As they described these desires, they identified barriers that they felt made it more difficult for them to achieve their desired states. They also talked about the ways in which the GSW workshops made it possible for them to overcome those barriers.

Reliance

The first category of approach describes the student's initial encounter with a new and rather alien land: the field of science that the student's course delineates. For many students the goal is to survive. It is an extremely anxious time, and the features of this new territory are unusual, more confusing than puzzling. Students feel they simply want to get through the course intact. As Claire, a first-year chemistry student, put it, "I used to be so nervous and think I was doing it wrong and just give up and leave blanks, 'cause I didn't know what I was doing." In the midst of this insecurity, the irresistible intention is simply to get clarity and shrink the confusion

Table 2.1 Student approaches to learning in peer-led workshops

Approach to Learning	Learning Intention	Constraints to Intention	Factors in Moderating Constraints
Reliance: Survive the course	Reduce anxiety; gain confidence	Fear of examinations	Friendly group Easy-to-approach facilitator Can make mistakes
Workshop as **"Refuge"**	Reduce confusion; gain clarity	Lack of confidence Lack of self-discipline and time-management skills Confusing instruction and content Uncertain focus	Examination-like problems "Forced" to spend time studying intensively Pointed toward key ideas Helped to get on the right track
Engagement: Engage with the course content	Reduce passivity; increase involvement	Watch rather than do	Encouraged to work actively through problems and discuss content
Workshop as **"Forum"**	Know why, where, and how to apply concepts rather than simply know them	Know principles but not why, how, where Misconceptions Not enough help/correction Do only basic problems	Discuss applying principles Misconceptions challenged Helped/corrected comfortably Higher-level problems
Independence Learn how to learn	Become a better learner rather than simply learning	Do not know what you do not know	Increased metacognition
Workshop as **"Studio"**	Develop an integrated system for understanding concepts	Limited set of problem-solving tools Concepts stand alone	Exposure to others' approaches Integrate diverse concepts

Source: Adapted from Micari, M., and Light, G. (2008) Approaches to learning in peer-led undergraduate science, technology, engineering, and mathematics workshops. *International Journal of Science Education* 31(13), table 2, p. 1726.

in students' knowledge of the main concepts and ideas confronting them—frequently through rote memorization—and thereby to slowly improve their confidence in that knowledge and in the process reduce their anxiety. Claire expressed relief at achieving this state. "This quarter," she said, "I am definitely just more confident in what I am doing, and usually am on the right track. And even if it's not all the way right, at least it's partial credit, so I did some of it right. So, I'm a lot more just confident, I guess." For such students, it should be remembered, the land of their science course is not simply new and different and baffling; it is also perceived as hostile. Exams, tests, and grades could bring them down at any minute. It can often feel like a sort of scientific D-Day. Students cannot afford to get "off track." Even "partial credit" gets you the next couple of feet of beachhead.

Students who describe taking this first approach talk about their reliance on the GSW program. They portray the workshop experience as something akin to a refuge on which they could rely for assistance toward achieving their goals of clarity and confidence: "Being in the program gives me a set time where I could study, and, knowing myself, I don't study too much on my own," Omar, a chemistry student, told us. The opportunity to take refuge and develop learning strategies with others and an approachable facilitator is a particularly important feature of the program for students in this category: "It's actually figuring it out with someone else," confirmed Mark, another student taking chemistry, "that's helpful." Beginning to understand the value of working with peers is a vital first step in understanding how science progresses. It is also a noteworthy discovery, particularly against the background of a higher education system that persistently asserts the primacy of the individual thinker as the focus of thought and learning.

Surprisingly, for students who take this approach—for whom getting the right answer is paramount—the GSW program really comes into its own as a secure place in which to publicly make mistakes. "We are all comfortable with making mistakes in front of each other," said Pallavi, yet another chemistry student. "Before, we wouldn't talk unless we definitely knew the answer, but now," she continues, "we don't really care anymore if we are stupid in front of each other, because we are all on the same page." In a strange and hostile land, it is wonderful to find others like yourself struggling to survive.

This point—that we all make mistakes, that it is all right to make mistakes—is critical to the development of a science sensibility. "Real science," noted Dudley Herschbach, the Nobel Prize laureate for Chemistry, "recognizes that you have an advantage over practically any other human enterprise because what you are after—call it truth or understanding—waits patiently for you while you screw up."[10] The students taking this first approach are beginning to understand the critical point that making mistakes is a constitutive part of doing science.

Engagement

With the first approach to the experience of learning science, we left our student learner on the "shore" of a somewhat forbidding new world, nervously searching for intelligibility within a maze of extraordinary ideas, concepts, formulas, and methods, on a quest to develop more confidence in her ability to navigate them clearly. She had found welcome refuge in a peer experience upon which she relied to achieve her goals. The second approach to learning—engagement—picks up where the first approach left off. This approach is characterized by an intention to go beyond merely establishing clarity in the scientific content and concepts presented in the course to *engaging* with them. Students taking this approach want to make sense of these new ideas and concepts for themselves. They are not content to remain observers on the "shore" of this new world, simply knowing the "that" or the "what" of the content—undertaking, as another chemistry student described it, "more than just memorization." They want to go deeper into the "how" and the "why" of these concepts to engage science, she continued, in ways that make you "feel like you know more than just the equation. You know where to apply it in the real world." Learning science is "really getting comfortable with the material and knowing why and where to use it." The recognition of this astonishing difference in the nature of what the learning of science is or should be—particularly in the context of a formal fact-laden course—is a considerable achievement. Liam, a biology student, provides a vivid example of this experience of knowing a huge amount of information—the "what" of science—but having no real idea of what it actually means or what to do with it:

> For this class, you have to know things about DNA replication. So, we know all the enzymes that are involved; what we don't really know is if someone asks us how a poison inhibits . . . DNA replication, where is that in DNA replication? It's kind of like, "I don't know what you are talking about!" . . . Even if you know all the information, you don't necessarily know how to apply it by doing problems.

It is not enough, however, to simply recognize the difference between knowing a concept and understanding how to apply it. Actively pursuing this understanding of learning science needs to follow. Sadly, students in this category report that the demands of the formal course situation more often than not constrain them from acting upon their new perspective on science. Time and density of information intercede. "Sometimes the class goes quickly, and you're copying the information down," begins Ana, a chemistry student harboring a desire to understand, "and also trying to think about it before you ask a question that is really obvious. So you don't want to stuff everything in your mind," she says, but the constraints are too great and she admits that "simply stuffing everything in is what I end up doing."

This unhappy quality of having to surrender to the memorization or "stuffing in" of facts and information is frequently a feature of this *engaged* approach to learning science. Danny, a physics major, described the experience in the following way: "Sometimes I know what is going on if I understand that stuff beforehand, but if I don't then basically the course becomes copying notes. You really don't understand what it is. It goes from the teacher's voice to paper, and that's as far as it goes; it never really sinks in." There is an inevitable sense of loss associated with the experience. In contrast to the first *reliant* category of students, these students are aware of what it is to really understand, so when it does not happen, they feel a natural sense of loss. With time and effort the information could have "sunk in" and made sense, but the opportunity was squandered.

Not surprisingly, students who take this second *engaged* approach to learning science report feelings about the science learning environment similar to those depicted in the accounts of the *reliant* category of students, feelings that, in both cases, constrain the development of their thinking. They both report, for example, feeling intimidated by the size of the class and uncertain about approaching the professor, or even the teaching assistants, for help. But they also report that their GSW workshop moderates these experiences—for instance, in the GSW, they feel no fear in approaching the peer facilitator for help.

This, however, is where the similarity ends between the two groups. For the second group the science workshop environment is regarded as less of a refuge for reducing anxiety and gaining clarity on the course materials and more of an intellectual forum for probing the course content for understanding and application. "I like it," a freshman calculus student concedes, "because we come in, we sit in a circle, and we actually go through each problem and discuss it and come up with ideas." And the peer facilitator ensures the opportunity for each student to understand or make sense of the concepts: "She'll ask us questions or present us with different ideas, and we'll try and come to the answer as a group." The key goal is to look at different ideas, probe misconceptions, and understand the ideas, to "really get into the meaning."

Most surprising, perhaps, is the discovery that many *engaged* students not only recognize the important distinction between learning for understanding or creating meaning and memorizing or simply reproducing meaning; they also appear to associate the former specifically with the role of the workshop and not of their textbook or class. "I think that part of the problem with the book," explains Mario, a physics student, "is that it's helping you just know the equations and knowing where to apply them." He continues: "I think the applicable part comes in class where they tell you where to *apply* the equation, and they explain conceptually what's happening in the book." Finally, he remarks, "The workshop kind of pieces the two together." In other words, the book presents the concepts and some possible applications, the class provides some conceptual clarity, and the workshop brings these two components of learning together, producing in students a deeper understanding. There is a sad irony here: the scientists who are master thinkers and learners of their discipline—indeed, that is why they are scientists and professors of science in higher education—frequently relegate themselves to the role of content provider, while the role of facilitating deeper scientific understanding and thinking is left to the students themselves.

The student voices embodying the second *engaged* approach to learning science describe a way of thinking about science that subsumes the first *reliant* approach, recognizes central deficiencies within it, and travels beyond it to gain access to the world of science through a concerted effort to understand it, to critically reconstruct one's own experience of the objects and materials and ideas with the intention of making sense of them. The workshop, as an intellectual forum, allows students the chance to expand their knowledge and to "come up with ideas" and let them "sink in"; to sharpen an idea and "apply it to whatever else you need"; to develop critical connections and "to piece things together"; and to work together openly and critically in that enterprise. The notion of making mistakes and challenging misconceptions[11] is more or less internalized as part of the process of making sense and understanding. "Screwing up" is part and parcel of the encounter with science.

Independence

Our look at student expeditions into the new world of science has so far revealed two distinct categories of student approaches. Students of the first category, *reliance,* have essentially located themselves on the "shore" of science. Feeling somewhat uncertain in the face of the alien concepts they are encountering, they see the peer workshop as a refuge within a hostile climate. Students in the second *engaged* category, on the other hand, have left the shore and journeyed more deeply into the dense regions of this world with a view to conceptually probing the key features of the territory. The workshop provides a forum in which they can sharpen their conceptual tools with peers involved in the same skirmishes, so to speak, but also with a more experienced peer who has been here before and can show them the ropes.

Students taking the third, *independent* approach to learning science hike further into this world. Their objective is not simply to understand key concepts in the subject; they also begin making sense of them and mapping them out in the wider scientific landscape. These students not only contrast the idea of learning as understanding with simply being able to reproduce a concept, they also recognize that to truly comprehend a concept is to be able to critically connect it to its larger scientific contexts and situations. As Kelly, a chemistry student, described the experience: "It is really being able to put things together, linking this concept to that concept and understanding the bigger picture." She illustrated her point with reference to learning about different chemical compounds. It is not sufficient to know the names of different compounds if, she said, "you don't really understand why there are prefixes, how the prefix of each element corresponded to how many atoms." Conceptual understanding goes beyond simply making conceptual connections, to include an understanding of how they play out in their wider scientific domain.

This example raises an important characteristic of this third approach to learning: metacognition, or metalearning. This kind of learning is defined as learning about learning.[12] These students actively explore and critique their own learning. Kelly reflected on her own learning of science concepts, saying: "It is hard to gauge whether or not you totally grasp a concept. I like to judge that I have learned something when we are given homework problems and I can do them and get the right answer. But sometimes it's a false sense of confidence. Just because you know the answer doesn't necessarily mean that you really understood it."

Recognizing the difference between reproducing and understanding a concept may be necessary for learning, but it is not sufficient. Critiquing one's own learning strategies and developing independently as a result is also critical. Nisha, an engineering student, expressed this in terms of reflecting on the different ways of thinking that she had observed in others and how that had affected her own learning.[13] "Learning is all about morphing it, or making it translatable, to other people, because not everyone has the same mode of thinking," she said. Indeed, she goes on to describe how the GSW workshop was instrumental in assisting this synthesis in her own learning. "When I don't get a concept even after the facilitator has explained it to me, a student in my workshop might come up with a different way too. So sometimes I get three ways. Then I adapt one of those ways to mine, or I might just take it as it is and just learn it that way." For students beginning to take this *indepen-*

dent approach to their learning, the GSW workshop becomes a conceptual science studio. While it is still an intellectual forum for sharing ideas and developing students' conceptual understanding, it also provides opportunities for deeper and extended critiques and conceptual experiments for learning science.

FACILITATING DEEPER CONCEPTUAL LEARNING

The three kinds of learning just described suggest a path toward scientific thinking and deeper conceptual learning. They should not, however, be regarded as a series of distinct stages through which all students must inevitably pass. Their journeys are typically much more multilayered and complex. These approaches to learning are best regarded as responses to the learning environments that students encounter in college science courses. Students respond to a course in ways they think have worked for them in the past and will help them pass the course and get the degree.[14] If a course does not require students to engage in the second and third kinds of learning, and if it does not provide opportunities for them to do so, for the most part they will not engage in them. Except for those very few "born scientists,"[15] students will engage in this scientific journey only to the degree that the college science environment encourages it. Ultimately, that means it will happen if the science faculty encourage it in their teaching.

The overall goal of a course, whatever the nature of its core content, should be focused on facilitating a conceptual understanding of that content. This is perhaps the most critical lesson from our study. And it cannot be overstated. The centrality of conceptual thinking in science is often not fully understood by students.

Science courses all too often send students very strong messages that conceptual understanding is not important. Indeed, the very way in which many faculty think about teaching indicates that they themselves are not aware of its importance.

In a parallel study to those we conducted with students on the GSW program, we looked at how science faculty understood and approached teaching. Many of the faculty who taught the science courses linked to the GSW program took part in this study.[16] The study found that teachers understood and approached their teaching in three different ways. The differences among these approaches centered directly on how faculty understood the nature of student learning and its relationship to teaching.[17] In this respect they mirror the student approaches to learning.

In the first approach to teaching the teacher essentially regards student learning as separate from teaching. It is not the teacher's responsibility. Teaching is concerned only with the ability of the teacher to transmit information. This *transmission* approach is regarded as teacher-centered. Faculty taking this approach feel they are teaching well if they "cover"—transmit—the best, most up-to-date, and relevant information in as clear and logical a manner as possible. The student's role is to receive the information and somehow learn. There is no attempt to help the student make sense of it. As one biology teacher expressed it to us, "Any time you are conveying information is teaching. Formal teaching is when there is somebody whose job it is to convey information, and that is what I do in my lab on a daily basis and that is what I will do in the classroom."

The second approach to teaching recognizes the connection with the student in the teaching process. It preserves the importance of the quality and presentation of the course content, but it pushes teaching beyond merely covering it to "uncovering" it for the student. Teaching consists of helping students acquire the course content, often, for example, through careful explanations and demonstrations. An engineering professor described this *acquisition* approach well. While undergraduates, he says, "are not picking their topics—I am picking their topics for them, and I am providing them with the theoretical underpinnings," he is nevertheless, concerned that his students acquire what he has given them: "I work them through some specific examples and then they have to take that knowledge and apply it to a different example in the labs and homework." He wants them to get the topic the way he has given it to them.

Science faculty who take the third, *engaged* approach push their thinking about teaching science to undergraduates even further. They are not simply interested in the quality of the material that their students need to learn; they are also concerned with the nature of that learning. Simple acquisition of the concepts is not sufficient; they are focused on facilitating conceptual development and change in their students' learning. They want their students to "discover" the content, to reconstruct it for themselves. Another engineering teacher put it as follows:

> I feel particularly strongly about using case studies because they enable students who are thoughtful and deep learners an opportunity to excel ... to try different approaches and focus on the underlying problem and on providing a set of recommendations that are practical and substantiated with thorough analysis.

Science teachers who take this approach focus on helping students develop the kind of scientific thinking that makes the science content meaningful in ways that go beyond merely something to be remembered. Indeed, as Eric Mazur, a Harvard physics professor known for his pioneering work in science education, remarked, "You can forget facts, but you cannot forget understanding."[18] These teachers design scientifically meaningful courses that begin to engage students as student scientists.

It is nearly impossible to help students achieve the kinds of scientific conceptual thinking we have been discussing without believing that teaching should focus on it. Indeed, faculty who take particular views of teaching into the classroom send tacit (or, often, explicit) messages to students about the kind of approaches to learning they expect their students to take. Transmission approaches to teaching suggest students take surface approaches to learning, whereas engaged approaches improve the odds that students might take deeper, more conceptually focused approaches to their learning.[19]

Fortunately, teaching beliefs and understandings are not innate or permanent. Faculty can and do change their thinking about teaching.[20] Indeed, they frequently hold different ways of thinking about teaching in different situations. As we saw in Chapter 1, science faculty often hold more advanced approaches to teaching—as the facilitation of deeper learning—when it comes to their graduate students and the peers they work with in their own scientific work. They need to find ways of facilitating that same deeper conceptual learning and thinking in their undergraduate students. The principles described in the following chapters will assist them in doing just that.

SUGGESTIONS FOR PRACTICE

- Go beyond teaching content. Focus on opportunities for students to actively work with the course content and reflect in depth on the quality of their learning. Engage students during class through questions, problems, and group activities.
- Help students develop the confidence needed to participate deeply in learning rather than just memorizing content. This often means discouraging competition among individuals, encouraging mutual peer assistance, and supporting students who struggle with material.
- Provide "forums" for students to share ideas with each other and "studios" for students to discover and build knowledge through problem-based activities; authentic, realistic projects; and exercises that challenge their misconceptions and prompt them to bring diverse ideas together.
- Help students develop their critical thinking abilities as well as their content knowledge—this helps them become better metacognitive learners.

Engaging Problems

The most exciting phrase to hear in science, the one
that heralds new discoveries, is not "Eureka!" ("I found it!")
but rather "hmm . . . that's funny."

—Isaac Asimov

"I'M NOT SAYING that the problems
are simple because, of course, I made mistakes," said Monica, a
second-year facilitator, reflecting on her experience of doing
conceptual-style problems in her biology workshop. "Often the way
I took to solve a problem was wrong. But I think that working on
conceptual-style problems is the way to understand the concepts."
She paused for a moment and continued: "And, I think it's cool
when you're able to understand them. That's exciting to me."

Asking good questions and engaging worthy problems is at the
heart of science. As Asimov suggests in the epigraph, however, that
excitement lies less in the solution than in the discovery of the problem. The popular understanding of science as a body of empirical
knowledge derived from the solutions to historically important
questions—Archimedes's famous "Eureka!"[1]—is only half the picture. The secret to engaging with science is spotting the problem

that stimulated the thinking in the first place. Whatever the precise nature of the problem, the excitement of "Eureka!" is preceded by a much more profound experience, the experience of observing something—a natural phenomenon, an experimental result, a wayward piece of data—recognizing it as interesting or "funny" or beautiful or strange, and then asking why or how or what. The excitement of science lies not in the finding of solutions, as satisfying as that may be, but in the finding of problems that are worthy of the human mind and scientific curiosity.[2] This excitement—not just the result of the discovery but the thinking behind the discovery—was what we wanted the Gateway Science Workshop (GSW) students to experience. And what we learned from them was that the quality of the scientific questions or problems that they encountered as undergraduates was vital to the development of their conceptual learning.[3]

The nineteenth-century Scottish physicist James Clerk Maxwell, famous for his discovery of the nature of electromagnetic waves, is reported to have expressed his curiosity about mechanical things and physical phenomena as a young child, asking, "What's the go o' that? What's the particular go o' that?"[4] The sheer wonder of witnessing the phenomenon is not sufficient for the inquiring scientific mind. It is wonderful in relation to the quality of the problems it poses or questions it raises. The mathematician and philosopher Bertrand Russell writes of a comparable childhood moment, this time about the "dazzling" experience of Euclid's axioms and theorems.[5] And while not all students are furnished with the remarkable intellectual curiosity of a Maxwell or a Russell, as part of our innate capacity for learning we are all endowed from birth with a natural aspiration to know, to understand, and to solve problems, particularly those related to our immediate experience. As any parent who has encountered the barrage of ceaseless "whys" that children ask in pursuing a subject will testify, we exhibit this ability from the very earliest days. At the core of this aspiration to learn is the innate capacity for creating and being stimulated by questions and problems.[6]

Unfortunately, in the traditional science classroom, the scientific inquiry into problems, which drives scientists and science faculty, is all too often lost. Despite the course "covering" the solutions and answers to some of the most important problems ever faced by our world, this kind of class rarely stimulates excitement, wonder, and awe in the student's mind. The details of the scientific discovery that students encounter are presented in the absence of the experience of discovery, and often without the sense that the solution is even worthy of discovery. Indeed, this is almost the definition of the undergraduate study of science in higher education—the accumulation of answers and solutions to unasked questions. The experience is akin to being given the answer key to a test without the questions.[7]

The key intellectual challenges that students confront in such courses are concerned mainly with strategic management problems about how to most efficiently achieve a good grade. Seeing an A on a transcript, while not a "Eureka" moment, at least brings a personal feeling of satisfaction. On the other hand, memorizing the structure of the atom, the structure of DNA, or a series of physics equations for an exam that leads to the "A" is essentially an empty experience.

Students do not have to engage with problems in science on a grand scale to feel the excitement of science. But the problem does have to provide the possibility of meaningful discovery, of being a problem worthy of investigation.

Monica's experience of the excitement of learning is reflected by nearly all the students participating in the workshop program. It speaks directly to the issue of motivation at the heart of learning, the difference between extrinsic and intrinsic motivations that distinguished between the surface and the deep approaches to learning, discussed in Chapter 2. And if problems are a necessary precondition of learning science, the quality of the learning is directly related to the quality of the problem at hand. Students are not excited by trivial questions with little conceptual merit but, rather, by those that inspire real thinking and curiosity. In this respect students are no different from their professors. "We are constant learners," remarked Jon, a GSW chemistry professor, regarding his own research. "We ask ourselves a lot of questions—'What if we know this?' or 'What if we know that?' Then we design an experiment around it, we build and test our hypothesis." This is what motivates the faculty. The same is true of their students.

THE ROLE OF PROBLEMS IN EDUCATION

The use of problems to stimulate and facilitate learning in higher and professional education has been recognized for some time. Indeed, problems characterize the very meaning of innovation in learning and teaching in higher education. They, and the educational theories they express, are at the heart of almost every major pedagogical innovation in science, technology, engineering, and mathematics (STEM) in the last fifty years: inquiry-based learning, challenge-based learning, case-based learning, project-based

learning, and active learning. The most prominent of these innovations is problem-based learning (PBL).[8] Originally developed in
medical education in 1961, PBL initiatives have spread throughout
the world during the past half century, spawning substantial changes
in curriculum reform in many disciplines, including the widespread
use of new educational methods in math and science education.[9]
While the nature of PBL implementation will vary among instructors, courses, and disciplines, its defining feature is simply "that the
starting point for learning should be a problem, a query or a puzzle
that the learner wishes to solve."[10] Other characteristic features of
PBL include

- problems reflecting real-world situations;
- students discussing the process cooperatively among
  themselves;
- students being appropriately guided by someone who
  knows the problem;
- students identifying their own learning needs, including
  the knowledge and resources they will require to solve
  the problem; and
- students applying this new knowledge to the problem and
  evaluating their learning.

Many of these and similar features have come to describe the
wide range of problem-oriented approaches to teaching designed
to enhance student conceptual and critical thinking as a way of engaging with course concepts and materials. Rather than absorbing
the course content through memorizing specific content and skills
(frequently called "plug-and-chug" skills) to answer problems, stu-

dents are presented with the problem first, usually a real-world kind of problem, and are required to find a solution to the problem. It is important to distinguish here between problems that are meant to probe and stimulate students' thinking and exercises (or problem sets) that are commonly intended to provide students with practice in solving certain kinds of standard science questions or particular types of equations. The former are focused on helping students develop a range of metacognitive and critical thinking skills essential to doing science. These are the reflective skills exhibited by the independent students described in the last chapter. They include questioning personal assumptions, reflecting on the nature of evidence, and exploring different approaches to problems and alternative explanations and solutions. They challenge students to inquire into the nature, core conceptual issues, and logic of the problem, as well as the kinds of resources (knowledge, information, skills, instruments, and people) necessary to construct solutions to the problem.[11] This problem-oriented approach involves working cooperatively with peers to solve or address the problem.

Not surprisingly, the learning objectives of problem-oriented approaches are very different from most traditional approaches to teaching. In the latter the focus tends to be on the acquisition of very specific content knowledge—of chemical bonding, for example, or genetic inheritance, or the properties of levers—and the skills for following specific kinds of prescribed procedures—such as solving an equation, for instance. In the former, in contrast, the focus is on the conceptual understanding of the appropriate content knowledge and skills to solve actual problems. Such a problem might be posed in a realistic situation in which students can envision themselves as real actors solving specific problems to answer a larger human dilemma. Rather than simply providing the genetic details of pedigree, for example, a biology professor we know engaged his students with the concept in terms of "a very rare disease that onsets later in life" and, with the help of a pedigree diagram of four generations, asked the students in groups to determine "the probability that the youngest individuals will both be afflicted with the ailment when they grow up."

Unlike PBL, where students are expected to identify and find the appropriate content required to solve a problem, other problem-oriented innovations provide the relevant content more or less simultaneously with the problems. In the GSW program, for example, the problems are encountered alongside the relevant concepts being presented in the lectures.[12] But the focus is less on plugging in the right fact or equation (which they have seen before) and more on identifying which concepts and approaches are critical to solving a new problem (which they have not seen before).

In his study of what the very best college teachers do, Ken Bain, who was involved in the early development of the GSW program, describes how problems characterized the teaching of our very best university teachers[13]—how, essentially, these amazing educators facilitated student encounters with problems. Whatever the teaching situation—a lecture, seminar, workshop, or lab—these teachers all turned it into a meaningful *learning* situation through five problem-focused elements. They started with an intriguing problem, indicated how that problem was relevant or important to a larger real-world problem, gave the students an opportunity to answer the problem, provided an answer to the problem (although this was sometimes left out), and, finally, left the students with another related problem.

The nature of these educational encounters—the value of the thinking and discussion stimulated and the quality of the student learning—is, to a large degree of course, dependent on the problems themselves. The student experience of learning begins with the problem. In GSW, after ten years of engaging problems across hundreds of topics in dozens of science courses, students' experience revealed key lessons for the construction of problems, lessons related to wording, structure, narrative, difficulty, and relevance, as well as the capacity for inciting interest, extending knowledge, deepening understanding, and provoking discussion.

THE EXPERIENCE OF PROBLEMS: LESSONS FROM STUDENTS

Early on in the GSW program, we would hear back from students that certain problems were "good," while others were not. Even if they did not always agree, students generally regarded a problem as good if it helped them understand the main concepts being presented in their lectures. But a problem was also "good" if it helped them prepare for midterms and final examinations or reduced the time they needed for study outside of class. Sometimes a problem was "good" if it simply showed the struggles that other students, or the facilitator, were having with the material, revealed other ways to look at a problem, or even just enabled students to connect with others who faced similar challenges with the material.

These informal observations led us to explore the students' experience of the actual problems more systematically. We asked all the facilitators to submit a report at the end of the workshop, rating the individual problems on how good the problem was in engaging students in a discussion of the key science concepts embedded in the problem. We also asked them to comment on their ratings. We analyzed those ratings and comments in order to identify which kinds of problems the students rated high or low and why, and to ascertain the key concerns held by students.[14]

While there were many problems that elicited mixed responses, overall the issues they raised about the experience of working with problems were remarkably consistent. These issues focused around three general categories—how helpful a problem was in

- promoting student knowledge of key science concepts;
- fostering a deeper understanding of those concepts; and
- facilitating a good discussion of the concepts in the workshop.

These features were often related. For example, problems that introduced key scientific concepts were also very useful for facilitating discussion. And problems that engaged students in lively discussion also stimulated a deeper conceptual understanding. But this was not always the case. Facilitators frequently reported that a particular problem was good in one respect but not in another. A problem "prompted good discussion," for example, but the "students had difficulty understanding" the key concepts discussed.

Promoting Knowledge of Key Science Concepts

A key theme of the facilitators' reports concerned the role that problems played in supporting student knowledge of key science content and concepts of the course.

1. *Reviewing Knowledge*

In some cases students' comments focused on the part the problems played in offering students a good review of content that had already been introduced in a lecture. A physics facilitator reported that a problem asking students to determine the free-fall time and end speed of a sphere dropped from a 145 m drop tower at a NASA zero gravity research facility "provided a straightforward review of an important concept that everybody understood." A chemistry leader described a similar problem as "a good review of material they had learned in class," as did a biology colleague, who applauded a problem for being "a straightforward question which really hit on the important basics."

2. *Extending Knowledge*

The students also reported the importance that problems played in extending the students' knowledge of a particular topic beyond what they already knew. One chemistry problem was described as having been well received because it "promoted an extension of what they already know about redox reactions," and another because it provided a "good segue into discussion about diatomic molecules, and touched upon important concepts." Problems that brought together different concepts—as a chemistry student put it, "with a good integration of multiple chemical concepts"—were especially appreciated. Indeed, one facilitator referred to a problem asking students about the competitive metabolism of ethanol versus methanol in the human body, in the context of the treatment of methanol poisoning that can lead to blindness, to be "my favorite question, and the group really liked it too; brings together a lot of different concepts." And this included those problems that provided opportunities to integrate "qualitative and quantitative" concepts.

3. Identifying Important Knowledge

Students also appreciated problems that helped them distinguish between those concepts that are important to solving a particular problem and those that are not. As a chemistry facilitator put it: "It is a good way to make the students weed out what information is important and what is accessory." This is a particularly important point, since students are often inexperienced at distinguishing between the core concepts they need to master and others with which they merely need an acquaintance.[15] This focus on identifying core concepts also has a strategic element to it, particularly if the problem reflected the key kind of questions that might be on an exam. Comments such as "very relevant, exam-type question" or "great exam-type question!" were frequently made by the facilitators.

These kinds of comments need not be regarded as typical of students solely interested in grades; after all, they naturally reflect the context in which their learning is taking place. It raises the much more important issue of developing exam problems that stimulate scientific thought and understanding. The comment of an engineering facilitator that "I really liked this week's workshop problems because they reflect questions that could actually appear on exams" is only meaningful if, for example, the exams actually contain real-world, conceptually rich science problems. An innovative chemistry professor addressed this issue by giving the following old exam question on his GSW worksheet:

> Suppose that a chemical spill in Milwaukee releases 100 L of a 0.1 M potassium chromate solution into Lake Michigan. As-

suming that Lake Michigan is roughly 100 m deep, 100 km long and 200 km wide, and that CrO_4^{2-} ions mix uniformly throughout the lake, how many CrO_4^{2-} ions from the spill would be in a 200 mL glass from the northern end of Lake Michigan?

While he asked them to do the calculation first, he then asked them to "criticize the assumptions of the problem; that is, what did the problem assume that is probably not true, and would that assumption have a substantial effect on the calculated answer?" While some students found it difficult, they ranked it very high in terms of identifying important conceptual material that might also be on an exam (4.74 out of 5).

4. *Clarifying Knowledge*

Problems that failed to help clarify knowledge were usually raised in negative facilitator reports of problems. Negative reactions primarily focused on the problems that provoked confusion in the students, especially when poorly worded. There were numerous comments, such as "the question was worded awkwardly," "the students got lost in the wording of the questions," and "could be made better by rephrasing." A problem describing electron donor acceptor complexes and asking students if the "bond in the Na/Cl ion pair is a donor-acceptor interaction," for example, was charitably reported by one facilitator as being "a little confusing, could have been worded better," whereas regarding the same problem her colleague simply said, "too confusing to explain." In some cases the confusion was less a result of poor wording than of clarity about how the students were expected to use the concept: "It's a great question," a biology student reported, "but it's not clear enough what to do with the issue at hand."

5. *Connecting Knowledge*

By far the greatest number of negative student comments concerned the relationship of the problem content to the students' existing knowledge. Frequently the students simply could not link the problem to the course: "Problem doesn't follow class content." Or, the links were so obscure that "it led," as one physics facilitator put it, "to confusion and blank stares." Even well-rated problems might be criticized in this way. An interesting chemistry problem asking students to use thermodynamic principles to assess whether or not treating methane with steam would be an economically feasible method for extracting hydrogen as an alternative fuel source was faulted for including "topics, such as fuel sources that the students were not familiar with, making [them] a bit more difficult for them to comprehend." We do not mean that problems should refrain from challenging students to extend their knowledge beyond what they are learning in the classroom or to make connections with new concepts. Indeed, pointing students within the problem to relevant material in the textbook or in another source will help fill in the gaps.

Problems focusing on material beyond the scope of the students' experience were especially acute when it came to cross-disciplinary concepts. Another chemistry problem was knocked for "involving lots of probability and background knowledge on experimental genetics that they don't have." And a quantitative biology problem was described as not working because it was "much more of a math problem than a biology problem" or for being "too physics-oriented." Again, the point is to construct problems that help students make connections to material they associate with other disciplines in terms of both what can reasonably be assumed to be part of their existing knowledge and in terms of the new cross-disciplinary con-

cepts in their course of study. It is the development of these connections that will support the development of students' conceptual
understanding.

Fostering Student Conceptual Understanding

A prominent theme in comments across all disciplines concerned
the role that problems played in fostering conceptual understanding. Facilitators from various workshops in chemistry, for example,
mentioned how certain problems "provided the students with a
deeper understanding of a topic only taught in class" or "helped to
facilitate understanding of isomerism." In some cases problems were
applauded for helping students make sense of science more generally: "This question facilitated understanding of experimental techniques and analysis methods."

1. *Identifying Misunderstanding*
Students often regarded problems as useful not simply for identifying
important concepts, as we saw in the previous section, but also for
detecting incorrect understandings of a concept, the kind of misconceptions, mentioned in Chapter 2, which often go unchallenged. A
chemistry facilitator, for example, reported that student understanding was facilitated with a problem that "revealed misconceptions in
basic chemistry." And the problem need not be complex. In this case
the problem simply pointed to a specific figure in the textbook and
asked the students to "critique it in the context of what you know
about the sizes of atoms and ions."

2. *Challenging Understanding*
Perhaps the most important and frequently reported feature of
problems facilitating student understanding centered on the level

of conceptual challenge that a problem poses. As a physics facilitator noted, "It was a hard problem, but I felt it really got the students thinking—the students were eventually able to grasp the concepts." Similarly, engineering facilitators commenting on a common problem noted: "These kinds of questions are always good to force students to really think about the material," and "it took a LONG time" but "excellent for truly understanding." The Lake Michigan chemical spill metaproblem (problem about a problem) mentioned earlier was also reported as an excellent example of a problem that stimulated conceptual thinking.

The difference between conceptual challenge and the challenges in acquiring new concepts is important to emphasize. The latter are rather low-level challenges in which clarity is the main obstacle to learning. Obstacles related to conceptual challenge, on the other hand, are often the key to understanding. Information perceived as not being connected to existing forms of knowledge was reported negatively in problems focused on knowledge acquisition. But new information—or new forms or information—in problems focused on understanding is often reported as helpful. A biology problem, for example, was reported as providing concepts that "help students understand the graph better and makes the problem far more functional and relevant to real information." And a physics facilitator reported the following problem as having a "useful visualization that was very helpful, of appropriate difficulty, and [which] induced thought."

> You are standing at the top of a tall cliff. You have two identical balls in your hands. You throw ball #1 straight up using you left hand and drop ball #2 directly down by allowing it to

roll gently off of your right hand; i.e., ball #2 has (roughly) zero initial velocity. Both balls leave your hands at the same instant of time. Which ball strikes the ground first? Which ball is moving faster right before impact?

3. *Stimulating Understanding*

The tension between simply acquiring a concept and understanding that concept at a deeper level was frequently apparent in the facilitators' reports. Facilitators recognized that problems that focused only on presenting content were usually *not* helpful for stimulating conceptual understanding. While basic reviews of the material were often appreciated, they did not by themselves stimulate deeper changes in student thinking. As one physics facilitator commented, "It was not much of a challenge; doesn't seem to test understanding." Interestingly, reports of problems confusing students to a moderate degree, on the other hand, were frequently seen as good for helping understanding. A problem on geometric series was described as "the most helpful of the three problems because it was a little more confusing and required more thought." Indeed, this facilitator went on to say, "This was a great problem." Confusion that is due not to poor wording or problem structure but, rather, to meaningful conceptual complexity has the power to stimulate constructive thought. Indeed, that is the key to thinking, to figuring something out. As Edward Teller—father of the hydrogen bomb—was reported to have said, "Confusion is not a bad thing; it's the first step towards understanding."[16]

4. *Illuminating Understanding*

Confusion may be a good thing, but not when it impedes understanding. The level of complexity and difficulty in many problems can simply be too much of an obstacle, as an engineering facilitator reported one question as being "a very challenging problem; students were lost." In many cases such problems were reported as requiring concepts not available to the students, as by this math facilitator about a math problem: "Difficult to do without a good grasp of the physics behind it." Another facilitator reports the same problem as being "really hard, none of us could do it," and goes on to add, "We gave up pretty quickly."

Of course, patience and additional hints, and a longer investigation of these problems, might have helped the students develop their understanding. For example, a chemistry facilitator reported similar issues with a problem asking students to "calculate the volume of empty space that the world population occupies." Aside from the almost philosophical question of "empty space," which here seems to be just bad wording, the facilitator reported it to be a "confusing problem; a lot of assumptions were necessary," but adds, "Students did not get this question right away; a lot of explaining was necessary." In this case the facilitator, with more time, hints, and illumination, was able to help the students develop an understanding of the concepts at play. Judging the conceptual "stretch" required and illuminating the experience through hints, clues, and additional information to enhance the students' understanding can often transform a mediocre problem into a very good problem.

Facilitating Workshop Discussion

The extent and nature of the discussion that surrounds a problem can be critical to the quality of student learning. As in the broader science community, the development and understanding of important science concepts are augmented by good dialogue and discussion between students and their peers. A good discussion of problems can foster critical and creative questioning skills among students, skills that students can and do internalize in their own thinking. Problems that do not promote discussion between students are unlikely to promote that critical, metacognitive level of internal discussion at the heart of thinking in the scientific mind.

Discussion was a prominent theme in the facilitators' reports. Time and again their comments distinguished between problems that, as one biology facilitator described it, "got them talking, and they all seemed to be on the right track" and others where "the question provoked very little discussion, or the students didn't know what to make of it." The following math problem, for example, which simply asked students to identify the surface parameterized under various assumptions, was highly rated (4.83 of 5) and highly praised: "Great problem. They worked through this problem easily, drawing and talking them all out with each other."

Identify the surface parameterized by $\mathbf{r}(t) = \,<s \sin t, s \cos t, s>$ if

(a) $0 \leq s \leq 1, 0 \leq t \leq \pi$
(b) $0 \leq s \leq 4, 0 \leq t \leq 2\pi$
(c) $0 \leq s, 0 \leq t \leq \pi$

1. Sequencing Discussion

The quality of discussion often depended on when the problem was raised during the series of problems discussed in a particular workshop. Some problems were natural discussion openers. Facilitators in math, for example, reported a problem being "fun; nice warm-up problem; good basic parameterization; these are all variations of the same basic problem." Similarly, a physics facilitator commented on a problem asking students to "plot the position, velocity, and acceleration of the ball" thrown straight up in the air with a certain velocity being "a good start, an introduction to general themes, and a confidence builder." The math facilitators reported on the sequencing of the problems, developing from easier to more difficult problems: "An excellent step-by-step walk-through; it totally made them think; parts A through C go in increasing order of difficulty and show students how to generalize from a specific case." They also reported on how the sequencing raised opportunities to engage students in discussion through comparison of key ideas in a problem: "You can compare and contrast with problems 1 and 2."

2. Situating Discussion

Facilitators also reported that situating the problem in terms of their students' prior knowledge—material that had been addressed in class, in readings, or in previous courses—was almost a prerequisite for a good discussion. A chemistry facilitator described a problem that stimulated a good discussion as having "promoted an extension of what they already know about redox reactions." But not every student in the group needs to have this prior knowledge for a good discussion. In a number of engineering workshops related to a lecture given at different times during the week, students whose lecture fell after the workshop had not had a chance to address the material in class. As an engineering facilitator remarked, "This topic hadn't yet been covered in the majority of the classes. Students were taking in and learning new info." Nevertheless, he and his fellow facilitators reported the problem as a "good problem, encouraged discussion; good for involvement" and a "good question, lots of discussion; could tell most kids were unprepared, but a few students carried the group through." A good group discussion requires the problem to be situated in the group's shared prior knowledge.

Situating the problem in the student's knowledge of and interest in real-world phenomena also helped stimulate discussion. It was "a good, real-life application," one of the chemistry facilitators explained. "It generated good discussion about the relationship between energy and the environment." This attribute of connecting to students' interest in and enjoyment of a science problem was frequently noted in the students' comments: "an interesting/different question that did make students think" and "funny scenario, everyone enjoyed it," in physics; "very interesting, required active participation," in biology; and, "a funny problem; we should have more of these, it keeps the students interested" in math.

3. *Engaging Discussion*

The facilitators' reports are full of comments about problems that tended to hinder student discussion. These also tend to be the same kind of features that hinder learning. As noted earlier, a critical impediment to discussion mentioned in all disciplines was the lack of meaningful challenge raised by the problem. Time and time again facilitators reported that easy problems impeded their attempts to engage their students: "Did not spark discussion; too easy; should have been more elaborate" (biology); "Very basic and almost too easy a problem" (chemistry); "Too easy for the kids" (math); "Not much of a challenge, doesn't seem to test understanding" (physics); "Too easy" (engineering).

In contrast, the facilitators reported that extremely difficult problems also undermined discussion. The following comments were typical of facilitators' comments on these kinds of problems: "A very challenging problem: students were lost and did not engage" (engineering); "It was too advanced; the students became frustrated and kinda gave up" (biology). Such problems may simply be too advanced for students, but in some cases support for discussion can be developed by breaking the problem into manageable chunks, using hints and providing the kind of conceptual toolbox mentioned earlier. In some cases, however, the facilitators reported problems in which discussion was virtually impossible. In such situations, discussion rarely got past the words—"they got lost in the wording"— and in some cases faltered because the wording thwarted the facilitator herself. As one chemistry facilitator explained, the problem was so badly worded that she simply found it "too confusing to explain." And then there were those problems that were too novel or interesting. An attempt to engage students through an unusual physics problem asking students to explain why "the motion of a sled on ice can be regarded as particle motion, but the motion of a diver, diving head first off the high board, cannot," for example, backfired: "Novel approach to introducing the concept and definition. Had to think about it," but "Students didn't know what to make of it"; or, "An interesting/different question that did make students think" but "largely provoked confusion, didn't go over so well." In such cases, having a colleague, a teaching assistant, or an advanced student simply pre-read a problem can quickly identify awkward or unclear ideas or wording that will stall a discussion.

The Goldilocks Dilemma

This exploration of how students experience problems raises an important dilemma—what might be called the "Goldilocks dilemma"—which most teachers and professors of science run into at some time or another with their students. When is hard too hard, and/or when is easy too easy? And what do "hard" and "easy" even mean? Indeed, the negative comments given earlier about problems being too hard or too soft illustrate the dilemma well. This problem is "just right," on the other hand, suggested different meanings. It could mean, as in the aforementioned chemistry and biology illustrations, that the problems challenged the students in a "test in reasoning" or pushed them to "think critically." It might also mean, as suggested in the engineering and physics illustrations, that the problem aided student learning with a "great intro" or through step-by-step support.

The Goldilocks dilemma raises what has often been described as the paradox of learning, one that goes back at least as far as Plato. How can one learn anything? How can you know that you know? If you do not know something, how can you evaluate whether what you are given or find out is even true?[17] What do you take as given, and what do you discover? Good problems address the inherent tensions in this paradox.

THE CONSTRUCTION OF SCIENCE PROBLEMS

Problematic Problems

As every teacher of science knows, the development of good science problems that challenge students in the best ways is a challenging problem in its own right. If solving problems is the application of creative science, the construction of good science problems is often a form of scientific art. Indeed, the inspired problem is as much a feature of the history of science as the discovery of the elegant solution—possibly behind Einstein's comment that "we can't solve problems by using the same kind of thinking we used when we created them."[18] Nevertheless, the experience need not be pure inspiration.

Over the program's ten years, our countless discussions with faculty about their approach to problem construction revealed the same general kinds of concerns as those raised by the facilitators. When asked about the ideal workshop problem for his students, a biology professor, for example, focused on paying attention to students' discomfort with workshop problems that did not directly connect to the content, timing, and style of the course:

> Ideally, it will be nice to have a person who is teaching the course writing all the GSW worksheet questions so that they can be done at the right time. Students also feel better when the questions are in the same professor style and are in the same style as the exam. A lot of it is cosmetics, but students get nervous about it when things seem unfamiliar.

In his concern that problems be similar in content and style to the course and exam questions, this professor focuses problem construction on contributing to a workshop environment that essentially *supports* student learning. Such an environment recognizes the element of "dependence" that students have on the teacher and the course in their learning and it looks to keep the course environment within the students' comfort zone.

In contrast, one of our chemistry professors likes to push his students beyond their comfort zone. He emphasizes the role of the problems in fostering "independence" in student learning, challenging students to think about the concepts and how they might be used in ways that go beyond how they are presented in the course lectures.[19] In response to similar concerns from the students, that "the questions are too hard and don't have anything to do with what the course is about," he asked the students and their facilitators to take a conceptual "toolbox" approach to help them see how the problems are related to the key ideas being raised in the course.

> The problems, of course, have something to do with the course, and students are solving the problems in an environment that is truly supportive: there are four or five people plus a facilitator, and a discussion is going on. So we want to use complicated problems. We asked the facilitators to ask the group before each question what concepts the problem uses. Then they have them work through the problem and at the end ask them what concepts they used. When you have a problem, open up the toolbox and work on selecting the ones that you are going to use to solve the problem.

Rather than redesigning what might seem at first pass like unfamiliar problems to the students, this professor found ways to support them in linking the science concepts with which they were more familiar to the unfamiliar conceptual complexity of the problem.

These two approaches to problem construction illustrate the paradox of learning raised earlier: the importance of linking the problems to the students' prior knowledge and at the same time challenging them to extend their learning beyond the familiar and the comfortable. The tension displayed here describes the essential characteristics of the students' journey from a surface to a deeper approach to their learning—to engage in scientific learning.

This tension permeates the key components of a problem. Despite their many forms and guises, all problems are characterized by three main components:[20] what is known, what needs to be known, and how to solve what needs to be known. It is essentially a journey with a beginning point, an end point, and a means of getting from the former to the latter. Each component may be more or less clear and simple, or obscure and complex. At one extreme are problems in which everything is rather clear and simple—these are frequently the kind of problems that dominate the exercises presented in a typical course. The known is given to the student as is the means for solving the problem (an equation or a formula, for example). These types of problems are essentially exercises and can usually be solved through rote application, with little scientific thinking. At the other extreme are what have been referred to as "ill-structured problems"— the sort that life tends to throw at us—in which all three components are complex and somewhat obscure. These problems fall in the very challenging "encouraging independence" approach to problem construction. A great part of solving these problems consists in reducing the obscurity and managing the complexity of all three features of the problem. It is frequently more difficult to figure out where you are and where you want to go than it is to find out how to get there.

The art of good science problem construction consists of judging the tension between clarity and simplicity (support) and obscurity and complexity (challenge) with respect to these three components of problems. Some problems demand much more thinking from the students in establishing where they are, what they actually know or need to know to go about solving the problem, and what concepts are important. Others introduce complexity in the second, what needs to be known, component. There may be multiple alternative ways drawing on different concepts to get to a solution or multiple steps that need to be worked out. Still others stress the complexity of the solution, noting possible different solutions and the contexts in which these different solutions may or may not be appropriate. Decisions about the problems presented to students may also be carefully calibrated with respect to the aforementioned three components within a series of topic-related problems—a sequenced set of problems. The different degrees of support and challenge that problems present to students can be adjusted over the problem sequence with, for example, confidence-building support problems early on and challenging problems coming later.

Constructing Problems

While the challenge of constructing science problems does not have a straightforward solution, the GSW experience has resulted in useful guidelines for faculty. But they are just that—guidelines. At best they may increase the likelihood of creating a meaningful experience for improving student learning of science. These guidelines are focused on four main features: the level of difficulty, the level of relevance, the level of interest, and the level of discussion.

1. Level of Difficulty

As we have seen, the level of difficulty of a problem is largely a feature of the balance between simplicity-clarity and complexity-obscurity. Students like learning challenges, but they need to be meaningful, conceptual, and within students' capability to solve individually or as a group. The problems should not be seen as remedial and must not mainly be a review of very basic material. Students need to see that they and their abilities are respected. Any problem that involves the simple "plugging" in of information and "chugging" through the problem is to be avoided (except perhaps as a warm-up), particularly in group situations where more people simply get in the way. On the other hand, problems should not be so obscure that the unknowns are impossible to clarify and/or the problem is well beyond the students' conceptual level. The problems should

- be at least "one step up" conceptually from ordinary textbook problems and/or from course assignments and exam problems;
- focus on the key concepts or big ideas that are essential in understanding the specific topic or course;
- help reveal common students' misconceptions, conceptual traps, or knowledge gaps;
- be conceptually rich, requiring the application of more than one concept for solution;
- help students discover the connections among multiple concepts and how their integration leads to more advanced material;
- help students make connections between textual, mathematical, and visual representations of a concept;
- encourage students to think beyond the familiar problem setting and transfer their knowledge to be applicable in different settings;

- include multipart problems with increasing conceptual depth; and
- contain a conceptual "toolbox" of key concepts, as well as hints and clues about approach.

Not all problems, of course, can simultaneously address all of the aforementioned points. The challenge posed by problem sets or worksheets, however, can be calibrated to range from easier to quite difficult in such a way as to include most of these features. In addition, the level of conceptual challenge of the problems can usually be extended if the problems are being discussed and solved by a group with a trained facilitator.

2. Level of Relevance

Students are more likely to engage conceptually with a problem or set of problems if they view the activity as relevant and meaningful to what is happening in their lives at the time. This will most likely be related to their performance-related needs and expectations of the course, although it might also be related to a future course or program or in some cases to future professional work. Whatever the case, the problems must not be seen as simply extra and unrelated work. In this respect the problems should be created to

- help students understand a difficult concept from the course text and readings;
- expand on concepts or methods stressed in class;
- tackle common questions asked or identified in class;
- illustrate key concepts related to lab activities;
- address misconceptions that came to light as students worked on previous problems;

- illuminate the key concepts that will be assessed on their exams; and
- help students make sense of current science-related social issues.

3. *Level of Interest*

Good problems can be the first portal for enhancing students' interest in the sciences. A good point to remember is that if the problem is not of any interest to the teacher, there is a good chance it will not interest the students either. Where the first two features focused on the nature and structure of problem content, this feature focuses on the problem's style, in particular, how to make the problem context-rich as well as concept-rich. Problems that engage student interest

- help students discover connections with "the big science or social picture";
- ask students to think about examples and counterexamples of the same concept/principle;
- connect problems to ongoing research or ideas and examples of future scientific advancement;
- engage real-world problems—real problems situated in everyday-life situations;
- embed an interesting narrative or story;
- frame a realistic scenario; and
- are often personal, starting with "you . . ." (as in, "You are looking at . . ."), or with a friend or member of your family ("Your sister has been hired to . . .").

4. *Level of Discussion*

All of the characteristics of good problems identified previously play a pivotal role in the facilitation of group discussion among students. Clearly a problem that is not relevant to the experiences of any, or only to a few, of the group members, or does not interest them at all, is going to have trouble stimulating a good discussion. Similarly, the level of difficulty needs to be such that the problem is able to engage the most advanced student while not alienating those for whom the concepts and material are new. Regardless of student level, the problem must be such that its solution can be understood and appreciated by all members of the group. When designing problem sets that will promote discussion and interaction among students, include problems that

- are concept/principle-oriented rather than procedure/ formula heavy;
- have no instant or quick solution but, rather, require students to wrestle with it for a longer period of time;
- contain multiple parts with varying levels of difficulty that can encourage wider participation;
- can be solved through multiple approaches and in multiple ways; and
- vary in difficulty, and ensure the most challenging problem is not always at the end (so often not addressed) or so close to the beginning that it takes up all the time.

Designing and creating problems can be a very gratifying and intellectually stimulating process—much like discovering new and interesting problems in the field of science. Some of the best problems even come from the "hmm, that's funny" experience a teacher often has when reading student papers and exams. That experience may arise from the way in which many students go about solving a problem that is unusual, from a student misconception of a concept that continues to pop up in class, or from unanticipated results on an existing conceptual inventory or test.[21] It may also arise through a simple conversation with a student or group of students. Finally, the best way to "construct" a problem could be to simply choose it very carefully (and perhaps modify it) from an existing open-source database.[22]

The finding of good science problems is part of science itself. Good problems, really good problems, are just as important to the progress of the scientific enterprise as any practice in the history of science. They are the key to scientific discovery—discovery cannot happen without them. Similarly, the finding of good problems for students is the first step to their own discovery, to their learning. It opens the door to, as the English chemist Cyril Herman Hinshelwood put it, "the imaginative adventure of the mind seeking truth in a world of mystery."[23] And it will have an incalculable impact on the future of our world.

SUGGESTIONS FOR PRACTICE

- Kindle interest: Create problems that reflect authentic, real-world scientific issues and that feel meaningful to students.
- Reveal relevance: Design problems that students can see are important to progress in the course and connected to issues in the world.
- Connect knowledge: Build into problems opportunities for students to seek new knowledge and apply it.

- Engage discussion: Develop for a group-learning context problems that will engender discussion and debate.

- Probe misconceptions: Design problems that, if solved incorrectly, should challenge assumptions and/or reveal basic misconceptions students might have.

- Promote critical thinking: Construct problems with several approaches or alternative solutions, or which require making connections between multiple concepts.

FOUR

Connecting Peers

Tapestries are made by many artisans working together.
The contributions of separate workers cannot be discerned in the
completed work, and the loose and false threads
have been covered over.

—Sheldon Lee Glashow

A GATEWAY SCIENCE WORKSHOP (GSW) student recently repeated to us what her professor said on the first day of class, in that time-honored science tradition: "Look to your left and to your right. Three out of ten of the people you see around you will not be in this room at the end of the term." Clearly dismayed, her eyes wide, she said, "I don't know if he thought that was going to motivate us, but all it did for me was make me scared to come back the next day!" Perhaps without realizing the impact of their words, faculty essentially tell students: "We don't want all of you." This is not to say that these faculty take some perverse enjoyment from seeing students fail. Rather, the culture of competition is so solidly established in science education that it is difficult to see beyond it from within the walls of an academic department. Individualism and independence are prized in our culture. And, in academic culture, particularly in science education, they are probably even more highly valued.

Part of the GSW mission has been to moderate the tendency in academia toward individualism and competitiveness by introducing collaboration. Indeed, during many of our initial conversations, faculty conveyed their skepticism about the value of student collaboration: "They won't want to help each other," they said. "They're competing for grades, so why would they share their own problem-solving techniques?" The irony here is that much of that competitiveness is generated by a grading system that allows only a certain percentage of students to succeed.

It is true; students *do* often shy away from collaboration. When chemistry facilitator Asam first joined us, he was skeptical about our efforts to promote collaboration. He was the most vocal of the group in challenging our reminders that collaboration promotes learning more than intense competition does. Competition motivates students, he maintained; without it students would risk slacking off. But in an end-of-year reflection note, he told us, "The competitiveness in chemistry here drives students to work for grades rather than learning. I want to make my GSW session *different*. In my group, students participate with each other rather than competing. Our goal is to learn as a group. If they end up getting A's in chemistry in the process, that's great, but it's not the point."

LEARNING THE WAY SCIENTISTS LEARN

One highly skeptical faculty member told us that an artificial environment is being created—that faculty are setting students up for failure, and that because students are being "coddled" in the GSW groups, when they get out into the real world they will be in for a sorry surprise. Yet the GSW environment more closely resembles the "real world" of collaborative science than do the traditional course structure and culture.

Many of the GSW students, even those who have had extensive science experience in high school, do not have a realistic image of the importance of collaboration in scientific work. When we ask students for their image of the practicing scientist, they say things like "Scientists spend lots and lots of time in the lab," but they almost never mention that scientists are in the lab *working with other people*. An expert panel on science education[1] once reported that science is "too often viewed as the retreat of the lone genius." Indeed, research studies looking into how young people view science demonstrate that many hold the belief that scientists work in relative isolation.[2] They grow up learning about the achievements of individual scientists—Galileo Galilei, Benjamin Franklin, Thomas Edison, Marie Curie, Albert Einstein—with little understanding of how discovery now occurs in scientific communities.

Scientists cannot work in isolation. The preeminent American chemist Joel Hildebrand described precisely this kind of collaboration in his biographical memoir of fellow chemist Gilbert Newton Lewis. Under Lewis's leadership at the University of California, Hildebrand recounted,

> there were no divisions within the department in either organization or spirit. All met together to discuss chemistry, organic, inorganic, or physical, alike. . . . Anyone who thought he had a bright idea rushed out to try it out on a colleague. Groups of two or more could be seen every day in offices, be-

fore blackboards or even in corridors, arguing vehemently about these "brain storms." It is doubtful whether any paper ever emerged for publication that had not run the gauntlet of such criticism. The whole department thus became far greater than the sum of its individual members.[3]

While competition fuels discovery, taken too far it can threaten the fruits of this collaborative enterprise. Students can become overly competitive, particularly in the "weed-out" courses that scare them into cramming lest they land on the wrong end of the curve. Term after term, GSW students complain about the intense competitiveness. Many see it as a fact of life, something they will have to put up with until they make it through the other end. But for many talented others, it makes the prospect of continuing in science less attractive. This sort of intense competitiveness has been shown in the research time and time again to be a harmful factor in learning environments.[4] Richard Light,[5] for example, in interviews with more than a thousand Harvard undergraduates found the same phenomenon: undergrads feeling an intense sense of competition for grades in science courses and avoiding science for this reason. In fact, the higher the competition, the more students cheat. So students, professors, and the institution at large all bear the burden of high levels of competitiveness.[6]

These competitive environments create what is known in social psychology as "negative interdependence"—individuals within a group believing that they can achieve their goals only when other members of the group do *not* achieve their own. By contrast, cooperative environments promote *positive* interdependence, or the sense that one achieves one's goals *because* others in the group are also achieving their own. Each person's success promotes the success of the group. In fact, research bears out the advantages of cooperative groups, which tend to solve problems more effectively than do competitive groups.[7] In the words of Sharon, a GSW biology student:

> I get the most out of the sessions when the atmosphere is one of collaboration and a desire to learn the concepts, and not just to perform well on tests. The nature of the science courses at Northwestern is one of competition due to the presence of a curve. But the GSW sessions provide a momentary respite from those where students come and work together to learn the material, rather than stressing out about performing better than each other.

We should take a moment here to distinguish between productive and unproductive competition. The sort of fierce, individualistic competition we have been talking about, which often characterizes science courses (particularly at highly selective schools), clearly has undesirable effects on students. But there are other kinds of competition. For instance, *intergroup* competition, or competition among small groups, has been shown in the research to motivate individuals to work cooperatively and to strive for success, without the sense of individual failure that characterizes more individualistic environments.[8] And, not surprisingly, this is most often the way professional scientists compete.

These lessons have not been lost on the world of science education, from individual faculty members to policy makers. Increasingly, *students learning together* has become a feature of science, technology, engineering, and mathematics (STEM) curricula around the United States. In fact, the National Science Foundation has funded large-scale programs (such as peer-led team learning (PLTL), process-oriented guided inquiry learning (POGIL), and Workshop Biology)[9] that incorporate small-group learning into the curriculum and turn traditional lecture-based science courses into collaborative learning environments.

WHAT DOES "GOOD GROUP LEARNING" LOOK LIKE?

Of course simply collaborating does not mean one is collaborating well, or benefiting from the collaboration. Collaborative learning will not work well if there is little support for it from the instructor—and support can range from providing time and space for groups to meet to "training" students on how to work together effectively. Collaborative learning will not work well if all students are underprepared, or if only some students participate actively. It will not work well if teachers fail to give students clear, meaningful tasks to accomplish.[10]

It is also clear, however, from research on the GSW program (see Chapter 1)—and from the vast body of research that has been conducted on collaborative learning—that under the right circumstances, students who work together do well. They perform highly on assessments, stick with their classes, and feel good about the material they are studying.[11] But what are those "right circumstances"? Even with excellent goals, material, support, and leadership, an array of other factors will influence how well a learning group performs. The leader's personality, the personality of the group members, the mixture of skill level and advance preparation in the group, the gender and ethnic composition of the group, and even the physical environment and time of day can have an impact on the group's performance.

When we first started the GSW program, we trained peer facilitators to promote collaboration and in-depth discussion in the groups. (We will elaborate on the facilitator training in Chapter 5.) Initially it was easy to monitor this: we had only a handful of facilitators and groups, so we could regularly check in with facilitators and visit groups to see how they were functioning. But after several years we began to wonder whether the groups were holding to these guidelines—and, indeed, whether these guidelines did help students learn. So we ran a two-year observational study, observing 159 GSW learning groups, comprising 646 students.[12]

In the first phase of the study, we were interested in simply identifying the key differences among groups. After observing a number of these groups, we noticed that there was a division among the groups in two respects. First, while in some groups the facilitators encouraged the students to actively participate, in others the facilitators acted more as information givers, doing most of the talking themselves. For instance, some facilitators would seem to purposefully hang back, giving students lots of time to think and respond, while others tended to jump in and answer questions themselves. Second, while in some groups students went beyond their assigned problems to explore deeper meaning and make conceptual connections, in other groups students stuck to the worksheets, moving on to the next problem once they had arrived at a correct solution. For example, in some groups we heard lots of "why" and "how" questions—Why do you say that? How did you get that answer? How is that approach different from this one?—while in other groups, the answer was simply a prompt to move on to the next question. We used these two dimensions to form a four-quadrant group typology (see Figure 4.1).

		Group Interaction Style	
		Facilitator-Directed	Collaborative
Problem-Solving Approach	Basic	Lecturing	Organizing
	Elaborated	Instructing	Guiding

Figure 4.1   Four Approaches to Facilitating

Note: For a fuller description of the development of the group typology and the resulting observation instrument, see Pazos, P., Micari, M., and Light, G. (2010) Developing an instrument to characterize peer-led groups in collaborative learning environments: Assessing problem-solving approach and group interaction. *Assessment and Evaluation in Higher Education* 35(2): 191–208.

We called the groups with the facilitators who took an information-giving approach "facilitator-directed" and the groups with more active participation "collaborative." Groups that stopped discussing once they had reached the right answer were described as taking a "basic" approach, and those that went on to explore concepts as taking an "elaborated" approach. By putting the two dimensions together, we came up with four facilitator approaches in the groups: lecturing, or giving fairly straightforward information on how to solve problems; instructing, or giving a more elaborate explanation of how to solve problems; organizing, where there is a focus on getting the students simply to work together to run through the problems; and guiding, where the facilitator organizes the students to work together but with the goal of exploring the material beyond what is required by the problems.[13]

Based on these distinctions we developed an observation guide that enabled us to "type" a large number of groups. Once we had categorized the groups, we looked to see whether students in one type of group did better in their courses than students in other types of groups. And, indeed, we found that students in groups that we had classified as "lecturing" earned the lowest grades.[14] In other words students in groups where the facilitator took charge rather than encouraged students to participate fully, and where the group was satisfied to get the right answer and move on, did not fare as well in the course as the other students.

In general, the greater the participation and the greater the elaboration of concepts, the better. And there is no lack of empirical research to support this.[15] The learning literature is clear that in order for students to benefit from learning together, they must

- be *actively involved* in their own learning;
- work with *relative independence,* being guided—but not led—by instructors;
- engage in open *discussion, question and critique* one another's ideas, and *reflect* on their own ideas; and
- engage with material at a *deep level* rather than superficially.

MAKING KNOWLEDGE ONE'S OWN

As we saw in Chapter 2, to learn effectively students need to construct their own knowledge. Learning does not happen because teachers and authors feed data to learners; it happens because learners engage with authors, teachers, and peers—and engage with *themselves* to effectively manage the process of their own learning.

Peer groups benefit students because they expose students to a wide range of thinking styles, approaches to learning, problem-solving strategies, and ways of understanding the course material. Sara, one of the very first GSW math students, said, "If you hear someone's idea and you can't really understand it, someone else might try to explain it another way." Rasha, another student, in physics, elaborated on this:

> I think the whole reason group learning works is because people are able to take the information that they learn and take a different angle to it than somebody else's. . . . One thing about knowledge is that when you're able to approach it from many different angles, you're able to get a better understanding of it.

This "one thing about knowledge" is critical. Anybody who has had the experience of suddenly seeing something in a new light, and realizing they had not fully grasped it before, will understand this concept. When we learn, we are comparing our old perspectives and approaches to the perspectives and approaches we see others using, and we are making decisions about which we ought to keep, discard, or reshape.

To benefit further from the group, learners need to help one another work beyond their current capabilities in order to progress—to provide the "scaffolding" that enables learners to construct knowledge, but not so much that the "constructing" is being done for them.[16] In the GSW program, peer leaders play this critical role (which we will explore further in Chapter 5). They are close enough to the students' own developmental level to be able to provide empathetic, relevant support, and—an added benefit—they provide a model of a student who has "made it through" the course successfully, helping to boost a learner's self-efficacy, or the sense that she or he can make it too.[17]

Returning to the group-type model, GSW students in the best-functioning groups—in which the facilitator takes the "guiding" approach—are doing the following:

- *They are responsible for their learning* in ways not usually found in the traditional course experience. This happens partly because the GSW is a voluntary program: students take part because they want to. They are also responsible in the sense that there is no teacher telling them what to do; they are collaboratively guiding the process themselves.

- *They are working to develop their own knowledge* rather than being "given" knowledge from a teacher. This learning-centered approach, in which the student creates meaning for himself or herself, is contrasted with the more traditional "transmission" model, in which the teacher "sends out" knowledge to be acquired by the student.

- *They are processing information at fairly high levels* rather than simply remembering facts. A solid foundation of knowledge is important, but more important is understanding that knowledge and what to do with it. We designed the GSW to engage students in the same kind of thinking that their professors engage in, albeit with less complex problems.

- *They are listening to and considering multiple approaches* and multiple ways of understanding the material and evaluating these. Just as scientists do, students benefit from seeing how others approach problems. They may ultimately decide not to take those approaches, but simply by considering them they are diversifying the set of tools they have for approaching any problem and broadening the way they understand the problem itself.

- *They are reflecting on their learning.* The act of working through problems together, out loud, and with critical feedback is also an act of reflection on learning. Rasha, the student who talked about approaching knowledge from different angles, underscored this: she was talking not just about learning but about *metacognitive* skill—skill at managing your own process of learning. Looking at how others approach problems, she says, not only helps you solve the problems but also helps you "get past why you can't figure out what you need to do."

FOUR KEYS TO A HEALTHY LEARNING GROUP

One of the stickiest questions we have faced in developing the GSW program is how to ensure the quality of the small-group dynamic. Facilitators often come to us concerned that some members do not contribute, that others dominate, that cliques seem to be developing, that the men contribute but not the women, or that some group members do not show up regularly.

In fact these problems are common to groups of many kinds. Group dynamics are tricky (to say the least), and we have no one-size-fits-all solution to offer. Instead, we train facilitators in group dynamics, so that they will be better equipped to recognize and address problems—or at least to know when to ask for help.

More than anything else, groups need clear goals, appropriate material, adequate support, and solid leadership. We have seen these four factors—whether by their presence or their absence—make the difference between a group whose members feel enthusiastic, contribute actively, and learn at deep levels and a group whose members see the group work as yet another task to complete, unsure of exactly why they are participating.

Clear Goals

One of the GSW math facilitators recently commented that in her groups there are always students who "don't really want to put a lot into GSW; they just expect it to give them a better grade." Some students view the program almost as a sort of medication, something you "take" to acquire the intended effect. As another facilitator put it, "In each group there is one person just sitting there, like, 'Explain it to me. Teach it to me.' I almost wish that we could specify before we start the group: If you are going to be ready to do the problems, sign up for this group. If not, there is another group over there for you."

But we do not have a two-tiered program: we expect all of our students to be ready to learn. The unrealistic expectations these facilitators described can cause problems for the student and for the group: the student is disappointed and may not want to stick with the program, or may disengage, and this in turn diminishes the motivation and enthusiasm of the group.

Group members need to know why they are coming together. If an instructor says to the group "Get together and study these problems," are the students supposed to focus on finding the answers? On finding the best approach to working through the problems? On identifying alternative approaches? On more deeply investigating the concepts within the problems?

When the goal is deep learning, it is difficult to manage students' expectations, particularly since most of them have been trained to expect a transmission approach, where the teacher transmits information and the student receives it and repeats it back to the teacher on the exam. It is important to counter that model from the start. We tell students that joining the program does not guarantee a better grade but, rather, if they work hard and take full advantage of the group they should understand the material at a deeper level. We also have facilitators talk to students on the first day of the workshop about the fundamental goal of the GSW program—to engage students in the deep-level processing of problems—and to tell them that while they may be reviewing course content here and there, the purpose of the sessions is *not* to prep for exams.

Appropriate Material

As we described in the last chapter, one of the quality-control checks we use is a weekly problem-evaluation form. After his or her session, each group facilitator submits a form assigning a score to, and commenting on, the worksheet problems. When the problems do not work well, the group does not function well. When facilitators say, for instance, "Problem 3 was really confusing and nobody understood what to do," or "Problem 5 covered material that nobody has studied yet, and they got frustrated and couldn't do it," they also tend to tell us that the group was not as productive, did not have as much energy, and simply did not run as smoothly as usual.

On the other hand, when faculty provided the groups with problems that were challenging and *conceptual*—more than just "plug-and-chug"-type problems—the groups were much more energized and active. Conceptual problems require students to do more than simply memorize formulas; students need to be able to use formulas in novel ways, and understand how particular formulas or concepts are relevant in a variety of situations, to solve the problems. As one GSW engineering student told us, "The problems were often difficult, but they helped you to understand the concepts. It was more than just *put this number in and solve it*. You had to think about how to get to where you can put a formula together."

Adequate Support

In end-of-year surveys and interviews with students, *support* figures prominently among the factors that either promote or hinder a good group-learning experience. Students frequently say things like, "My facilitator really guided me through some hard problems, and that made the experience great!" or "I got so much great advice about what classes to take, how to apply to med school—that was an invaluable part of the GSW experience," or "My facilitator made me feel comfortable trying to answer questions in the group." But the value of support becomes even more evident when support is missing. From time to time, a student may say something like, "My facilitator really did not help us through the problems, and we often felt stuck," or "Sometimes the group did not communicate well, and the facilitator didn't seem to know what to do," or "I felt intimidated to participate because other people talked all the time, and I wish my facilitator had done something about it."

We think about support for groups in three ways: individual support, interpersonal support, and academic support.

Individual support. Individual support provides group members who are struggling with material with another source of help. For instance, some first-year students in the GSW have not taken the high school AP classes that many of their fellow group members have taken, and these students often find themselves feeling overwhelmed in the group discussions. We talk continually with facilitators about the importance of staying alert to how their students are experiencing the workshop—if they are quiet, why is that? Are they struggling with the material? Did they not do the reading? Are they intimidated by others in the group? We tell facilitators to offer support— through conversation after the session, an extra one-on-one meeting to clear up confusion, a referral to a professor's office hours or to a tutoring program. When facilitators are unsure of how to help, we are happy to step in—but more often than not, the facilitators are able to handle these situations, and they enjoy it. "Facilitating was a really good experience. To be someone's mentor puts a lot of responsibility on you," said Damien. "They put a lot of trust in you."

Individual support becomes especially critical when stereotypes come into play. Stereotyping works in both directions: students might feel they are stereotyped as less able and thus feel added pressure to live down the stereotype, or they might feel that they are stereotyped as more intelligent and feel added pressure to live up to it. Many GSW students have spoken openly about this. Alana, a physics student, told us:

> I was a student in a workshop, with a male Indian facilitator. Everyone else was all male Indians except for me and one other girl. It was weird. It was so bad in the beginning. I was like, "I've got to switch out of this!" I was really intimidated. Indian guys are known to be really smart, at least, stereotypically.

Other students had the opposite concern, that somebody might see them as less able because of a stereotype—and this is when stereotype threat[18]—the worry that you will confirm a negative stereotype about your group and a subsequent drop in performance level—comes into play. Courtney, a facilitator in engineering, said:

> As a facilitator . . . I felt they wouldn't think I am as good because I am black. It is not an issue, but I just felt that it might be. . . . You get stereotypes about who is good at science. . . . You can see some premed African Americans, but you don't see too many engineers. That's why I thought the students will think that I wasn't good enough. But I found that they don't think so.

Interpersonal support.   Consider the group led by Ryan, one of the senior facilitators in biology. Ryan came to the GSW office one afternoon early in the fall quarter looking weary. He told us that his group was "really not meshing well." After a little probing we learned that in this group of six there were two women who were close friends and who tended to sit and work together, interacting very little with other group members; that one group member was always way ahead of the rest and sometimes made condescending comments about others' wrong answers; that one was often late or absent; and that the last student in the group simply seemed perplexed at this strange dynamic—as Ryan was himself.

We suggested some fairly simple remedies: have the students pair off with different partners to split up the two friends; remind students repeatedly that giving a wrong answer is just as valuable as giving the right answer, as long as the group uses that wrong answer to figure out how to make corrections; and talk to the often-late student about the negative impact of her tardiness on the group (and on her own ability to remain in the group, since too many tardies or absences can mean expulsion from the program). Ryan tried these approaches—along with some others. At the end of the term he reported that his group had greatly improved. And his student evaluations reflected that improvement: all six reported having liked the group experience, and two added comments that Ryan had helped ensure that everybody felt comfortable participating.

Academic support.   Several years ago one of the organic chemistry professors called us, frustrated, to say that he thought the facilitators needed better training in the subject matter. In his weekly meetings with them, he saw them struggling, and he was hearing from his students that the workshops were confusing and that the facilitators did not appear to understand the material well. We also talked with the facilitators themselves and found that many felt that the preparation sessions with faculty felt rushed, so that they were leaving confused and frustrated that they did not understand the material better. We decided that the facilitators would benefit from longer, or at least slower-paced, preparation sessions spending more time on each problem, even if that meant going over fewer problems. We also asked that group of facilitators to spend more time reviewing the material before their workshops. By the end of the term, the facilitators felt more confident in their workshop sessions, and the students' concerns had eased. This experience also taught us the value of open lines of communication in an academic program that has multiple players.

The support the GSW offers may be especially valuable for underrepresented students and women. In a small interview-based study we conducted of twenty-six GSW students, we talked with students about what it was about GSW that they valued most.[19] Students' answers fell into two main categories. All emphasized the GSW's role in helping them master material, but while some talked only about this, others also highlighted the importance of the comfortable social environment in allowing that mastery to occur. For some students, feeling comfortable and supported by peers appeared to help make mastery of the material more possible. Of the nine students in that category, only one was a majority-group student (defined in the study as white or Asian/Asian American). Seven were minority-group (defined as African American or Hispanic) women, and one was a minority-group man. These findings echo a good deal of other research showing that for students from underrepresented minority groups, social integration and academic integration into the learning community are especially critical.[20] In fact, the comfortable GSW environment may mitigate the stereotype threat effect by reducing competitiveness, encouraging mistakes as part of the learning process, and emphasizing the value of contribution to the process over getting the right answer. The ample research on stereotype threat has shown repeatedly that when group identity is made salient—whether through direct mention of group differences, by the task being viewed as high-stakes, or by the task being described as a test of natural ability—people who are members of groups stereotyped as deficient at a task will perform more poorly on that task. This effect has been demonstrated in children and adults, in men and women, and across ethnic groups. Among the educational practices that have been suggested in the literature as likely to counter stereotype threat are environments that encourage cross-group friendships, role models belonging to the student's identity group, an emphasis on learning rather than on performance, high expectations, and affirmation of students' potential to learn.[21]

Solid Leadership

Peer learning groups need leadership, direct or indirect. In some cases this leadership might come from the course instructor, who should establish clear learning goals and provide appropriate material and support, and in other cases the group might have an assigned leader, such as the peer facilitators we use in the GSW program.

Leaders can take a variety of approaches, ranging from very directive and structured to much more laissez-faire. Neither of these extremes is wrong; the key is to match leadership style to the learning environment. In the GSW we want to move facilitators toward the "guiding" quadrant of the four-square model, so we encourage them to err more on the side of coaching from the sidelines than providing direct instruction. David Jaques, in his highly regarded book on group learning, talks about this difference in leadership approach in terms of a continuum ranging from "information-giving" to "echoing," or using open-ended questions to help the group refine its own direction.[22] We tell GSW facilitators that as part of an over-all "guiding" strategy there may be times when they will need to take a more traditional information-giving approach, for instance, to ensure that everyone has basic material when group members have not adequately reviewed ahead of time. But, as much as we all would occasionally like someone to simply give us the answers, most students know deep down that the best teachers help them find the answers themselves—and those students appreciate it. As one of the GSW biology students told us very enthusiastically, "I love my facilitator! She's awesome; she's really cool. She didn't feed us answers, but she guided us. Intellectually, I felt challenged."

THE NUTS AND BOLTS OF LEARNING GROUPS

In this section we offer some suggestions—based on lessons we have learned—for establishing learning groups that truly help students learn.

How Can Students Be Motivated to Join?

When students decide not to join the GSW, or when they start and drop the program in the first weeks, we always ask them why they made that decision. By far, the number-one answer we hear is "I didn't have time for it." Many students feel so overwhelmed by their courses and other obligations that joining a learning group seems like just one more activity taking them away from time they need for studying. But we have found that, in the end, a study group can actually help students *save* time by making their study time more effective and efficient. In one of the very early studies of the GSW program, Wendy Born and her colleagues found that GSW students actually *decreased* the amount of time studying outside of the workshop and still did better in the course than the students not participating in the GSW did.[23] Once students have been with the program for a while, they almost invariably say that the study time in the group was more valuable than solo study time would have been.

Who Should Participate?

Since we had always had some concern that the GSW might erroneously be perceived as a remedial program, a year or so into the program we began to informally canvass students about their perceptions of whom the program was meant to serve. Some students seemed to think that the GSW best served struggling students, while others held the opposite belief—that the GSW was for advanced students, and that it was *hard*.

In reality—as we touched on earlier in this chapter—learning groups can work well for everyone, provided the group is a healthy one. In fact, there is a real advantage to including people with a variety of backgrounds and perspectives in a problem-solving group. One of the salient themes that emerged from the focus groups and interviews with GSW students was *the value of being exposed to other perspectives*. One of our interviewees, for instance, told us, "You just get to hear different [ideas] when you're working through a problem. Sometimes you hear one person who thinks to solve it this way, and it's wrong—but that's a *good* thing, because you get to see everyone's thought processes and why things don't work out a certain way." This student is on to something: being asked to take a new perspective on a problem, whatever sort of problem, is productive even when that action does not lead to a solution. The more different "takes" a student has on a problem, the more likely she or he is to understand why some work better than others, and which ultimately will work best.

Skill-level diversity can also be an asset, although it is often not viewed that way. The research shows that when students with different skill levels work together, less advanced students tend to do well in groups where there is a greater mix of skill level, while more advanced students tend to do well in all kinds of groups.[24] In mixed-skill groups, less advanced students get to ask questions and hear explanations from more advanced peers, and more advanced students get to "teach" the concepts, reinforcing and elaborating on their own knowledge. To take advantage of the benefits of group diversity, students may need to overcome certain barriers that diverse groups can present. For instance, GSW facilitators sometimes report that less advanced students feel intimidated and reluctant to participate, and more skilled students feel frustrated over having to slow their pace to help other group members understand the ideas. A skilled leader can help the group navigate these roadblocks. We encourage facilitators to, for example, occasionally pair less and more advanced students so that one student gets a one-on-one explanation and the other has an opportunity to talk through his or her ideas, have less advanced students work at the board while others guide them through a problem, or provide review and extra coaching for less advanced students when necessary. And providing group members with some instruction on how to effectively support one another—probing for reasoning behind answers, for instance—ensures that all students feel comfortable sharing their ideas.

Student diversity—in all senses of the word—also plays a critical role in *who participates* in the groups. Students who have less background or feel less skilled in the subject matter, students who are shy and feel uncomfortable being in the spotlight, and students who are in the minority in terms of their gender or ethnicity—may be reluctant to participate fully. Ethnically diverse groups may have to overcome more interpersonal challenges than less diverse teams do,[25] and a number of educational studies have shown that people who may feel marginalized in a group—for example, ethnic minority students or women in a mostly male group—participate less than others.[26] In more everyday terms, people may simply feel less comfortable in a group where they do not see other people who are like them. As physics student Kristie put it: "I think just the comfort level is higher in a group of all girls. Like I sometimes feel like we have the same kind of feedback and communication styles."

The good news is that diverse learning groups *can* be productive for all their members, and with relatively little intervention. Biology facilitator Mailee, who is Asian, said, "I think in the beginning maybe the Asians felt more comfortable talking to me." But, Mailee added, "I think by three or four weeks in, it doesn't matter anymore; we are kind of all the same." Creating an open, friendly atmosphere, modeling respectful and constructive feedback, and giving everyone a chance to be heard are a few simple things the group leader can do to help ensure that all students succeed in a diverse group.

How Big Should the Groups Be?

At one point we had a situation in the GSW physics groups that underscored the importance of group size. The physics department, in an effort to engage students by providing multiple learning environments, told students that they had two choices: they could either sign up for teaching assistant recitation sections or join the GSW program. Much to the department's surprise (and ours), we were inundated with registration requests. Our program coordinator badly wanted to accommodate all of the students who wanted to join the program, and so we turned no one away—but this meant that some of the groups comprised up to a dozen students.

Our mistake quickly became apparent. Within the first week, we heard from facilitators and students alike that the groups were not functioning well: some students said they did not have the opportunity to speak, others complained that the conversation was difficult to control, and facilitators simply felt overwhelmed by the number of students for whom they were responsible.

We wasted no time recruiting more facilitators, but the message hit home: twelve is too many. Conventional wisdom holds that the ideal size for a peer learning group is five to seven students. Although only a small amount of research supports this claim, and although some research suggests that groups of fewer than five work well,[27] the five-to-seven rule of thumb makes sense. With fewer than five or so students in a group, you run the risk that all of the students will struggle with the same kinds of problems or have the same misconceptions—so little learning would take place. With more than seven or so, the group can easily become unwieldy and unbalanced, with the more confident or assertive students stealing the show.[28]

What Are the Ground Rules?

At a recent facilitator training session, we asked how many in the group had developed ground rules for their workshop groups, which is something we suggest at the beginning-of-year orientation. Nobody raised a hand. We were dismayed: Why had they not taken our advice?

We probed a little and learned that many of the facilitators felt sheepish about devising ground rules: "I'm not their teacher; I'm their age," one said, and another chimed in, "Yeah, it would just be really awkward to do that." Others said they felt that the groups did not need ground rules—that they would know how to behave, and if there were problems, they would "just handle it."

Some groups "click": the chemistry among members is such that the group functions well without any effort explicitly devoted to group maintenance. But most groups need some guidance about how to work effectively, and when problems do occur, it is not at all easy to "just handle" them. As we noted earlier in this chapter, a solid set of ground rules is the best way we know of to provide this guidance. When facilitators told us they felt embarrassed about imposing ground rules, we realized we had not sufficiently made the point that the ground rules can be (and really should be) developed by the group itself. Typically this happens at the first group meeting and should address the group's expectations around how group members will behave and interact with one another. For instance, we tell our facilitators to say something along the lines of "Okay, what are the expectations we all have of one another?" and group members might agree that they should all come prepared, will show up on time, will provide only constructive critiques of one another's ideas, and will help ensure that no single person dominates the conversation. In our experience, when all group members participate in developing ground rules they are likely to all feel invested in upholding them. There are a number of techniques for creating ground rules, but one that works particularly well is to have each

group member spend a few minutes remembering positive and negative group experiences and jotting down what she or he thinks
made those groups work well or not so well. Then, based on what
students have written, we suggest that facilitators have group members collaboratively devise a list of "dos and don'ts" for the group.
Some of the facilitators spend a good chunk of the first session talking with group members about good group-work skills, such as
asking productive questions, giving constructive feedback, taking
turns effectively, and listening actively, and, while they have to give
up a little bit of group time to do this, they uniformly report that
the discussion pays off later.

One of the ground rules we set for the groups is mandatory attendance (with allowances for excused absences) for the full term.
Groups need time to gel, and that will not happen if group membership changes from week to week. There is a great deal of research
on small groups that shows that groups have life cycles and, like living things, do not mature until some development has occurred. In
newly formed groups, individuals tend to trust one another less,
be more self-focused, and base their judgments of one another
more on stereotypes than is the case in more mature groups. Mature groups are also better able to resolve conflict and complete
challenging tasks.[29] So while one-off groups can work well with
quick in-class exercises, learning groups need sustained and regular membership.

What Should the Group Do if Things Go Badly?

Groups are, in a sense, living things, and so even with the best planning they sometimes experience growing pains. Through conversations with GSW peer facilitators, we have found that the most

critical problems that arise in the groups include varying levels of preparedness among students, students feeling intimidated to share their ideas or admit that they do not understand, and the variation in students' learning styles or preferences.

Students with varying levels of preparedness. Most typically, students in the GSW are at approximately the same level of understanding, but it is not uncommon to have one or two students who are much further ahead of, or further behind, the others. This can lead to negative feelings that undermine group effectiveness: intimidation and reduced self-confidence among less advanced students and frustration and annoyance among more advanced students. As we mentioned earlier in this chapter, mixed-ability groups offer certain advantages, but these cannot be realized unless the group is managed carefully.

In the first instance the group facilitator needs to be paying attention to the student who seems to be zipping through the material, who is working at a fairly "normal" pace, and who appears to be struggling. If there is an imbalance, the facilitator can take steps to restructure the group. As mentioned earlier, a common approach is to break the group up into smaller groups or pairs. Such pairs or groups can be mixed so that the student further ahead guides the other student, or they can be more uniform so that students who are at about the same level are working together at their own pace. Both arrangements can be effective, but success depends on the difficulty of the material, the mood of the group, and the group's history. When the material is difficult, pairing more advanced and less advanced students can help, since two less advanced students working together may wind up feeling stuck. When the material is more straightforward, or when there is a facilitator nearby to offer guidance, homogenous pairs may work well—with the particular advantage that less advanced students can experience success in arriving at the correct solution. We recommend that facilitators vary the approaches they take so that students are sometimes in more uniform and sometimes in more mixed pairings.

Another technique that many facilitators find works well is to use one student's questions to help the whole group. As a biology facilitator told us in speaking about students who are "lost," "I tell them, 'show us where you got lost, where you got hung up,' and then I help the others explain to them their train of thought, their processing, really. We'll work through it so that the person then understands."

Students feeling shy about sharing ideas or worried about demonstrating a lack of understanding. Even though most students tell us that the GSW small-group setting is much more comfortable than the large-class environment, a number of students still feel nervous about answering questions out loud in a group. This reluctance can stem from a variety of factors: being introverted, not having done the reading, lacking confidence, lacking prior preparation, and so on. In a survey-based study we conducted among GSW students, we found that about 10 percent of students felt more than mildly concerned about looking bad in front of the group, and that about 5 percent felt more than mildly uncomfortable in the groups. We also found that students who felt intimidated within the group were at greater risk for dropping out of the program and for not doing as well in the course as the other students.[30] To counteract these tendencies, we encourage facilitators to try to learn something about what the root causes of students' reluctance are by, for instance, engaging them in informal conversation after the session. Promoting a comfortable, open atmosphere where mistakes are encouraged can increase the odds that students will participate actively. As one of the facilitators put it, "I think that we've got that kind of atmosphere where saying 'I don't know' isn't this horrible thing any longer, because everyone at one point or another has stumbled upon that." And a biology student told us, "At first I was embarrassed to ask questions, but now I see that it's okay to ask questions, because other people get stuck on the same thing."

When all of the students, even the "best" ones, occasionally fail to answer correctly, each has permission to fail. Just as scientists need to allow room to fail in running experiments, students need permission to fail as they face the challenges of learning. As Thomas Edison is often quoted as saying on the merits of failure, "I have not failed; I've just found 10,000 ways that won't work."[31] Students will have the freedom to fail only when the group encourages active involvement—the "guiding" quadrant in the group-type model. Groups in which students feel they should simply follow a leader's direction, or in which they are not asked to push beyond simply getting the answer, do not encourage the healthy risk-taking that promotes learning.

Instructors should be creating environments where failing is *valued* as a vital part of the process of learning and discovery. Group facilitators can do this by modeling failure themselves (trying to solve a very challenging problem in front of the class, for instance); by rewarding students for their failed attempts and noting how the failure helps move the group along ("That was a great effort, and it helped us all understand why the X principle does not apply in this sort of case, and when it does apply"); and by explicitly asking for failed attempts ("I expect you to fail from time to time. If we aren't doing that, it's a sign that we're not trying hard enough"). Ideally, we would develop in students the attitude demonstrated by Jonathan, a GSW physics student:

> I *wish* the other students would critique my stuff. I love criticism. Especially in math and science, because if I was doing a math problem one way and somebody has another suggestion or wanted to show me why I was doing something wrong, I'm sure they'd have a very good reason.

Students' varied learning preferences.   GSW facilitators frequently tell us that they struggle with trying to please everyone in the group, for instance, when some students want to simply talk through a problem and others want to discuss how the problem relates to real-life situations, or when some students want to work individually and others want to work as a whole group. They ask us if they should be trying to tailor their approach to students' learning styles.

Many different learning styles or learning preferences are identified in the educational literature, and many models exist to help explain how people differ in the ways in which they learn. Some of these models are considered more valid than others, but what is clear is that people tend to take different approaches in learning situations. Some enjoy debating and eagerly participate in group discussion, some prefer to read or reflect quietly before participating, some enjoy working in front of the group, and others prefer to work on their own.

But facilitators (and instructors) cannot tailor their teaching approaches to each student's desires, nor should they. Students themselves are often unaware of how they learn best, and even if they are aware, they will benefit from trying out new approaches.

Our advice to facilitators is to (1) vary the approaches they use in the group so that everyone has a chance to use a variety of approaches, and (2) make this practice explicit to group members. By using a number of different approaches, students enjoy using the ones with which they are most comfortable, but they also nudge themselves to try unfamiliar or less comfortable approaches. This can help them become more adaptable learners and may offer the additional benefit of helping them learn new things in new ways. In doing so they are developing the important metacognitive skills we described earlier. For instance, an efficiency-oriented student who wants to stick to the problems on the worksheet may very well begin to see new connections if he is persuaded to adapt concepts from those problems to real-world issues. And, in contrast, the student who always looks for the big picture (for instance, how a concept relates to other concepts) but ignores some of the details can become a more efficient and effective learner by being pushed to work carefully through each of the problems. Further, if the leader explicitly tells the group that they will be using different approaches, and that some people may be more or less comfortable with each, she sets up realistic expectations and avoids some of the frustration students can experience when faced with a learning task that runs counter to their natural preferences.

Some years ago the Committee on Science, Engineering, and Public Policy of the National Academy of Sciences published a report noting that "science is inherently a social enterprise—in sharp contrast to a popular stereotype of science as a lonely, isolated search for the truth. With few exceptions, scientific research cannot be done without drawing on the work of others or collaborating with others."[32] Just as scientists can experience an internal struggle between the desire to work independently and the practical need for collaborative work, college students can feel frustrated working in groups when working on their own is logistically easier and encouraged by a culture of competition. What persuades professional scientists to work collaboratively is the knowledge that to get their work done successfully, they need the exchange of resources, critique, and inspiration that comes with collaborative work. The GSW program is one larger-scale attempt to create such an environment that mirrors this professional reality. But more modest efforts within and outside the classroom can also make a difference. An informal study group, say, that meets before each exam can help increase the chances for success of each of its members beyond what each could do studying individually. And that is the real goal of collaborative work: to create something greater than the sum of the individual contributions of each member.

SUGGESTIONS FOR PRACTICE

To enhance group dynamics:

- stress collaboration rather than competition;
- provide support and leadership;
- keep learning groups relatively small (five to seven, as a rule of thumb);

- help learning groups develop ground rules for participation; and
- ensure learning groups have clear goals.

To encourage engagement with problems:

- create diverse learning groups so that students are exposed to multiple perspectives, and so that less experienced students can benefit from their more experienced peers;
- allow peer leaders to provide "scaffolding" to push students beyond their current capabilities;
- create learning groups that dig deep into problems;
- ensure that the group, and not just the group leader, is actively engaged in problem solving; and
- provide groups with high-quality material that will prompt engaged discussion.

FIVE

Mentoring Learning

> When I ask an educated person, "What was the most
> significant experience in your education?," I almost
> never get back an idea but almost always a person.
>
> —D. C. Tosteson

WHEN GATEWAY SCIENCE WORK-
shop (GSW) student Prasad told his facilitator that he was thinking
of dropping out of the program, we knew about it within the hour.
The facilitator, Abby, left the workshop group and walked directly
to our building, climbed the stairs, stepped into the middle of the
GSW office, and exclaimed, "One of my students wants to drop, and
we can't let him!"

After finding a seat for Abby and talking through the situation,
we learned that Prasad was feeling overwhelmed with a heavy
course load and pressured by extracurricular obligations, and that
the GSW seemed like one of the few things he could take off his
plate. We suggested that Abby talk to him about the pressures he
was feeling but also reinforce the benefits of the GSW and ask
whether there was anything else he might first be able to eliminate.
Ultimately, Prasad decided to temporarily give up a leadership role

in a student club and stick with the GSW, and he ended up doing well in his courses that term.

Abby's concern for Prasad was not unusual. We see facilitators develop real bonds with their students and a real sense of responsibility for their academic and personal well-being. As mentors, that is what they should be doing. We cannot train them to care, but quite often that is what happens. Through the training we do provide, the weekly experiences they have with the students, and their own leadership instincts, over the year the facilitators become genuine mentors to their students.

We have tried hard to make sure that the GSW provides high-quality mentoring to undergraduates, and much of our motivation comes from our knowledge that without the GSW, most of these students will not receive much, if any, true academic mentoring during college.

For professional scientists, mentoring is critical. As graduate students and postdocs, scientists develop close working relationships with senior faculty who coach and advise them, and as practicing professionals they often continue these relationships and develop new, more mutual coaching relationships with colleagues. All of this happens within a community of practice (see Chapter 6), with the senior "core" of the community developing those who will someday occupy their place. For undergraduates, though, genuine mentoring relationships are generally restricted to the lucky, well connected, or exceptionally talented.

But that is beginning to change. Mentoring has recently taken a more prominent position in science education (and higher education generally), and it is increasingly an explicit part of what students of science are expected to experience throughout their training.[1]

The more mentoring gains prominence for aspiring scientists at all levels, the more access undergraduates will have to it. Undergraduates who receive effective mentoring are more likely to finish college, to do well in college, and to enjoy their college experiences.[2] Mentors help mentees develop, assess, and reach academic and professional goals, and they provide social and emotional support. In peer-learning situations in particular, the research demonstrates that good mentors provide value by encouraging students to focus on learning, helping students see what they do not understand, supporting them in developing their understanding, interacting with them about learning tasks, and providing them with more general, personal kinds of support.

WHAT IS MENTORING IN A
PEER-LEARNING CONTEXT?

When we first began to talk to facilitators and faculty about mentoring, we kept hearing variations on the same question: "What do you mean by mentoring?"

Mentoring is so widely talked about and written about, in so many different settings and at so many levels, that it has become difficult to pin down just what sort of relationship it refers to. A 2009 review of the literature found more than fifty definitions of mentoring.[3] It occurs in academic settings, in the workplace, and in the community, and some people use it as almost equivalent to *teaching*, while others consider true mentoring to occur only when the two people share a very close relationship. Plenty of general mentoring frameworks are available in the scholarly and popular literature, but none of these fits our particular situation: peer-led, small-group learning in the science, technology, engineering, and mathematics (STEM) disciplines. So, a few years into the program, we began to develop a model of what effective mentoring looked like in the GSW.

THE ROLE OF THE MENTOR IN A
PEER-LEARNING ENVIRONMENT

To develop our mentoring model we spoke to students and the peer facilitators who served as their mentors. We individually interviewed twenty-nine GSW students, and an additional thirty facilitators,[4] from all of the GSW disciplines, in part to learn how they understood this relationship. We asked them a range of questions about their experiences in the GSW, but in particular about the value the facilitators brought to students, about how the facilitators influenced students' learning, and about the nature of the facilitator–student relationship generally. Based on what they told us, we identified six critical and interrelated components of mentoring for peer-facilitated learning.

We fleshed these out and now use them as our own model of mentoring. The six, shown in Figure 5.1, are guiding, shaping, modeling, prompting, relating, and caring. Two of these—guiding and shaping—involve the mentor influencing students cognitively, for instance, helping them see how to think through a problem more logically or deeply. Modeling and prompting, by comparison, address the behavioral realm of learning, for instance, with a mentor helping to motivate students to work through problems, and by demonstrating effective techniques. Finally, relating and caring allow the mentor to forge interpersonal bonds with students that promote students' persistence and positive attitude toward the work they are doing.

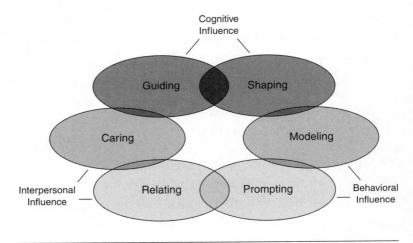

Figure 5.1   Peer Mentoring Roles

Cognitive Activities: Guiding and Shaping

Guiding is what most students probably first think of when they picture peer facilitation. In the GSW, the facilitator-mentor guides students through problems by providing "scaffolding"—offering support and clues but not giving the answer away. This kind of guiding characterizes the preferred approach in the facilitation framework we presented in Chapter 4. In guiding, the facilitator forces students to work out the answer for themselves. The key here is to provide students with all of the information they need in order to be able to solve problems on their own—information that the professor may not have time to give, or even think to give. As one of the students plainly put it, the facilitator "says extra stuff that the professor didn't say." One reason the facilitators may more readily do this is that they are closer in experience level to the students than the faculty are. In fact, because problem-solving support must be cognitively "within reach" for students to be effective, a peer facilitator who is only just a bit more advanced is in some sense the ideal guide.[5] Anna, a biology GSW student, explained, "Facilitators are much more at the level of the students than the professor is. . . . He has a PhD and much more knowledge, and his thought processes are just not at the same level." And because they are in a small-group setting and can focus on a handful of problems, peer facilitators are in a perfect position to coach students through solving a problem, which means that students engage actively rather than passively when they take in information.

Shaping is the activity that most enables students to engage in the alternative perspective taking that is critical if small-group learning is to be effective. Facilitators expose students to new ways of looking at a problem, to new approaches for solving the problem, and to new ways of categorizing information within a larger set of ideas and then help them reshape their mental models to incorporate these new ideas. They do this by sharing their own perspectives, by encouraging students to share their ideas, and by getting students to try out these new ideas and approaches. Joseph, one of our chemistry students, talked about the value of the facilitator encouraging students to share different problem-solving approaches: "Everybody has different ways of solving a problem. If you hear someone else's and you can't really understand it, someone might try to explain it another way. And you get it," he said.

Exposing students to new ideas is one thing; doing this in ways that will shape their understanding is another. Moving students from misconception or confusion to clarity is, in large part, an art, and most facilitators find that they become more skilled at it with practice.[6] It can also feel awkward for the facilitators, especially given that they are about the same age as the students they are mentoring. Dan, an organic chemistry facilitator, had another take on this, having come to realize that his role as a facilitator-mentor was to push students beyond "getting the answer" to really questioning their deeply held conceptions:

> When I first facilitated, I would explain how you should think about the problem and the concept behind it, but I didn't focus on whether the students had really accepted and understood this change. Now I realize that if they still thought their point of view was correct and did not see why, in some instances it did not work; I had not done my job. What I plan to do from now on is to discuss every student's preconception to the problem. That way, the whole group can discuss why some preconceptions are wrong and why some of them can be used to approach the problem.

Challenging students' ideas can be uncomfortable for a peer (and even for faculty). Frankly, it is easier just to get them to the right answer than it is to dig into why they had the wrong answer in the first place. But, as Dan rightly points out, going only halfway is completing only half the job.

Behavioral Activities: Prompting and Modeling

Prompting is what happens when facilitators give students the gentle push they need to engage and stay engaged, even when the content becomes difficult—moving students beyond where they are comfortable. Many of the students talked about facilitators "making us think," not letting them get away with sitting passively through the two hours. One student, Lila, offered a lively description: "My facilitator is really good. He knows when to push. . . . If I ask for help on a problem that I can do, he will say, 'Come on, you know you can do it!' But at the same time, if I really didn't know what I was doing, he'd explain it to me."

One of the organic chemistry facilitators, Jeff, talked about how difficult "prompting" students can be, and how much the facilitator's own enthusiasm plays a role in making it happen. He said, "I've realized how hard it is to get students to think outside of the box and to get them interested in other ideas connected to problems. What helps is that *I* enjoyed learning about whatever I am facilitating. I am actually excited about connecting the ideas together. Part of teaching is to get the group excited, get them in a positive mind-set."

Modeling happens when facilitators demonstrate how the students might approach their work, from solving a problem to studying for an exam to making decisions about graduate school. It is critical here that the facilitator-mentor is honest about his/her processes, so that students understand what real challenges and successes look like. One of the biology facilitators, Fanyu, talked about wanting to demonstrate his own enthusiasm for the subject matter in a paper he wrote for the facilitator training course. He asserted, "The facilitator must take on the 'role model' position, must show genuine interest, curiosity, and motivation in the subject. I try to provide students with anecdotes about the material to help them remember. This gets them interested, and it shows them that I am personally committed to biology." And Adrian, a physics student, said this about his facilitator: "I think that, more than just her understanding of physics, I can learn a lot from my facilitator, just from her study habits in general. For example, I can tell that she's a

person who knows how to manage her time. . . . Her overall understanding of how to do well in a class has really made me admire her
as our facilitator."

Interpersonal Activities: Relating and Caring

Relating occurs when facilitators present themselves *as themselves*—
sharing their own successes and failures in the academic world and
developing genuine relationships with students characterized by
trust, empathy, and acceptance. GSW student Ben put it this way:
"My facilitator is very nice. At the beginning, she always asks 'How
was your weekend?' She gets us very relaxed, and then once the
work actually starts, she kind of leads us." Students also frequently
talked about how much they valued facilitators' openness, and the
honest information facilitators provided about their own experiences as students. But this does not always come naturally for facilitators. One of the math facilitators, Julia, talked about the deli-
cate balance required here: "It's one of those things where you have
to find the right balance. I want to make it seem like, yeah, this is
hard material. I'm not perfect; I don't know all of it either. But at
the same time, I didn't want them to get discouraged . . . to have
them lose their faith in my ability."

Another facilitator, Paul, shared similar sentiments: "I think it's
important to let my students know that I struggled with some of
the material as well. I'm not a great math genius. I just enjoy teaching it." And Jinwoo, an organic chemistry facilitator, shared this:
"There have been times in the workshop when a concept came up
that I was confused about, and I started struggling in front of the
students. The incident was a total blow for me. I felt that I didn't
know the material well enough in front of them. But then, I think it

was also good, because it makes them see that this is hard material and that I am not expected to be an expert." While not knowing the answer was initially embarrassing for Jinwoo, he later saw this as a liberating experience for both his students and him—for his students, because they would recognize that, indeed, the material is difficult, even for advanced students; for him, because the group would understand that he was not a comprehensive knowledge storehouse. Finally, Rebecca told us: "I like to tell students about my own difficulties with the material when I was taking the class, and what helped me succeed. I do this because I once had a role model who did this, and it . . . helped me be more confident in myself." Demonstrating that successful students persevere through difficulty is especially important for students who lack confidence, or who may be vulnerable to stereotype threat (discussed in Chapter 4). And when role models present themselves as real people, they can promote students' beliefs that they too can succeed in the courses.

Relating can also mean that the facilitator is interacting with students about more than just the problem sheets. Facilitators provide information about the university, about professors and courses, and about applying to graduate or medical school. And because they are interacting in small-group settings, they do this all in a way that is tailored to the students' own circumstances. Paula, one of our chemistry facilitators, described the pleasure she felt in knowing that her students wanted to come to her for advice. She proudly told us, "One of my students has questions because he wants to be a bio major, but he's not sure which concentration he wants, or should he do an econ major as well. So, he'll leave messages to call him back with my advice." Raj, a physics facilitator, echoed this: "It's really fun for me," he said, "when the students can relate to me more than just as students. I like it when they come to me with other problems, their concerns and questions. I really enjoy helping them out with course questions or professor questions."

Caring occurs through all of these other activities, but it is important enough to stand on its own. Caring means helping students overcome anxieties and failures, providing them with direction and helping them shape their goals, and helping them believe that they are capable of doing the difficult work required to meet those goals.[7] Students emphasized caring perhaps more than any other of the qualities as being critical to a positive GSW experience. They talked about facilitators being genuinely invested in their learning. "He makes sure you understand," said one student. "When she asks for questions, she really means it," said another. "She took time to explain, to make sure I knew what the problem was about," said yet another.

Caring comes naturally for the facilitators, since they were all GSW students once themselves and know the value of the program. They empathize with the students' struggles and want to help. For example, Nicoletta, an engineering student who later became a facilitator, wanted to help students believe in themselves: "I think one of the most important ways to help students in the workshop—and I know the reason I did the workshop—is *confidence*. A lot of the kids in workshop have the ability to do these things, but they assume they can't. And they assume they're struggling. And, sometimes, they're very close, and, it's that little bit of confidence they need to avoid test anxiety, to perform better." Chitra, a chemistry facilitator, wanted to offer a low-pressure alternative to office visiting hours: "The workshops make students feel like they have a facilitator they can rely on, as opposed to a faculty member. It can be intimidating to just walk into a professor's office and be like, 'Hey, I have some questions!'" Peer facilitators are an additional, more accessible, and more comfortable resource for students. Simply knowing that their facilitators care seems to motivate students, even those who feel lost and confused, to persist.

Key to this peer-mentoring framework are the interrelationships among the areas. Addressing only one or two areas is not necessarily helpful and sometimes can be counterproductive. For instance, caring and relating as a friend without prompting students to move forward and guiding them effectively might help the group bond but will do little to improve learning. By the same token, prompting and attempting to shape understanding without relating and caring can produce feelings of intimidation in students—and increase the chances that students will withdraw intellectually or literally. Recall that in the GSW survey-based study we noted in Chapter 4, students who felt intimidated to participate in the groups dropped out of the program at higher rates than other students.[8] Peer mentoring is most effective when facilitators pay attention to all of the areas and, indeed, how each area influences the others (hence the overlapping areas in the mentoring diagram). When mentors relate, caring comes more naturally; when they care, they can prod without being seen as aggressive; when they guide rather than tell, they can more effectively shape students' thinking; and so forth.

Using this mentoring framework, we developed a "dos and don'ts" list for our peer facilitators. Using the information we had gathered earlier from students about their positive and negative group experiences, and by observing workshop groups ourselves, we sketched out what good and not-so-good examples for each of the mentoring roles would look like. These are listed in Table 5.1.

Table 5.1   Mentoring dos and don'ts

	Cognitive	
	Don't	Do
Guiding	Tell students how to solve problems; solve problems for them	Give students the tools to work through problems on their own
Shaping	Close off conversation by labeling a response as wrong and moving on without discussion of how and why	Encourage students to share ideas and perspectives and offer constructive critique to one another

	Behavioral	
	Don't	Do
Prompting	Give the correct answer after a student has gotten it wrong; answer rather than letting the group answer	Continue to ask a student to try after she or he has given an incorrect answer; wait long enough for an answer
Modeling	Regularly express fatigue with the problems	Demonstrate enthusiasm for the problems, even in the face of difficulty; demonstrate trying different approaches to a problem

	Interpersonal	
	Don't	Do
Relating	Avoid demonstration of any academic anxiety	Talk openly about anxiety before a hard exam the day before
Caring	Limit discussion to course material	Chat before or after the session about personal interests, professional goals

Source: Adapted from Light, G., Cox, R., and Calkins, S. (2009) *Learning and Teaching in Higher Education: The Reflective Professional.* Thousand Oaks, CA: Sage.

It is easy to see the contrast between the "do" and "don't" approaches, and students and facilitators see it clearly. Why, then, do facilitators occasionally veer into the "don't" side?

Lack of comfort with their role as facilitator-mentor is a major factor. Many are not ready to give up some of the direct authority and distance that helps them feel in control. Just as is the case for beginning teachers or beginning teaching assistants, beginning facilitators feel nervous, unsure of whether they will come across as smart, whether they will be able to develop and maintain a good group dynamic, and whether the students will respect them. Often their default approach in the face of these anxieties is to pull back, to try to show only the part of themselves that demonstrates competence with the material, and to avoid any situation that might reveal otherwise.

This is all very normal. We do not expect facilitators to jump in on the right-hand side of the chart. Going through some self-image-related anxiety is a necessary part of developing as a mentor. Rather than try to suppress it, we talk with facilitators about it. By the end of the year, with almost no exceptions, the facilitators feel good about having waded through that awkward first phase, and they emerge feeling much more comfortable in their mentoring skin.

TRAINING FOR EFFECTIVE MENTORING

While our facilitators are highly motivated to improve as mentors over the year, they too need mentoring. They come to us with little (or often no) prior knowledge of teaching and learning issues aside from what they have gleaned as students themselves, which may or may not be in line with the approach we want them to take.

In our first year we trained facilitators very informally. There were just a handful of them, so we were easily able to meet and talk about peer learning, provide them guidance, and offer a few readings on group facilitation. As the group rapidly grew past a hundred facilitators, however, we realized that this informal model was no longer feasible. We also recognized that we could not create a standard sort of course—say, one that met three mornings a week—since the vast majority of the facilitators had very full schedules already, and requiring them to commit to yet another time slot might turn many away from the program. We also did not want the training to be a one-off experience, or even a one-term experience, since facilitators held their positions for a full year. We settled on a year-long course, one with only a few regularly scheduled meetings but plenty of small-group, individual, and online communication. To get around the problem of the large number of facilitators, we began to use senior facilitators to act as coaches for small groups of facilitators all working in the same course. These paid senior facilitators receive their own training, in the form of quarterly development meetings and regular coaching from GSW staff. Each is responsible for one group of five to seven facilitators, and in addition to playing a leadership role at the facilitators' weekly meetings with faculty, these experienced senior facilitators observe the facilitators in their groups and provide feedback, coach the facilitators through a research project they do as part of the training course, and are generally available for support to facilitators throughout the year.

———

Although we still hear the occasional grumble, the vast majority of facilitators tell us that they value the training course and that it provides them with important information and an opportunity to reflect on their development as mentors.[9]

The training program for facilitators has six key learning goals:

1. Develop understanding of the science, math, or engineering content as well as knowledge of how to facilitate students' learning that content.
2. Become familiar with, and critically reflect on, pedagogical theory and research.
3. Gain knowledge of the dynamics of small groups.
4. Gain practical facilitation skills.
5. Develop inquiry skills by engaging in research on practice.
6. Reflect on practice and develop self-evaluation skills.

For the first goal we want facilitators to continuously improve their understanding of the subject matter, or their *science content knowledge*, as well as to develop and practice the skills that allow them to help others understand that content, or their *pedagogical content knowledge*.[10] As any new teaching assistant quickly learns, simply knowing the material well does not mean one can teach it well. Teaching the content well requires learning how students understand the content, what kinds of misconceptions they have, what kinds of errors they are prone to make and why, and what methods work best for helping them construct a deep understanding of the material. Facilitators begin to develop this pedagogical content knowledge by watching faculty and senior facilitators coach students through the problems in their weekly preparation meetings and refine the knowledge through their own facilitation practice.

The other five goals are a bit different. While they are linked to the first—facilitators cannot be good mentors without content knowledge—they address areas critical to facilitation that those weekly content-area preparation meetings do not address, at least not explicitly. To meet these goals we ask facilitators to engage in a range of activities geared toward developing as teachers, coaches, leaders, and group facilitators. For instance, facilitators do readings on educational psychology, small-group dynamics, and group facilitation and write short, reflective papers in response to these. We also require facilitators to engage in reflection on their own practice, in the form of essays and discussion in response to feedback they get from students and observers.

This reflection is worth considering more fully. So often professors and teachers do not have the time to reflect on their work, on how they do it, on why they do it that way, and on how well it works. In order to make meaningful improvement on practice, we all need to engage in this sort of purposeful reflection from time to time. For those who teach, reflection often comes in the form of research on one's own teaching—looking systematically at how different teaching practices impact students and student learning. Our facilitators engage in this very practice: in groups, they develop a researchable question related to the practice of facilitating learning in the STEM disciplines, and they review literature, develop instruments, collect and analyze data, and present results at a public forum. Groups have investigated the effect of additional facilitator preparation on student understanding, of cofacilitation on group dynamics, and of student anxiety level on student satisfaction with learning in the groups, as well as a wide range of other questions.

The facilitators may not realize it at the time, but they are engaging in a sophisticated professional practice, one that university professors themselves are often reluctant to take on—looking closely at one's own teaching and how effective it is. And in the end the vast majority put together high-quality projects that attest to their own deep understanding of, and interest in, teaching and learning.

THE MENTORS' DEVELOPMENT AS LEADERS AND AS LEARNERS

It is often said that one does not really learn something until one teaches it.[11] Almost without exception, facilitators tell us that what they gained as facilitators was greater than what they gained as GSW students. In fact, in a recent survey we distributed to former facilitators, 100 out of 126 (79 percent) agreed that having been a facilitator promoted their learning more than any other academic experience in college. A characteristic comment came from math facilitator Rachel:

> I think GSW benefits the facilitators even more than the students. It's not only that we are solidifying the math. We are the people most directly involved in the GSW process, in terms of hours and being involved in every step of it. It allows us to get involved in the subject in a way that is really unique that you can't do in any other way. It's the little control that we have over what gets taught and how it gets taught. As a facilitator, I have learned so much about how *I* need to be taught.

To look more directly at this issue of mentor development, we investigated the ways in which the peer facilitators benefited from their involvement in the program.[12] Through surveys, focus groups, and interviews with approximately one hundred facilitators, we identified a range of valuable outcomes of the facilitation experience, falling into three broad categories: academic, leadership, and career oriented.

Academic Development

Facilitators told us that they had come to more firmly grasp the content of the courses, not just the ones in which they were facilitating but in related courses as well. They attributed this to having spent extra time reviewing that material—material they had already learned when they took the class but that, they now realized, they had not fully understood at the time (even though they had all done well on course exams). One of our facilitators explained it this way: "Having the close contact with the professor, going through [the material] in a small group, and then going out and teaching it really helped reinforce the material that I had kind of learned before. But now I understand it much better."

Facilitators also gained an understanding of the discipline more holistically. They explained that they had had to bring disparate ideas, often from different courses, together in order to better explain concepts to students, and that this had given them a better "big picture" sense of the field. As a physics facilitator said, "Concepts come together because you are drawing . . . connections in order to make it easier for the students to understand, and when that happens, you start understanding it better."

Another area of cognitive development was problem-solving ability. Facilitators became much more aware of the ways in which they approached problems, and they were better able to critique those approaches. One highlighted this self-awareness: "I guess in going through your own problem-solving strategies," he said, "you kind of understand yourself better and see how you tend to approach things."

Leadership Development

This area encompasses communication and teaching skills. Facilitators talked about gaining confidence with public speaking, which they saw as linked to being better able to "read" the audience (in their case, the students), and thus being more skilled at communicating to them effectively. They also talked about simply feeling more skilled at explaining their ideas out loud: "Before the 'facilitator thing,'" said a chemistry facilitator, "I was not that great at explaining myself or explaining the concepts that were in my head. They were there, and I could understand them well for me, but for other people, I couldn't push it out there and give it to them. So, being able to do that in the workshop was number-one helpful."

Facilitators also felt they had become skilled at making the best use of the problems and asking effective questions, and at knowing when to lend a hand and when to step back and let students take over. And there was an added benefit here—they felt they had come to a more realistic (and forgiving) understanding of what it means to be a teacher. A biology facilitator told us, "As a student, I thought a facilitator would always have the answers if I didn't. Now I know that I don't have all the answers, so I see it as more that we all work towards the answer . . . together."

Career Development

Not surprisingly, facilitators put a lot of emphasis on the professional advantage that facilitating would afford them. They valued the experience for having prepared them for placement exams and for giving them professionally applicable skills, such as leadership and teaching skills. Physics facilitator Ivan said, for example, "I was doing the premed track as it is, but I think facilitating opened up a possibility that maybe I would like to teach medicine at some point. It gave me a little bit of hands-on experience in that, and I like what I've seen."

In a separate study[13] we looked at whether the facilitators' confidence in key leadership areas changed over the course of the year in which they facilitated. We surveyed 166 facilitators at the beginning and end of the year and found that they had made statistically significant gains in confidence in the following areas:

- keeping the groups satisfied, motivating students, and managing group meetings well
- managing a group in which one student dominates
- solving problems that may emerge in the group and solving interpersonal conflicts
- explaining complex ideas from the STEM course and helping students work through problems
- adjusting the workshop when things do not go as planned

As they are developing as learners and as individuals, they are also developing as teachers. In fact, in an in-depth qualitative study of eighteen GSW facilitators,[14] we found a trend toward more sophisticated approaches to facilitation. Of those who began with the kind of "teacher-centered" approaches we described in Chapter 2, approaches that focus on the facilitator's ability to transmit information rather than on the students' learning, nearly half moved clearly into more learning-centered approaches by the end of the year. And our longer-term evidence suggests meaningful change in the way these facilitators think about learning and teaching. In interviews and in essays they write as part of the training course, we have repeatedly seen facilitators describe a process of reconceptualizing what teaching and facilitating should be.

In all these ways facilitators become better mentors as they move through the year. Take Dana, a physics facilitator. Dana told us that one of the most important things she had learned as a facilitator was how to get students to think creatively about problems—to go beyond a tried-and-true approach to solving them. She said, "I've learned when and if to give my students clues or answers to questions and how to make them think about the different steps of the question. I've realized how hard it is to get students to think outside of the box and to get them interested in other ideas connected to problems." Thinking "outside the box" is something that is often lacking in the classroom, especially when students are asked to follow prescribed formats and where deviating from that plan can set a student up for failure.

Jonas, one of the math facilitators, drew an important distinction between a traditional lecture and a more group-oriented approach as he talked about realizing that the way things had always been done was not necessarily the best way: "In high school," he said, "it was always the teacher in front of the classroom writing on the blackboard, lecturing to the class. And by being a facilitator, I learned that that may not be the best way to teach. You don't need to stand in front of the classroom to be effective. Oftentimes, the most effective way is to kind of have the circle group, where you're not elevated above any of the students, and it's more of a discussion rather than a lecture." Jonas made a key point here when he talked about not being "elevated" above the students. We do not want to suggest that teachers are equal in all ways to their students, or that they should give up their authority in the classroom, but the research demonstrates that when teachers engage *with* students, rather than talking *at* them, more productive learning occurs.[15]

Janet, a biology facilitator, talked to us about having learned that students get stuck in their own misconceptions, and that it can be tricky to "undo" those misconceptions. She said, "I've learned that it's really hard to lead people to the right answer. When they have a wrong set of ideas, it's very difficult to get the idea out of their head without being mean about it. In terms of actually leading someone, it is a struggle between telling them the answer or telling them that they are just wrong and actually helping them."

Enrique, another chemistry facilitator, talked about the same issue Janet struggled with and found an approach that seemed to work. "I have learned to . . . engender gradual conceptual change," Enrique said, "rather than immediately rejecting a student's answer as incorrect and providing the correct one." Enrique is basing his approach on the idea that in order to be motivated to seek a new conception, students must feel dissatisfied with the conceptions they currently hold, and that it is the job of the teacher (or facilitator) to prompt this dissatisfaction, which typically comes through creating cognitive conflict in the student. Students must first see that their conceptions do not make sense given other information they know to be true; after that they will be motivated to seek correct conceptions.[16]

Finally, Annie, a math facilitator, talked about gaining skill in questioning in order to prompt students to think about the problems in such a way that they arrive at the right answer. "I think one thing I have learned to do better," Annie told us, "is if someone doesn't understand the concept, then I'll try to ask them questions that would hint at the answer." And she adds: "That's something that you don't really do anywhere else. This is kind of a unique thing to GSW, and I've honed that skill, being able to ask the people a question that would help guide them to the answer."

Dana, Jonas, Janet, Enrique, and Annie are all actively engaged in reflecting on their facilitation in order to improve it. They are developing mentoring skills that will benefit their students, and benefit *them* as they move on in their careers.

And many of our facilitators do go on to teach in one form or another, whether as physicians training medical students or interns, as college STEM faculty, or as classroom teachers. In a recent survey we sent to ten years' worth of graduated facilitators,[17] 65 percent said they planned to pursue, or were pursuing, some form of teaching. Whatever the case, they are developing an increasingly complex understanding of what teaching and learning are all about, and this will serve them well in their professional lives.

GSW'S IMPACT ON THE FACULTY APPROACH TO MENTORING

In the university, mentoring is not generally considered one of the essential functions of faculty members, particularly not the mentoring of undergraduates.[18] And most faculty members do not mind: they are under pressure to get grants, do research, and publish, and it is these things, not mentoring students, that figure greatly into tenure and promotion decisions. As a rule, faculty members do not establish mentoring relationships with students, and, indeed, very few faculty members have received any sort of training on how to be an effective mentor.[19] As a result, relatively few undergraduates in the United States receive real academic mentoring, and when they do it may not be the sort of mentoring they were hoping for: existing research shows that many students are dissatisfied with the mentoring they receive at the university.[20]

That ought not to be the case. There is no reason university teaching cannot be thought of as mentoring. If the job of faculty is *not* to guide, shape, model, relate to, prompt, and care about their students' learning, then what is?

A mentoring-oriented take on teaching aligns with the engaged, learning-centered approach to teaching we described in Chapter 2. Learning-centered teaching can be contrasted with student-centered and teacher-centered teaching. In learning-centered teaching, the ultimate goal is to promote change in the student. Teaching is understood as dialogue, with students bringing their own knowledge and ideas into the conversation. Student-centered teaching is geared toward the student acquiring knowledge from the teacher; good teaching from this perspective means presenting the material in such a way that the student can acquire it. Teaching that is teacher-centered views the student as a passive receptor of information; teaching "happens" when information is transmitted.

Table 5.2 describes what these three approaches in STEM disciplines often look like in practice. We should note, though, that it is the conception of teaching, and not the practices used, that defines the teaching approach. For instance, it is possible to use lecture

Table 5.2 Teacher-centered, student-centered, and learning-centered practices

Common Practices in Teacher-Centered Teaching	Common Practices in Student-Centered Teaching	Common Practices in Learning-Centered Teaching
• Pure lecture • Emphasis on memorization • Exam-based assessment, often graded on a curve • Goal is to ensure that the students have the information they need to move to the next level in the discipline	• Lecture includes opportunity for students to ask questions and clarify confusion • Students read text and/or related readings to reinforce and contextualize lecture • Teacher may use classroom time to assess students' understanding • Evaluation based on ability to apply concepts rather than memorization only • Goal is to ensure that students gain important information and understand key concepts	• Lecture may be mixed with discussion and small-group work • Students try to solve problems/answer questions before hearing the answer • Students may engage in inquiry-based or creative projects to gain a deeper understanding of projects, solo or with peers • Goal is to help students develop their knowledge, understanding, and ability to learn effectively within the discipline

Source: Adapted from Light, G., Cox, R., and Calkins, S. (2009) *Learning and Teaching in Higher Education: The Reflective Professional.* Thousand Oaks, CA: Sage.

very effectively to engage students actively in learning but, more typically, pure lecture is used in a teaching-centered approach.

Often it is easier to change students' and peer facilitators' attitudes about teaching than it is to change their teachers' attitudes. Faculty members are much more firmly embedded in the academic and institutional culture of a university, and teaching and learning are a core part of that culture. But—and we have seen this happen—even the most orthodox believers in the traditional method can change if they are given time and space to fully consider the alternatives. As we saw in the study of teacher change reported in Chapter 2 (which included many of the faculty who collaborate with us on the GSW) faculty who took part in a year-long faculty development program often reported meaningful change in their thinking about teaching—beginning with teacher-centered conceptions and ending with student- or learning-centered conceptions of teaching.

While the GSW is not a faculty development program, we have seen that many of the GSW faculty do experience change in their thinking about teaching, taking on a more student- or learning-centered perspective than they had before. We heard this repeatedly in interviews we conducted with faculty in the first several years of the program.

Some told us that working with the GSW reinforced their existing student- or learning-centered beliefs about teaching—that teaching should be interactive, and that in order to learn, students need to deeply engage with the material. This reinforcement is not at all trivial, especially in a climate that essentially rewards faculty for taking teacher-centered approaches, as is too often the case in STEM departments. Lee, a young chemistry professor, for instance, told us that the GSW had prompted him to take action on previously held student- or learning-centered beliefs that had, in a sense, remained dormant. He said, "I've always felt that students learn best when they talk amongst themselves, but GSW has reminded me of these values. In the past I never encouraged group work, but now it's my first recommendation."

Other faculty felt they had been more directly affected by the GSW. Jeri, an engineering faculty member, said that the GSW had prompted her to broaden her thinking about teaching. "[The] GSW gives us a way to make the course more challenging and stimulating. I'm a bit less linear now. The program has made me more aware of different types of learning that can go on." And Nate, in chemistry, said that being involved in the GSW had opened his mind to other new teaching approaches, especially those that would motivate his students. "I'd always envisioned myself just reading and regurgitating facts for a big lecture class, but a colleague showed me the potential for creating a lesson with so much more interaction with the students. It really blew me away—it was a lot of fun. The students seem to love it, and they show up to the lectures— even the one right before the holiday break!" Another chemistry professor, Lev, saw a very direct impact: "I am getting much more relaxed in teaching," he told us. He also spoke of the program's impact on the quality of his assignments and on his ability to gauge students' learning level: "I'm using better problems that tell stories than before. I see by the way the students respond whether there is a connection with a certain problem or example."

Several faculty members also spoke of the benefit to their departments. Natalie, one of the math faculty members, put it this way: "I really feel that the whole department is benefiting. We have some of the facilitators coming back to teach. One big benefit is that these students really are more involved with the department—and that's very refreshing for everybody."

What comes through most clearly in these comments is the emerging centrality of the student. As faculty engage in a broader community of practice through participation in the GSW, they are also beginning to adopt teaching practices that pull them away from the individualistic paradigm and toward the relational. To put it plainly, they are thinking less about themselves and more about their students. They are beginning to think in terms of mentoring students, and not just pouring knowledge into them. They are beginning to take into account what students bring in terms of preexisting knowledge, as well as goals, motivations, and anxieties. They are trying to work with students to improve their learning and not just to master a set content area. And they are beginning to allow students to know them as people rather than simply as fonts of knowledge. Teaching that resembles good mentoring is teaching that does not assume that the teacher has all the knowledge and that the student is a blank slate. Rather, it positions knowledge as, to some extent, a product of interaction, including that between teacher and student.

Whether from a peer leader or from a faculty member, mentoring comes down to two basic elements: a focus on the learner rather than on the teacher, and a focus on the learner as a whole person rather than merely a mind to be filled. When learners receive high-quality mentoring, they have the potential to develop more fully than they could in the classroom alone, gaining not just knowledge but also an understanding of what that knowledge means for them as people. They are learning how they can link the knowledge to what they already know, and how they can build on it to develop as learners and professionals. Good mentoring allows learners to develop critical personal and interpersonal skills that will benefit them well into the future. And, finally, good mentoring prepares another generation of mentors, and if the trends in higher education continue, these future mentors will find themselves highly sought after as critical teaching resources within the university.

SUGGESTIONS FOR PRACTICE

- Ensure that mentors understand that they are not there to tell students what to do or how to do it but, rather, to help students find their way to solutions.
- Teach mentors to pay attention to the cognitive, interpersonal, and behavioral dimensions of learning.
- Train mentors—good mentors know something about pedagogy, about group dynamics, and about facilitation, in addition to the STEM content.
- Pay attention to the mentors as well as to the students—peer mentors benefit too, and their learning should be nurtured.

SIX

Creating Community

Scientific research is a social act. It is not a solitary struggle
between "nature" and the human mind, as accounts of the
heroic scientist would lead us to believe, but instead
entails relations within a community of scientists and a
community of minds seeking recognition and consensus.

—Daryl Chubin and Edward Hackett

AS A GENERAL RULE, undergradu-
ates are considered observers of, not participants in, the academic
community. Professors and professional scientists are the community, since they are engaged in the real work of the community; students are spectators until they are well enough developed to join
the team. In fact, the language we commonly use often suggests
that students should be actively prevented from joining. We offer
"gateway" courses that provide access to more advanced study only
to those meriting it (as demonstrated by their course grades, whether
or not these genuinely reflect the ability to succeed); we "weed out"
students in difficult entry-level courses so that only the best per-
formers will thrive; and we hear students talk about "killer classes"

that leave only the most hearty standing to take the next step toward joining the scientific community.[1]

DEVELOPING THE GATEWAY SCIENCE WORKSHOP COMMUNITY

From the outset the Gateway Science Workshop (GSW) program was concerned with developing a more inclusive, well-functioning science community open to undergraduates at the very beginning of their studies. It was guided by the influential work of psychologists David McMillan and David Chavis,[2] who proposed a model of community that consists of four important levels. First is membership in a group that provides a *sense of identity;* second is the *influence that the group has* among individuals, and vice versa; third is the *fulfillment of needs,* such as status needs, that comes through membership; and fourth is the *emotional connection* that comes through a history of experiencing significant events together.

To gain a *sense of identity,*[3] students need to feel a part of a group of people committed to "doing" science (or math, or engineering) and through this group draw a sense of themselves as people dedicated to the same pursuit. That involves, for instance, the faculty engaging the GSW facilitators as assistants in science, committed peers of sorts, helping them with their educational work. In turn, the facilitators are encouraged to foster GSW students' sense of identity in the workshop groups by having their students get to know and support one another. Indeed, we often hear that students become friends and keep their groups intact well into the future.

To be *influenced by and influence the group,* students need to have regular and genuine contact with faculty and teaching assistants, as well as with other undergraduates who are seriously committed to science, technology, engineering, and mathematics (STEM) pursuits. To count as genuine, this contact needs to be more than students listening to teachers. Students need to participate fully in conversations about the work of the discipline. When peer facilitators meet with science faculty to go over the week's problem sheet, they are urged to do more than listen to a brief lecture and then work through the problems on their own. We want them to ask questions, get answers, provide feedback (for instance, on reasons they felt certain problems may not work well), and receive coaching about how to best help fellow students "get" the problems.

To allow for students' *needs to be met*—needs such as a sense of purpose, and for academic and emotional support—facilitators provide positive feedback and constructive critique. They work to ensure that all students leave the workshops feeling better about the material than when they entered. We also ask facilitators to pay attention to the students as individuals, watching for indications that a student may not understand or may feel discouraged, and take action to remedy that. And we offer the same support for facilitators, meeting with them regularly to identify potential problems and providing senior facilitators who can monitor and coach them.

Finally, to provide an *emotional connection,* we promote group environments that feel safe—we know from many, many conversations with students that this is most often the way they do feel in their sessions. We train the facilitators to develop a comfortable group atmosphere so that students will be willing to try, even if it means failing, and to share their own academic anxieties (about exams, graduate school, and so on) and their excitement (about a high exam grade or a successful grad school application), so that students will understand that it is normal to have academic highs and lows. We also provide food for the groups, giving facilitators a snack allowance they can use at their discretion, and they all tell us that food does indeed seem to make people feel friendlier.

A key impetus for developing this model of community in the GSW program is to combat the frequent feelings of isolation that many students feel, particularly in the first years. Trudging from one large lecture class to another, feeling indistinct among the masses, students may struggle with anonymity and isolation. Take June, for example. As a chemistry student, she often felt alone in her struggles in science courses. Her fellow students were so worried about their own grades that they offered her little help in studying. The GSW community, however, offered needed support. June told us during an interview, "The sciences can be really hard and even sometimes discouraging. So to be with peers who are going through the same thing, and seeing facilitators who have gone through it and can empathize—it really helps." Punctuating her statement with a sigh of relief, she added, "I think GSW is a really great support system for students."

Scientists, of course, rely on support as they progress in their professional careers. Professional societies, peer-reviewed journals, academic conferences, research groups, web-based discussion communities, and even informal groups gathering for dinner and "shop talk" are all examples of support systems that professionals deem indispensable for finding success. "If scientists were prevented from communicating with each other," the National Committee on the Conduct of Science wrote, "scientific progress would grind to a halt. Science is not done in isolation," the report continues, but "takes place within a broad social and historical context, which gives substance, direction, and, ultimately, meaning to the work of individual scientists."[4] Just as scientists do, students thrive on that kind of personal and professional support.

COMMUNITIES OF PRACTICE

In the earlier quotation, the National Committee is describing what has been called a *community of practice*.[5] The term describes the "collective learning" of a large group of people "created over time by the sustained pursuit of a shared enterprise."[6] Communities of practice value not just the learning that happens in formal settings but all learning, including the sharing of knowledge in hallways, in dorm rooms, and in dining halls. Students, for example, are continuously teaching one another how to understand the material, how to study, how to relate to faculty—in short, how to be science students.

A thriving community of science practice comprises multiple participant levels. At the community's core are the senior scientists and science faculty. They are deeply engaged in pursuing the goals of the community and also understand the breadth of the community, what its various parts are and how those parts fit together. At the next level are junior faculty, who are just as fully engaged in science work but may not be as fully integrated into community networks as are senior faculty. Next are postdocs and graduate students, who are becoming fully engaged in the work but still rely on faculty to provide guidance, and who are only beginning to have some interaction in community networks, such as professional organizations. At the next level are senior undergraduates, who may be working in labs or on real projects but are simultaneously learning from graduate students and junior and senior faculty. At the periphery, looking in, so to speak, but not generally given access, are new undergraduates.

A vital feature of a flourishing community of practice consists of the two-way relationship between the participants on the different levels: senior professors mentoring outward their junior colleagues, for example, who gain inward access to professors' knowledge and expertise. And this reciprocal mentor-mentee dynamic occurs at all levels of the community, with participants playing both roles in different situations. Faculty provide mentoring—coaching, support, and guidance—to postdocs and graduate students, and faculty also mentor one another. Postdocs and graduate students, in turn, provide mentoring to undergraduates. In this way postdocs and graduate students act as liaisons between senior faculty and undergraduates, helping to bring students further into the community. Of course, faculty can also mentor undergraduates directly, although in many institutions this is not typical.

A second key feature of a community of practice is that all members are engaged in meaningful community practices. The students may be junior-level participants, but they are *legitimate* participants engaged in learning the actual values, practices, and norms of the profession. This is often referred to as *legitimate peripheral participation.*[7] Their participation is peripheral because they are on the periphery of the community. They are not yet engaged fully in the essential activities of the community and do not yet have complete knowledge of it, and, in fact, they may not even realize that what they are engaging in is preprofessional training.[8] But their participation is also legitimate, because they are engaging, even if at a very basic level, in the real questions and problems of greatest interest to the community.

We often encounter faculty who say students are not operating on the same plane as faculty and so really cannot be considered members of the same community. And certainly faculty are doing work that is far beyond the capability of most undergraduates. But a community has room for multiple levels of expertise. In fact, were this not the case, communities would die out and new membership would be impossible. Students and faculty *do* share a fundamental set of goals: scientific problem solving, scientific literacy, scientific thinking and learning, and teaching and mentoring.

Unfortunately, most college education is not structured to encourage legitimate peripheral participation. It is peripheral but typically not legitimate. Faculty make up the science community, and students sit on the sidelines trying to absorb as much knowledge as they can. This knowledge is usually filtered so that students learn isolated pieces of information but not the big issues and puzzles these pieces are related to, or with the manner in which their professors approach those puzzles. Rarely do faculty, for instance, share with their undergraduate students the details of their own research or the hurdles they must overcome just to get a research project off the ground, let alone fund it and ultimately publish meaningful findings.[9] Typically, students and faculty do not interact apart from the classroom,[10] which often limits interaction to a simple speaker-audience member dynamic. And this is all the more unfortunate, since we know that meaningful interactions with faculty, particularly informal interaction with faculty outside of class, are among the key factors associated with student success.[11]

Certainly there are exceptions: many students do engage with faculty outside of the "speaker-audience" setting. Such opportunities can be as mundane as office hours or as exceptional as dinner at a faculty member's home. The critical element is the nature of the relationship that is conveyed through such personal interactions— the recognition of the student as a legitimate member of the community. Some students even earn highly sought-after positions as lab assistants, which may give them more access to the big-picture activities of their professors, and on occasion a student may even become part of a project and a research paper.

THE GSW COMMUNITY OF SCIENCE

The GSW program is designed to encourage legitimate peripheral participation within a community of practice. As shown in Figure 6.1, the course faculty are at the center mentoring senior facilitators, who in turn mentor facilitators, who are "on the ground" mentoring student peers. New undergraduates (the student participants) work on the periphery, but as full participants in the sense that they are engaging in solving problems in the same manner in which faculty members themselves solve problems: by working through them piece by piece, giving and receiving feedback on their problem-solving approach, and sharing their "results" with a group of peers for critique. Undergraduate student participants are brought into the community by virtue of having close access to an older peer facilitator. As Natalia, one of the math facilitators, described it, her goal with students was

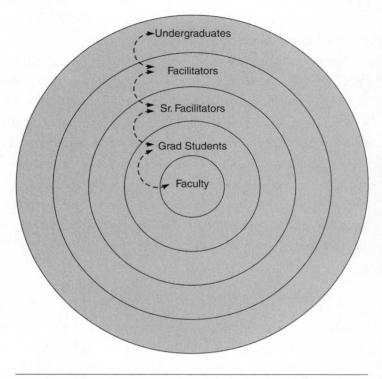

Figure 6.1   The GSW Community of Practice

just to kind of create a community where we can bond by
talking about college. You know, "Oh, yeah, this professor
does these kinds of problems; I found them really difficult." I
always encourage kids to think about a math major or minor—
even if they don't do it, just something to think about. I think
it helps them look at it in a broader scale, once they start looking at the other classes that the math department teaches, to
kind of see where what they are doing has a place.

Such interactions not only help to create ties among students but also promote in undergraduates an important sense of belonging to and identifying with the department and discipline.

The community also provides a mechanism for two-way communication, so that student questions and concerns are communicated to facilitators, who can pass them along to senior facilitators, who in turn can pass them along to the faculty. These last three groups—facilitators, senior facilitators, and faculty—all have the authority to make adjustments as necessary. For instance, students provide feedback to their facilitators twice a quarter, and, based on this feedback, facilitators very often make small but meaningful changes to their group sessions—maybe by providing more opportunity for pair work or by encouraging quieter students to take a more active part in the discussion. Facilitators provide feedback each week on the problem sheets developed by faculty; this feedback is channeled back to faculty, who then know which problems (if any) were problematic and thus can alter them. And senior facilitators have direct, regular access to faculty through the weekly meetings both attend.

THE IMPACT ON STUDENTS

In our work with the GSW and its spin-off program, Science Research Workshop (SRW), we have interviewed dozens of students, conducted dozens of focus groups, and surveyed several hundred students to ask what they feel they get from belonging to the GSW community of practice. Based on this information we have identified five key benefits that both the students and the student facilitators report they have received.

Seeing the "Big Picture"

As students become acquainted with the larger concepts and questions that concern the discipline, they begin to make deeper connections among ideas. In the traditional model, by contrast, students are typically removed from the professional practice of the faculty, meaning that they lack access to the larger context, the pressing and overarching questions and practices that frame the content the teacher is striving to convey to his students.

Faculty are well aware of how the principles they are lecturing on fit together to apply to real-world problems of science or engineering or medicine that impact people's lives. The individual topics covered in a course fit together, like interlocking puzzle pieces, in the service of helping to answer larger questions in the field. It may be that there are many other puzzle pieces necessary to answer the question, and it may be that the question has already been answered; nevertheless, it is a question critical to the development of the field. By contrast, students often lack this perspective. They see this very same material as isolated bits of content to be learned in order to do well on a text, not connected in any meaningful way other than the organization of a book chapter, and not working together toward addressing larger issues in the field. As a result, they often find it difficult to retain knowledge of facts (even if they successfully memorize them for an exam), and they are unable to link concepts and ideas to create broader meaning or to deeply understand the content areas they are studying.

One of our first-year students, Josh, talked about an experience that highlighted this student-faculty difference: During a unit on force and motion in his physics class, Josh felt uneasy, because although he felt he would do well on the exam, he did not really have the "sense of things," as he put it—the feeling that he understood the material at a deep level, and how it fit into some broader context. Josh went to his professor during office hours, and they talked for twenty or so minutes about applications of the course content to real-world problems. At the end of that meeting, Josh reported, his unease had lifted, and he felt more confident going into the rest of the course material.

Josh's experience is strongly supported by research. Brain-based research on learning over the past two decades has endorsed the critical importance of learners making connections and findings patterns among ideas.[12] And research on expertise has identified making connections as a critical difference between how novices and experts in a community approach problems. Novices characteristically overlook meaningful patterns in data and miss opportunities for applying knowledge in real-world situations.[13]

As we saw in Chapter 3, the GSW program encouraged faculty to bring the problems to life and provide a bigger picture for students by connecting worksheet problems to research or to real-world problems. Indeed, one of the math professors recently worked with colleagues in chemistry and biology to revamp her department's worksheets to help students make important interdisciplinary connections. And faculty see immediate, tangible benefits of this approach: students perk up when the material feels relevant. One of the chemistry faculty members talked to us about the deliberate effort he had made to bring his world—the broader world of research and application—into view for his students. "This year," he told us, "I did a little bit of going back to the primary literature, coming up with questions that were actually directly related to research."

Students appreciate these efforts. As one facilitator said when asked for the greatest benefit of the GSW, "It's when you really understand what all these different questions are asking, and just how those ideas lead to the everyday world."

Demystifying the Faculty

To many of the students we talked with, faculty are mysterious and unreachable. Students described feeling terribly intimidated about asking professors questions in class, e-mailing them, or—most fearsome of all!—going to faculty office hours. In a thriving community of practice the professor is not the unapproachable figure on the podium. She is humanized, becomes a flesh-and-blood person, one in whom a student might see a little of herself. When students can interact comfortably with faculty, when they are invited to see faculty as whole people, with senses of humor and warmth and their own professional struggles, they suddenly feel more at ease in their own academic roles. They are able to more easily envision themselves in the professional role they might one day like to adopt.

Grant, one of the peer facilitators and a junior biology major, had long felt frustrated with the lecture hall environment because it felt so formal, so devoid of enjoyable, interpersonal interaction. For him the GSW environment was an antidote to this formality. Grant told us, "I enjoy the faculty contact because once a week you get to spend time with a professor and a group of about eight other people, and you just get to know the professor. It's laid back, and we joke around. The classes at this school, most of them aren't that small, and usually you are going to be lectured. Maybe discussion, but you are never really laid back and joking around."

A GSW physics facilitator, Hasim, echoed the positive sentiments that informal opportunities to see faculty outside of work provided. "I have noticed that a lot of facilitators have been able to talk to the professors about various aspects of their lives outside of GSW," he told us. "I thought that was really nice. Just to be able to ask advice, and have time to talk about something outside of GSW. You don't have to talk about the class work in particular; you just talk about just general things coming up in your life."

Accessing Informal "Wisdom"

Belonging to a legitimate community of practice offers students access to the everyday "wisdom" that more seasoned members have but seldom share in a formal way. Rarely, for instance, would anyone type up guidelines for "How to make it through organic chemistry with Professor So-and-So" and post them on the corridor wall. Community members simply accumulate and share this knowledge over time through being active in the community. Often that sharing happens in haphazard ways: during a chat a student has with a professor while waiting for the elevator, or with a fellow student he bumps into during the professor's office hours. The GSW program helps make it a little less haphazard. As one of the chemistry facilitators, Tom, explained, "I'm taking classes I want to take, and I want to help other people have the same situation. I offer my help with advice for med school stuff too. I just feel like I'm like, like a big-brother type figure." Tom understands the importance of the informal knowledge it takes to succeed, often best communicated through informal conversations—brief, invaluable encounters that help initiate newcomers into the community. A GSW student recently mentioned to us that in the GSW she learned things about how to succeed in science that were "not as commonsense as you'd think." Commonsense knowledge is easy to come by. It is the elusive knowledge that often separates those who succeed from those who fall out of the community somewhere along the line.

Acquiring Tacit Knowledge and Skills

It is within communities of practice that students can also gain access to the tacit knowledge that other members have. This benefit is of particular value to students who come to college with less advantage or less experience in academic environments. Tacit knowledge is the knowledge that is not formally available to members of the community but, rather, is part of what people "just know."[14] As scientist-philosopher Michael Polanyi has written, "We can know more than we can tell."[15] For example, students who have had the benefit of years of guidance in studying effectively have a sense of how to study well; students who attended high schools that offered science enrichment programs simply have a feel for lab work; and students who have parents or other relatives who are professionals in a science discipline simply recognize what being a scientist "looks like." Jeremy, a GSW biology student, talked to us about feeling he lacked the independent study skills that other students had already developed upon arriving at college:

> In high school it's a lot different because classes are so structured, and the teachers are there to monitor your progress the whole way through. Whereas here, you're really responsible for knowing the material. And that's a big change for me. And it makes it harder to do well, especially when you thought

you were doing well before. I see some people excelling, because they know how to study on their own. They know; they can manage their time well and stuff like that. And *not* being able to do that as well as other people is kind of intimidating.

Students like Jeremy who arrive at college without the kinds of experiences that develop strong science learning skills can read up on these topics or can be told something about them, but until they gain experience they will probably not have the feel for them. The trouble is that when students lack this background experience, they can easily get left out of the community of practice. This can be an especially important issue for underrepresented students—even those at the top of their high school classes and entering with high test scores. They have lacked access to academic and professional resources and networks for developing key tacit skills and knowledge.[16]

Bringing all interested students into the community can help ensure that tacit knowledge gets passed around. Students who have not yet gained this knowledge can interact with students who have, and with graduate students and faculty who are experts in it. But these interactions need to be promoted: students need to be provided with structured opportunities to talk with and observe others in ways that will encourage the sharing of tacit knowledge.

Navigating Science

For many students who aspire to become scientists, doctors, engineers, or other science-related professionals, the "way into" the profession is not clearly marked. This is especially true for students without parents or other mentors who are already in the community and can help guide the way—again, more often the case for students from racial/ethnic and socioeconomic backgrounds traditionally underrepresented in science. Aspiring professionals need practical guidance on how to navigate those often bumpy roads, fraught with obstacles such as "weed-out" courses, tough competition among peers, placement exams, intimidating interviews and applications, and very real financial costs. In an inclusive and well-functioning community, these roadblocks would take a very different shape: rather than large and difficult hurdles that only the advantaged or very strong willed could overcome, they might look more like steps to be climbed—with effort, but also with guidance.

At the most basic level, access to guidance on how to navigate science allows students to feel like genuine members of the community. As a GSW facilitator put it, "You know, it feels good when the teacher says, all right, *all of us engineers,* we need to think like this. You just don't hear phrases like that back home." This student is beginning to develop a community identity, reflecting the highest conception of what learning is: *changing as a person.*[17] Feeling included in the professional group, in a way that they never have previously, takes students a very long way toward believing that they can, in fact, one day fully belong to that community. This experience, as we will see in the next chapter, is particularly salient for students who engage in research communities.

These five ways in which students benefit from community—by situating the key problems and questions of the community, by rendering the senior members of the community more knowable and human, by providing the informal "wisdom" and information held by the community, by illuminating the tacit community knowledge, and by opening the roads by which the community is navigated—

bring students and faculty together and enhance the learning experience for students. But this kind of student-faculty engagement does not happen easily. To develop healthy communities of practice, faculty must engage in the same principles of academic dialogue that undergird thriving research and teaching communities in the sciences and elsewhere: a commitment to supporting and encouraging new members and to helping them develop as professionals, to bringing into the community those who are traditionally left out, and to continually reflecting on and improving one's own research and teaching practices. This requires a shift from the traditional, individual-centered orientation of academic practice to a more relational approach that puts the community, rather than the individual, at the center. When faculty and students interact as members of the same community, students fare better.[18]

WHO GETS TO JOIN THE COMMUNITY?

Even in communities of practice that are seemingly well functioning, there is often an invisible dysfunction: the absence of certain groups of people from the community, or from core levels of the community. For decades or longer, for example, women were not actively welcomed into certain professional communities such as engineering and law, and certainly men were excluded from others, for example, nursing. These absences leave gaps in the community's collective power, since people with different life experiences will bring different knowledge, skills, and perspectives, and this variety creates greater potential for the profession to prosper.

Developing learning environments that open our communities of practice to undergraduates is only part of the challenge of who gets to join. There is unequal representation in the undergraduate representation in the sciences based on ethnic identity, gender, socioeconomic background, and other demographic characteristics. For instance, between 1997 and 2006, on average only 8.2 percent of bachelor's degrees in science and engineering were awarded to African American students and only 7.1 percent to Latino students.[19] In 2006 women earned less than half of all bachelor's degrees in earth and physical sciences, only a quarter of all degrees in math and computer science, and less than a quarter in engineering.[20] A student's socioeconomic background also is an important factor in his or her success in higher education,[21] and this appears to be especially true for racial minority students. We also know that parental influence is a key factor in students' persistence and success in science study.[22] Couple these figures with the finding that even the *perception* of a lack of support or of any sort of discrimination on campus can hurt students' chances of success in the sciences[23] and it is easy to see how students who self-identify with underrepresented groups may be less likely to become fully fledged members of the scientific community.

So how do we better represent all of these groups? This is not an easy question; in fact, many research and community-based organizations, national and international, are devoted to providing answers to it. Still, at the very local level, there are some proven practices. As we noted earlier in this book, in many cases underrepresented students in the GSW program show even greater gains than do students from well-represented groups. This suggests that underrepresented students who join the GSW can be better positioned to make their way into the core of the community than those who do not join. One probable contributing factor to this improvement is the sense of connection that the GSW provides students. Vincent Tinto, a leading scholar on college student retention, has pointed out that one key factor that runs through all of the research on student persistence in higher education is *engagement*.[24] Students who are involved in the academic life of the university, and who feel engaged in that pursuit, are more likely to stay in the academic community. For underrepresented students, engagement and belongingness are especially important, particularly at more selective colleges and universities, where for students it is more difficult to feel one is "on the inside." Joining learning communities (such as the GSW), particularly those that offer ethnic diversity and opportunities to get advice from more experienced students, can boost the sense of belongingness for underrepresented minority students[25]—indeed, for all students.

Another factor that appears to be important for integrating women and underrepresented minority students into science communities of practice is the social relevance of the subject matter they are studying. Several studies have found that women and girls, as well as students from underrepresented minority groups, are often more drawn to science for the social benefit it can offer than out of an abstract interest in science. Several studies have found women to cite social relevance—for instance, projects to improve clean water supply in developing countries—as a critical factor in drawing them to a science field.[26] Indeed, women who are especially oriented toward social advancement tend to be deterred from their interest in pursuing science careers.[27] The better integrated students are into the university science community, the greater chance they have of hearing about, talking about, understanding, and taking part in work that promotes the positive impact of science on people's lives.

Aside from the sense of belonging it affords, engaging in a community of practice provides access to role models who can help solidify and shape students' developing academic and professional identities. And while this is critical for all aspiring science students, it is often especially important for underrepresented minority students.[28] One of the African American facilitators, Melanie, understood this well. Melanie extended her role beyond facilitating learning to promoting an image that would offer inspiration to her students: "Being both a minority and a woman, one of the best things I can do as a GSW facilitator is act as a role model for my minority and female students, to show an example of a minority female student who was successful in the course." Another facilitator, Erica, told us, "In all my years of general chemistry, organic chemistry, biology, and physics, I have yet to have a professor who is not a Caucasian male. Having facilitators of different genders and races is important because they can serve as success examples for other students. I know I looked to my female biology facilitator as a role model." Indeed, role models are effective in both increasing students' self-efficacy—their belief that they can do well on a given task—and in reducing stereotype threat (discussed in Chapter 4).

Becoming more fully integrated into an academic community can also help alleviate some of the pressure that underrepresented students often feel about acting as representatives of their identity groups. One African American GSW student, Danielle, who was interested in a science career, told us, "In terms of representing

African American ladies on this campus, I feel somewhat different and somewhat like I have a duty to uphold our image academically. Sometimes you feel that you don't know how other people view you, and so you don't ever want people to have the excuse of saying that you didn't belong here. You know that how you perform really speaks for itself, you know, as an individual and also as the group that you want to represent." Although Danielle does not explicitly talk about the stress that accompanies the pressure she describes, the research on stereotype threat suggests that the stress resulting from trying *not* to confirm a stereotype can hinder performance. Feeling a genuine part of the scientific community can help tone down this stress.[29]

So, for underrepresented students, the stakes are often higher, meaning that feeling part of a thriving and meaningful community of science can offer richer rewards. But for all students, becoming a legitimate member of the community of practice makes meaningful learning more possible.

HOW DO WE DEVELOP HEALTHY, THRIVING COMMUNITIES OF PRACTICE?

Between the pressures to pursue research and the very large class sizes that many science faculty face, they very understandably may feel unable to focus on their students as individuals. As we have seen, undergraduates and faculty generally do not interact much outside of the classroom. A number of institutions have begun to structure experiences that help bridge the faculty-student interpersonal gap. For instance, some institutions offer honors or residential colleges, such as Northwestern's Residential Colleges, which typically feature a small student-faculty ratio and opportunities for informal interaction with faculty; small learning communities, such as the University of Michigan's Michigan Learning Communities; or programs bringing faculty and students together socially, such as the faculty–student dinners offered at Columbia.[30]

While these sorts of programs can be extremely effective at building community, they require fairly significant effort and resources. Individual faculty, and even individual students, can take much smaller steps toward the same goal and achieve solid results. Through the GSW experience, we have collected a number of fairly simple ideas for building community in STEM disciplines. Some of these ideas come from students and facilitators, some from faculty, and others from actual "experiments" that students and faculty have tried and benefited from. What follows are just some examples of these small grassroots efforts that were felt to be effective in promoting a sense of inclusion and belongingness among students and, ultimately, to promote learning.

WHAT FACULTY CAN DO

Faculty-student interaction can be increased by doing the following:

Hold group office hours.   One of the GSW physics faculty members told us that he had been inspired to do this after seeing how well the GSW students fared in a small-group setting. A faculty member teaching a lecture class of up to, say, one hundred students can hold small-group office hours, hosting five to seven students at a time. These meetings can focus on a particular topic, or they can be open sessions in which students bring their questions. Either way, all benefit from hearing others' questions and ideas, as well as faculty members' explanations.

Encourage students to take advantage of regular office hours. Especially in large lecture classes, only a very small percentage of students typically take advantage of regular office hours—one of the best ways to get to know faculty. Students may feel intimidated to visit the professor—facilitators frequently remind us that going to office hours requires a certain amount of bravery. In fact, the students most in need may be those most reluctant to appear during office hours. Research shows that students considered at risk academically are less likely than others to ask for help, as are students who feel that seeking help poses a threat to their self-esteem or sense of identity.[31] Students need to be reminded that the professor is there to help them, and that the vast majority of faculty members feel encouraged when students do show up during office hours. The message should be that students are expected to take part in the community and take advantage of office hours.

Go to recitation. With very large classes, faculty can periodically attend recitation or discussion *sessions,* taking ten or fifteen minutes at the beginning of class to field questions from students.

Answer questions virtually. Some faculty feel they cannot take up class time to answer all the questions students have, so they have devised efficient ways to answer questions using e-mail or the Internet. One approach we have seen used is to gather questions from students and, via a class e-mail list or web-based courseware, provide answers to two or three of these questions a week, posting or sending the same message to the whole class.

Require study groups.   A chemistry faculty member who had been involved with the GSW for a year or so began requiring his students to form study groups, telling them that "being a lone wolf won't work in this course." Students resisted initially, but they later found the groups very valuable. Such groups can also be used to help students delve deeper into key course topics, with each group charged with producing a short presentation or an innovative study guide for all members of the class. The faculty member provides guidance for the group, perhaps meeting with each group once to offer feedback on a draft document.

Share a meal.   When we asked one of the GSW facilitators what would help him feel more in touch with the professor, his reply was, "Well, like, if we maybe went to dinner with him or something," and then he laughed. This idea seemed almost ridiculous to the student, but many faculty members do this sort of thing all the time—this does not require a big time commitment and does not need to be a big out-of-pocket expense. Meals can be at a dining hall or even potluck style. And the group can (and should) be small. A faculty member might, for instance, announce that there will be one or two meals during the term, and that the first five or six students who send that professor an e-mail to sign up will be included.

To introduce students to the larger questions of the field, the following can be done:

Let students learn about faculty research.   As we will see in the next chapter, a very popular feature of the SRW program is the opportunity for students to hear from faculty about their research. In the SRW this happens as part of a larger program, but faculty members can take more informal opportunities to talk to students about their research and how it relates to topics students are currently studying. This might be done periodically, taking just a few minutes out of each class, or the faculty member can hold a special session for a certain number of students, perhaps over lunch, to discuss research and to answer students' questions about it.

Keep the class current.   Almost all of the GSW faculty have talked to us about their efforts to bring the events of the day into their classes to help students see the relevance to their own lives of whatever content they are studying. For some faculty this is just a quick reference; for others it is a more involved assignment. An engineering professor, for example, used the well-known traffic congestion problem on the street outside the classroom building as the basis for an assignment that asked students to analyze the problem and propose solutions.

Have students do the work.   Another GSW professor, in biology, assigns students to find articles (either from the popular press or from academic journals) on research linked to the course topics, and then asks them to post summaries and comments on the course website.

Bring in topical guest speakers.   Some of the most enthusiastic descriptions we have heard students give of their STEM class experiences relate to guests the professor has brought in to talk to students about research or other projects in which they are involved. Students gain perspective by hearing a new person talk about what they have been learning, and students vicariously experience the guest's enthusiasm for the subject matter.

To reduce high levels of competition among students, the following can be done:

Avoid grading on the curve.   GSW students overwhelmingly complain that curve-based grading increases levels of competitiveness among them, which makes it less likely that they will be willing to develop a mutually beneficial community where they help one another. Grading on the curve also means that no matter how many students we help stay within the community, there will always be a certain percentage that get left out—meaning that our efforts are effectively in vain. Most important, grading on the curve does not necessarily tell faculty which students have learned the most.[32]

Encourage students to help one another.   Faculty have done this in different ways, by helping students set up study groups, by allowing them to work together on low-risk assignments or in-class activities that require a group answer, or simply by asking them to compare notes at the end of the class period.

Make collaboration commonplace.   In the GSW program, for instance, faculty often highlight for students the fact that they collaborate with their own peers on research. As another biology professor told us, "I show my students random articles from science journals and say, 'Look, this was not written by just one person.

Many articles have many authors.' It shows them how collaboration in the sciences really matters." Faculty can also model collaborative behavior in the classroom, for instance, by joining groups of students as they work through problems, acting as a real, but more experienced, member of the group. They can also speak openly about their own concerns over high levels of competitiveness among science students.

Create opportunities for friendly, group-based competition. Such competition is generally healthier than individual competition and promotes teamwork. One of the GSW faculty members created groups that engage in friendly competition in math classes through the use of "clickers," the small, handheld devices that enable students to display their answers to questions on a screen that everyone in the classroom can see. Students divide into teams and work together to solve problems, and the winning team gets a small prize. Discussion is lively, and students are motivated to talk their ideas out and get to the right answer.[33]

KEEPING THE COMMUNITY TOGETHER

Developing the GSW community was one thing—keeping it together through the natural flow of changes in faculty, staff, grad students, and undergraduates was another thing altogether. Communities have a way of coming unglued if someone does not actively work to keep the various parts well connected. Even as we write this, we are thinking about ways to maintain ties: ties between the facilitators and the faculty, between the students and the program, and between the program and the departments. Keeping these connections strong requires regular communication, careful listening, and genuine attention to what each stakeholder needs. For instance, several GSW students recently approached us to say that they were having trouble communicating with their facilitator. The students felt that the facilitator was not adequately answering their questions, or passing them along to the course professor when he was not able to answer them himself. In this case there was a breakdown in the crucial bridge that facilitators create between course students and faculty. We talked with the facilitator and learned that he was feeling overwhelmed by a heavy course load and also felt embarrassed about not knowing the answer to students' questions and thus was hesitant to go to the professor for help. We arranged for a cofacilitator to work with him for a few weeks to ease his load a bit, and we reassured him that we do not expect facilitators to have the answers to all student questions—and, in fact, that the most successful facilitators are the ones to ask for help when they do not know the answer. A few weeks later, the facilitator was feeling more able to balance his workload, and the students in his group reported feeling more satisfied.

This is one example of the kind of small, regular effort that is required to keep a community like the GSW afloat. Keeping a close eye on the community's "glue"—patching small tears in the relationships that hold it together—goes a long way toward avoiding more significant ruptures later on. Once created, a genuine, thriving community of scholars and learners needs regular upkeep. Students (and faculty) come and go, new projects absorb people's time, and soon the thriving community is faltering. Getting together regularly to talk about how things are working, providing support and training for community members, and assessing the effort more formally

on a periodic basis are all necessary to keeping a community flourishing. We will address all of these in more depth in Chapter 8.

SUGGESTIONS FOR PRACTICE

- Bring students into the broader departmental community
  by creating opportunities for meaningful engagement
  with faculty and graduate students.
- Find ways to help students and faculty get to know each
  other, for example, an invitation to discuss a problem, an
  informal question-and-answer session, or a shared meal.
- Consider what kinds of informal wisdom or tacit
  knowledge some of your students may lack, and make that
  information available to them.
- Provide opportunities for students to learn the ins and
  outs of working toward a science-related career.
- Reach out to students from groups that are underrepresented in STEM, and welcome them personally to take
  part in discussions, activities, and the like.
- Increase opportunities for collaboration among
  undergraduates and between undergraduates and
  graduate students and faculty.

SEVEN

Doing Research

My brain is open.

—Paul Erdos

IN CHAPTER 2 we talked about the different stages in the journeys students experience in the Gateway Science Workshop (GSW) program. For some the journey was just beginning. They described a reliance on the program to help them survive their courses. Other students described the workshops as helping them engage more critically with science concepts. They did not want to stay on the "shore" as merely observers of this new world. They wanted to go beyond the "what" of the content to the "how" and "why" of it. Finally, there were those independent students who indicated an interest in traveling further into the terrain, toward a more complex understanding, by mapping out the broader relationships among many concepts. In this chapter we explore how we used the workshops to extend this journey even further.

In 2007 we sat down with science faculty from different disciplines and looked at how we might draw upon the principles of the GSW program to help students experience science more fully early in their college careers. We wanted students to do real science work.

And if they were going to do real scientific work, they had to get into real working labs.

While most science faculty were sympathetic, few thought this was practical. The idea of a freshman entering their lab and doing anything meaningful without becoming a disruption bordered on terrifying. Moreover, most faculty already had undergraduates in their labs doing research and recognized the benefits they provided for students.[1] As a rule, these students were juniors or seniors, had excelled in their courses, and had demonstrated an unusual aptitude for doing scientific research. Only a tiny fraction of the faculty members' lab mentoring was focused on students fresh off the high school boat, so to speak.[2]

While the focus on senior students makes sense, it is not the whole picture. In large part our question was about those students who had not yet committed to science and might not—not because they had no interest in science, but because they felt their early college course experience with science was boring.[3] Of course they were getting an artificial idea of science. And while many students see beyond this misleading picture of science, others receive this artificial depiction of science and decide it is not for them.

As we have seen, the GSW program alleviates some of this misleading experience of science by engaging students in some of the genuine experiences of doing science: challenging problems, engaged peers, helpful mentors, lively discussion, and a real community. These are important. They are not, however, the full experience of science and what scientists do. They do not take students to the edge of knowledge. The more we thought about it, the more we came back to the question of what scientists and mathematicians typically do. In which practices and activities do they engage to conduct their work? In the end it came down to the fuller and richer experience they get by "opening their brains" to doing research. And as Jon, the chemistry professor, reminded us in Chapter 3: "We are constant learners. We ask ourselves a lot of questions: 'What if we know this?' or 'What if we know that?' Then we design an experiment around it, [and] we build and test our hypothesis."

He goes on to acknowledge that to do this kind of "constant learning" he needs resources, particularly funding. And to get funding requires developing a research proposal that peer experts in the field believe meets rigorous criteria concerning the intellectual merit and broader impact of the science.[4] Indeed, as one scientist with comic leanings put it, "Contrary to what Asimov says, the most exciting phrase in science, the one that heralds new discoveries, is not 'Eureka!' or 'Hmm . . . that's funny'; it's 'Your research grant has been approved.'"[5]

So to push the boundaries even further, not only did we want to create a program that put freshmen to work in the labs of their professors; we also wanted them to earn their way into the lab—to write an original[6] research proposal to secure funding to work there. And they would need to submit it to an independent panel of science faculty to be judged through a rigorous, university-wide process of evaluation. We wanted them to experience the learning of science in the way in which scientists learned science, by engaging in the key experiences of science that lead to the discovery and the construction of new knowledge. This became the core idea of the Science Research Workshop (SRW) program—to ask students to become the best science students they could by becoming student scientists.

THE SCIENCE RESEARCH WORKSHOP PROGRAM

From the outset the SRW program was focused less on simply putting students into science labs and more on engaging them in the
scientific thinking and processes that would lead them to the lab.[7]

The Problem

Like the other student journeys we have described in this book,
this new journey begins with a series of science problems. Rather
than beginning with a given set of problems, like the ones used in
the GSW program, SRW students are required to identify a problem themselves, one they will address in a research project. In the
process they engage many other problems that will also need to be
addressed—for instance, what does an original science problem look
like, what field or topic will it be in, what is possible given the resources and time available, what labs are available, what will I need
to know or find out, where might I go to get help in identifying such
a question, and with whom might I collaborate in addressing these
questions?

The SRW student must also describe and justify her problem to
others in her two-to-three-page proposal for funding. Why this
problem? What makes this problem worth addressing? What has
been written about this problem? What scientific methods are best
used for answering this question? What lab resources will be used?
What expert assistance is available? Who is going to advise me on
this research? What does a genuine science proposal even look like?
Coming to understand the nature and importance of such questions
is a critical part of understanding science—and of becoming a member of the community of science.

At first glance the world of science that this challenge reveals looks, as one of the biology students told us, "inaccessible" and wholly "out of my league." For students who had only recently arrived on campus, the challenge looks formidable. Azim, a chemistry freshman, described it well when he told us of his first encounter with the program: "The processes of developing a project and writing up a grant proposal seemed astounding and nearly impossible to my naïve hands." Nevertheless, both of these students, and many more of their student colleagues, were excited by the challenge.

The Workshop: Small Groups

The students, of course, are not left to work in isolation. As with the GSW, the SRW program draws on the learning features of small groups (described in Chapter 4) led by peer undergraduate facilitators (see Chapter 5). It brings the students and their peers together in small disciplinary workshops to assist one another in developing their proposals.

The Workshop: Curriculum

The workshops are biweekly and designed to provide a carefully constructed scaffold around which the students structure their work. Each session in the series focuses on a particular theme and kicks off with a "science café." The science café consists of a thirty-minute talk and discussion in which science faculty share personal stories about their own experiences as undergraduates and graduate students starting out in research, as well as their current scientific research. Faculty are asked to discuss what excites them in science and what they find most satisfying. The science cafés are

also arranged to take students through the initial stages of the research process, from contacting a lab to writing a successful research proposal. Faculty will often provide insider information on
which labs to approach, who is doing research in what area, how
to identify and approach the lab, and which labs are willing to
host first- and second-year students.[8] This information is critical
early on: students must provide confirmation of a lab invitation by
the beginning of the following term in order to continue in the
program.

The science café is immediately followed by workshops designed
to provide students with a test site for trying out their own ideas
and developing their research plans. During these sessions students
work collaboratively to put together their individual proposals. The
topics of the workshops include strategies for approaching a lab,
identifying potential research topics and research questions, conducting a literature review, selecting research methods, using a
database, structuring a proposal, writing the proposal, doing an
oral presentation, and initiating the proposal review process.

The Workshop: Mentoring

The workshop groups are typically an hour and a half long and
composed of five or six students led by a peer facilitator. The facilitators are senior undergraduate students selected for their enthusiasm for science, their interpersonal skills, and their recent research
experience in a science lab. In many cases they have been facilitators in the GSW program with training in facilitation skills. Facilitators are close in age to the students but have recent experience of
actually doing science research. So they can and do give the inside

scoop on the faculty, the labs, the proposal development experience, and the different challenges to expect from each.

———————————

In all of these activities the sort of mentoring relationship we described in Chapter 5 plays a central role in the students' learning
process. Within the first few months of the program, these students are exposed to a wide range of science mentoring experiences.
In the science cafés the central community members, the scientists
themselves, begin to mentor students on the important elements of
doing science, providing them with a personalized overview of the
scientific enterprise and guidance in navigating it. In contrast, the
peer facilitators provide personal ground-level perspectives and
concrete support on plotting a specific course.

In addition, in the early months of the program the students begin
to engage with other people in the scientific community—particularly
the postdocs, technicians, and graduate students in the labs that
will be hosting them. These members of the community are particularly helpful in providing new viewpoints on the labs' research.
Finally, the collaborative nature of the program means that the
students begin to learn the process of becoming mentors themselves. Not only are they developing their own proposals during the
course of the program; they are also expected to help their fellow
students with their proposals, provide feedback on their ideas, and
share the results of their own experience to benefit the research
progress of their colleagues.

The Workshop Proposal

The workshop series culminates in a formal two-to-three-page written proposal laying out the student's rationale, faculty and lab support, and research plan and requesting funding for conducting independent research in a laboratory over the summer.[9] At the end of the workshop phase, students present their proposed projects to an audience of invited science faculty, postdocs, and graduate students who assess the student proposals with formative feedback. Based on this feedback, the students finalize their proposals and submit them to an independent undergraduate research panel for summative assessment. This completes the first phase of the SRW program. The next phase of the program, beginning with the external review and evaluation of the individual proposals, extends this experience more fully into the community. The students are now competing with students from across the university, most of whom are juniors or seniors, for research funding. Based on their scores from this panel[10] they may be funded by the university, by the college, by a specific department, or by funds available through the program. Almost all of the students who complete the program are funded.

At the point of notification, the successfully funded students leave the support structures provided by the SRW program and enter the science research communities of practice of their labs. They are now semi-independent science practitioners working on their own original research questions. And most of them have not yet begun their second year of college.

THE EXPERIENCE OF THE SCIENCE
RESEARCH PROGRAM

Determining the success of the SRW program presented different challenges from those described in Chapter 1 for the GSW program. The activities of the latter program were linked to very specific courses and course sequences. In that case measuring student performance in terms of exam scores and final grades was an obvious outcome to investigate, and so too was measuring student persistence in the respective course sequences. The SRW program, on the other hand, was not specifically connected to a course: grades were not a program goal. Rather, the SRW goal is for students to develop a more integrated understanding of science as well as skills and confidence in doing science research.

From this perspective, one gauge of the program's success was simply whether or not the students participated. We were quite sure it would initially pique their interest. Our early discussions with GSW students and facilitators about the idea of such a program had indicated so, but would any of them persist in staying with it? After all, this was a major commitment for which they received no grade, no credit, no payment, and no obvious strategic benefit other than the possible chance of summer research. And doing the program would certainly require considerable time and hard work. Nevertheless, in the first five years, 100 students completed the program, 87 submitted proposals, and 79 were funded and conducted their own research in labs.

The Impact of Science Research

While the evaluation activities will continue for some time, the data analyzed so far suggest that the program is enjoying substantial success.[11] Data gathered from students through surveys given before and after the program, through in-depth interviews, and through essays written after their lab experience indicate that the program has provided students with an added understanding of and confidence in doing science research.

The group of students who participated in the SRW program, for example, reported increased confidence in two general categories of research skill as compared to a control group of similar students who applied but for timing reasons were unable to participate in the program.[12] The first category of research skill focused on the students' conceptualization of research and included questions about following ethical principles in research, exploring literature in a topic, and conducting literature searches. The second category focused on students' reported confidence in carrying out early research tasks and skills, such as generating a researchable question, presenting a research idea orally or in writing, choosing a research design, and consulting senior researchers. In comparison to a control group of students, over the length of the program SRW students gained confidence at higher rates, and these differences were statistically significant. SRW students had a 14-point advantage (on a 100-point scale) over control group students on the perceived ability to conceptualize research tasks and held a ten-point lead on the ability to engage in early research tasks.

In some cases SRW student confidence levels rose even as the control group students' levels fell. When we examined tasks associated with students' confidence in developing a logical rationale for a research idea and for organizing their ideas in writing, for example, program students revealed gains in confidence of thirteen points, while the confidence of control group students fell by seven points.

The Experience of Science Research

By far the most rewarding (and often humbling) part of working with workshop students is listening to them talk about their experiences. We have interviewed nearly all of the SRW students, and in these interviews the sheer enthusiasm with which they describe their experience often tells much more than the numbers we use to portray that experience. They signal the kind of experience that may have a long-lasting impact, will assist in crossing into new frontiers, and will open new intellectual opportunities in science. The following two comments are wonderful examples of this kind of response.

The first comment is from Dena, a sophomore:

> To my great surprise, I felt as if I had become a part of a science community in which everybody shared the same passion that I had and were very encouraging. . . . I remember the thrill that ran through my body when Professor D. accepted me into his lab and I knew that I would stay at Northwestern over the summer even if I didn't get funded.

The second comment is from Drew, a freshman:

> I gained numerous tips, and more importantly, a positive mind-set from SRW. And never once did I regret following any advice I received from the professors and facilitators. I now have confidence in my lab skills and mannerisms, particularly

with genetics procedures. And all after only one summer? Pinch me, I must be dreaming.

While not all students expressed their experience of science research in such enjoyable terms, they did usually describe their experience in terms of new realizations about what science is and what scientific research is all about. Sometimes they described the experience in terms of it giving them a wider and more detailed picture of the life of science. Leanne, a freshman chemistry student, described it this way: "I was able to truly get a glimpse of what life as a researcher might really be like." Sam, a biology student, similarly described his new understanding of science: "This experience has made me realize that science and technology are both very dynamic and exciting fields," he said, "and that having a science career is both stimulating and fun."

These comments are particularly interesting in how they describe the dynamic nature of science. There are actual lives associated with doing science, and they can be interesting, meaningful, and enjoyable. It is a picture of science that contrasts notably with the passive portrayal students frequently receive of science, from even the most entertaining professor in a large science lecture class. For many students just the real day-to-day experience of life behind the stream of facts normally associated with science can be a transformative one.

1. The Research Lab

For most students, particularly freshmen, the research lab is mainly a place of mystery; students' perceptions are frequently acquired from television and movies. Popular renditions of research labs have little time to focus on the day-to-day research. Some students noted that just learning about these details was interesting. James, a freshman, told us: "By spending full, consistent workdays at the lab, I was able to see much more in depth into the entire organization, learning how chemicals are ordered or where shipments come in, for example."

Another student, Terrence, commented on how important these small day-to-day events in the lab can be, and how much impact they can have on the life of a researcher. "Often in lab, a single mistake can lead to exposure to hazardous material and cost anywhere between a day's work and a few weeks of hard labor. I learned to steady my focus (and my hand) and constantly be aware of my surroundings." He added, "Such is the way of chemistry; [I'm] now beginning to feel like a real member of the community."

2. Getting In

Most students really valued the opportunity to get into work in the lab. As we saw earlier in the chapter, some are astounded that it is even possible, and others, like Drew above, are over the moon, elated to be invited to work in a lab. Most students are thrilled to get a chance to become a meaningful part of this new world.

Time and time again the students told us about their appreciation for the program helping them get into a lab. Some students, like Jenny, a sophomore biology student, had already identified getting a lab as a college goal, but they had not figured out how to do it.

This workshop helped me to find a lab, which I was having some trouble with before I attended the sessions. I didn't really know how to approach different labs and whether the labs I was interested in actually accepted undergrads. Professor G.'s help in creating the list of labs that allowed undergrads was extremely useful, as I was able to narrow down labs by their work and whether it interested me, rather than whether they would accept me or not.

Other students might never have found their way into a lab. The idea was too intimidating. Typical were comments such as "The group setting of SRW was something I especially liked. After talking to the other members of our group, as well as our facilitators, I didn't feel as nervous as I had before about approaching a lab." This idea of a mutual support system of "companions" who helped each other along the way resonated very strongly in the report of another student: "There was camaraderie. We learned from one another that we can all be very resilient, we e-mailed a lot of lab PIs [principal investigators], many said no or never responded, but you keep trying. It was inspiring to be in things together, to stick it out and find a space eventually." The critical step of getting into a science lab is described, in these comments, as a mutual passage into the heart of the science community in which the students rally together to overcome the various obstacles that spring up in their way—fear, awe, and even the professors themselves.

3. *Listening to the Community*

If the failure of busy professors to reply to student requests was an obstacle, the professors' personal advice and encouragement were important sources of learning for students willing to listen. Listening to the community repeatedly surfaced as a critical factor in the successful experience of doing research. This was true for the broader professional picture as well as for specific insights into various aspects of doing science. For many it was the single most valuable part of the research experience. For young undergraduate students trying to work out what their future in a particular profession might look like, getting concrete ideas of what research in science might actually lead to can reinforce their decision to study science. In the words of one student: "The presentation given by Professor S. on what a science major can do after graduation was especially useful and enlightening. I learned what job options a bachelor's, master's, and PhD would allow for, and it reconfirmed my desire to pursue an advanced degree in science after graduation."

In addition to learning about future career possibilities, students cited the experience of listening to their professors' personal accounts of becoming scientists as highly valuable. These types of "sitting around the campfire with elders" stories are a classic source of inspiration and learning across most human communities. Shannon, a freshman in biology, told us:

> Hearing all of the individual professors talk about their career path and how they got to where they are now was really nice. Professor G.'s talk was very good: transition from being a TA, lots of twists in his path, told how he got a C in his molecular genetics course, almost failed, and now that's all the work he's involved in.

Learning in the community also comprised the inside experiences and insights of graduate students and postdocs, who are often available only through labs and, of course, of peer facilitators. Indeed, they were often the best source of information, especially with respect to doing the actual work. Asking faculty about their lives as scientists is one thing; asking them about the specifics of the actual research was another thing entirely. A student reported that "it is easier to talk to the facilitators (than faculty)" about the work because "I am not shy of asking stupid questions." Even remarks from faculty that no question is too stupid are not necessarily believed by the students or, for that matter, by the faculty themselves. In such cases the involvement of more junior community members is a definite plus.

4. *Working and Belonging*

Data from our conversations with the students supported the survey results (reported earlier) about their development of various research skills, as a biology student clearly notes: "Yes, definitely, we learned how to use databases; learned how to do a lit review of a topic area of interest; how to read, analyze scientific articles, to present my project to other students." But while these research skills are essential outcomes, their simple articulation masks more subtle and powerful changes that the students were beginning to experience.

The new skills and abilities that were learned in the program were often expressed by students in terms of how they helped them see themselves in the lab more generally. The skills opened up ways of making wider connections to the lab work. In response to a question about her learning on the program, for example, Lena, a biology student, referred to developing her scientific reading and writing abilities. "SRW really helped me in scientific writing and reading," she said in response to the question. She then quickly added why these skills were important, making explicit links to her work in the lab. "To design new experiments and overcome roadblocks in my lab work, it's often necessary for me to read papers regarding work with *C. elegans,* an organism, nematode, used by a large portion of my lab." There is a sense not only that she is learning important skills for doing specific experiments in the lab, but also that she is gaining a sense of her "scientist self" in her lab community more generally. What she is doing is what the lab, or at least "a large portion of her lab," is doing. She belongs.

For students, these beginning feelings of belonging in a lab are an important step toward seeing themselves as a meaningful part of science more generally.[13] In some cases these feelings were enriched by feelings of actually being able to contribute to the conversation. Consider the words of Avi, a biology student:

> In the SRW program, we discussed the significance of reading as many publications as possible in your field of interest. This activity not only confirmed my interest in circadian rhythms; it also contributed to my ability to have an intelligent conversation with members of the lab. Several times they would mention a specific mechanism or drug, and I would relish in the surprised look on their faces when I would refer to a paper with that particular term.

5. *Developing a Scientific Mind-Set*

The experiences of doing research and engaging with a research community were accompanied by a more profound change in the students' very idea of science. For instance, we heard comments like "This program has done a lot more than 'job-searching' and science-writing. It helped us make clear what it takes to be a scientist, what a scientist should be like, and why to be a scientist." The deeper and broader understanding of science and being a scientist expressed here—the development of the kind of positive scientific mind-set cited by the student quoted earlier—was an experience reported by a large majority of the students. They described expanding their perspective on science and talked very little about simply gaining science knowledge or content. As Henry, a freshman, put it, "Much of what I have learned this summer consisted of the attitudes and thought processes required by a successful researcher." Interestingly, as Henry became "more and more involved in research," he became increasingly aware of the broader scientific ways of thinking and understanding that underpin achievement in research, and he attributed them to "working in a research lab and taking an active part in the scientific community."

Other students were more forthcoming in what this new mindset included. One theme that arose in different guises was the recognition of science as being essentially process driven, fraught with ups and downs in which the kinds of results and discoveries dished out in lecture classes were the result of patience, time, and hard work. One of the chemistry students told us that while his summer research was a "rewarding experience," it was also a very "taxing" one in which he had to work "way over the required forty hours a week and nothing was going right." Science does not conform to the forty-hour week. It has its own rhythms and patterns that need to be experienced and learned.

These fundamental kinds of experiences where students are confronted with ongoing real-life problems with no guarantees of immediate result or success provide important lessons for every student. But for students in their first year of introductory science courses, where hard work is rarely seen as engaging in an extended process of deeper learning but is focused more on getting precise results, the right answers, every time, such lessons can lead to substantial changes in their intellectual development.[14] From sophomore Ted's description of his summer research experience, we can appreciate the kind of changes in understanding engendered by doing research for the first time.

I have learned of the humility that comes along with scientific research. In addition to being intellectually adept, researchers must also have indefinite patience and the ability to adapt quickly to change. During the first experiment I attempted several procedures found from literature searches; however, none of these proved effective. I became somewhat discouraged at the situation, but soon realized that this is exactly how research is done. Things rarely work out in your favor, and while irritating, dead ends such as the one I encountered are necessary to ensure the best final products.

If these examples stressed the thorny side of developing scientific understanding, these young researchers also described unexpected positive experiences that advanced their understanding of science. A large number of students came in with a very fixed, narrow idea about what could be done in science and came out with a far broader understanding. Chemistry student Anisha announced to us, for example, that science "can be a dynamic and flexible" endeavor where "you can pursue your own interests." The idea that scientists do not have to work on a set of boring topics, presumably like those laid out in traditional textbooks, was a genuine revelation to her. "You don't need to be stuck in a rut or on a subject that doesn't interest you," she continued, somewhat amazed that this was a real possibility.

Closely related to the aforementioned revelation was the realization of the importance of independent, critical thinking in doing science. While science requires care and rigor in its methods, it does not insist on slavishly following orders. The scientific mind-set is creative and independent, even aggressive at times.

The following remarks by chemistry student Carl illustrate this idea well.

> I was eager to put myself more or less in a submissive position in the lab, someone closer to a technician who follows the superior's orders than an independent thinker. Professor N. had kept telling me that I was not aggressive enough to do research, and after several weeks of unsatisfactory results, I finally understood what he meant and decided to take things on my own. I wish I had known to think independently earlier and that I was expected to have more confidence in my opinions and initiatives.

Science faculty often forget their own journey to independent understanding and thinking. They take for granted that it will simply happen for students over time, as it did for them. Simple ideas like giving students permission to think independently, let alone actively encouraging them to do so, can be an enormous revelation to students. Even our best teachers often just encourage their students to learn the material as given, assuming they can learn to think later, as if learning science in science communities is not a complex and creative thinking process.

A Brief Addendum

While student research was not the focus of the GSW program, as we saw in Chapter 4, the training of the peer facilitators in the GSW program provided them with an initial encounter with science education research. As part of their training, each GSW student worked on a group research project with other facilitators, investigating a problem in science education typically related to student learning and the learning environments of the GSW experience.[15] Unexpectedly to us, a number of these students found that the experience of science education research opened up their understanding of the field. One of our facilitators, Joel, described it this way:

> I enjoyed our topic of research and would love to pursue more research in the field of learning. As a student who is a science major, I was quite closed minded in the types of research I thought I enjoyed—typically science research, namely, biological research. However, blending science and research in learning blends two of my passions. It opened my eyes to a whole new way of looking at and approaching science and math disciplines which I was unaware of previously.

Like the previous students, he describes this new mind-set of what science is, and the range of questions that it might address, as arising through doing research. In this case, however, the experience of science as being dynamic and flexible in which one can pursue questions of interest arose through research on science education. While it is probably true that few students and scientists traditionally regard such research as doing actual science, research in science education has established itself as an important part of the work of many of our most brilliant and renowned scientists.[16] Indeed, the development of more rigorous understanding of the factors underpinning the improvement of science education has increasingly been recognized as critical to the future of science. And research collaborations of this kind among faculty, graduate students, and postdocs from both science and education have grown substantially.[17]

Completing the Journey

The student experience of research explored in this chapter depicts a further step in the journey into learning science that was described in Chapter 2. Previously we illustrated the assistance provided by the workshops in three distinct ways: as a shelter for those who were reliant on others for support in learning the new science concepts they were encountering; as a forum for those students wanting to engage critically with these new concepts; and as a studio for those wanting to independently create broader, more connected understandings of the science. Taken together they described different points in the development of the conceptual skills required of students graduating in science. The engagement with research emphasized in the SRW program takes that journey further. It is less an exploration of what science knows and more an exploration of what science does not know. It is doing science. As such, the SRW program is more than a "forum" or a "studio" for developing thinking. It is a "lab" for trying out ideas that engage the student in multiple intellectual, practical, and social skills while also contributing to our scientific knowledge.

UNDERGRADUATE RESEARCH ENVIRONMENTS

The goal of the design of undergraduate research environments is simple: provide students with the experience of actually doing science.[18] The realization of this goal, however, is more complex. The character of specific undergraduate research environments will differ greatly, reflecting the diversity that flourishes among the vast number of science, engineering, and math departments in the nation's colleges and universities. Many will happen, as in the program described earlier, during the summer. Others may occur during the academic year as formal courses, honors work, or separate independent studies, internships, or capstone projects. Others may take place as part of paid work or in volunteer and service opportunities, both local and as part of study abroad opportunities.[19] The final structure will reflect the opportunities and constraints that characterize the institution and its various practices. As unique as these programs and courses are, the opportunities for undergraduate research that these different environments offer should, ideally, share a number of core elements.

Content Must Be Meaningful

The principal elements of undergraduate research environments should mirror the features of our own scientific research communities. The main point here is the relationship of the researcher to the outcome of the research. The outcome is unknown, even to the program instructors and possibly to science more generally. It is important that the knowledge to be gained, however partial and limited, be original and potentially make a meaningful contribution.[20] This distinguishes the experience from the "right-answer" curriculum that dominates traditional science courses and traditional cookbook-type lab experiences in which students simply reproduce existing experiments with the goal of finding a predetermined answer. In effect, this means that the research tools—the basic knowledge and skills through which scientists engage the knowledge frontiers of their discipline—constitute the content of the undergraduate research environment. As such, in addition to actually doing research in a lab, the research environment should also provide students with guided opportunities to

- approach and engage the key resources (labs, scientists, technology, and materials) needed to conduct the research;
- identify and shape the research topic and question, including the rationale for the question, and its relevance, for example, to key local, national, and/or global issues;
- conduct a review of the literature;
- select the research methods to employ in the research;
- write up a proposal for doing the research;
- conduct the research experiments;
- analyze and interpret the data obtained from the research; and
- write up and present the results of the research (including an oral presentation, with feedback from instructors and peers where possible).

Structure Should Be Scientific

In the same way, the learning structure of the undergraduate research environments should also reflect the structure of scientists' own research communities. Perhaps the main idea here is that the research happens in a community. The researcher is rarely alone. Even in those cases in which the researchers may find themselves physically alone, they are working, writing from and writing to a community that will support their work, review it, critique it, and ultimately accept or reject it. For the most part the science research community works in groups and teams. Indeed, much of this book has focused on the important relationships and experiences that characterize these groups. Studies of the undergraduate research experience[21] have indicated that the structure of the most effective research experiences for students reflects actual science research communities in the following ways. Students are permitted to

- possess (and feel that they have) some real ownership of the research project;
- work in or be closely connected to actual science labs or research sites;
- collaborate with one or more peers in teams or groups;
- interact closely with a peer mentor—a student just a year or two ahead of the undergraduate with undergraduate research experience and training; in some cases, this may be a junior graduate student; and
- associate directly with the scientists—science faculty, postdocs, and senior graduate students—in the actual research environment.

Engaging Students

The most difficult task in designing authentic undergraduate research environments is often persuading students that they can actually engage in research, that research is achievable for them. Decades of experience believing that real science is something other people do have undermined student interest and belief in it as a possibility for them. The student who expressed previously that he felt that research was "inaccessible" echoed the sentiments of many of his peers. And he was one of those few students who gambled and tried it. What of the others who do not take the chance?

When we asked those students who did not participate, even when the program was made accessible to them, the answer was generally a question of time. This was also the main issue mentioned by students who started the program and then dropped out. Often, strategic students intent on attaining good grades do not feel they have the time to engage in an academic program for which there is no material reward or credit.[22]

What is more interesting is why the students who did take the program persisted in doing so. Much past research has examined why students have turned away from engaging in science, let alone engaging in science research.[23] We wanted to know which factors underpinned their motivation to continue in science and science research even given the constraints of time. We were less concerned with the innate personal factors[24] that might explain their motivation and more interested in the external factors that contributed to their interest in science research, factors that might inform the design of undergraduate research environments more generally.

Students in the program were surveyed and separately interviewed in some depth about their past experiences with science, in both their home and school environments, with attention to specific people and events that might have ignited an enthusiasm for science. The analysis of the data revealed six important factors that may have contributed to their determination to take the program:

- positive experience of science class
- exposure to science outside of class
- an enthusiastic science teacher
- a parent in a science-related profession

- positive media experience of science
- experience of science as connected to the concerns of everyday life

While these results have important implications for the design of early science experiences for students, they also suggest that the design of undergraduate research environments should not be created in isolation from more traditional science curricula in higher education. The experience of these environments—particularly the engagement of students in them—would benefit by meaningful connections to the science courses in which the students are engaged. And those courses would benefit by providing more explicit links between the science that students are studying and the three key aspects of science that engage students: the excitement of experimental science and research, the passion and questions of the scientist and science researchers themselves, and the sheer awe-inspiring impact of science and its potential in our everyday lives.

Not surprisingly the design of undergraduate research experiences leads inexorably back to the traditional college science course where the facts of science are served up and delivered. Through research, students get the opportunity to really "open their brain" and confront the facts, so to speak, at the brink of their formation as concepts in their minds. In the final analysis the practice and process of scientific inquiry require students to be taken to the edge of science where knowledge is created and science pushes nature to reveal itself to us. Here, in this cauldron, the critical and creative conceptual skills of tomorrow's world are forged.

SUGGESTIONS FOR PRACTICE

- Talk with your students about your research. Not only does this help create interest in research, but it also helps your students get to know you better.

- Bring examples of real-life research into your classroom whenever possible.

- Talk with students about the challenges and disappointments of doing real research. Many undergraduates have an unrealistic idea of research, believing it to be much less messy than it really is.

- Build opportunities to do authentic research both within and outside courses—hypothesis building, reviewing literature, conducting experiments, and including actual proposal writing and presentation of findings.

- Use peer groups to help students develop their research ideas and practices in a real community.

- Help students develop a science identity through working in a genuine research community with members at different levels of expertise helping one another.

EIGHT

Creating Lasting Change in the STEM Classroom

The best way to predict the future is to invent it.

—Alan Kay

"I DON'T HAVE MONEY, and I don't have help," a clearly frustrated biology professor told us. We were leading a discussion on course innovation, and as he spoke many in the room nodded in agreement. "I have ideas for pretty substantial changes in my course, but how do I go anywhere with them when I'm already resource- and time-strapped?"

The complaint is not uncommon. Many faculty would like to be innovative in their teaching, but they feel they lack the time and resources to make it happen. This chapter is devoted to helping faculty who find themselves in this position. We take the principles we have explored over the past six chapters and apply them to a single course or even to a single teaching session. Learning conceptually, focusing on problems, learning with peers, engaging in a community of practice, mentoring and being mentored, and engaging in research can all be incorporated into the classroom with a modest additional expenditure of time and resources.

This chapter will also examine how to *sustain* these kinds of pedagogical changes. Bringing new ideas and practices into the classroom (or department, or institution) is one thing, but ensuring they work and getting them to "stick" are more challenging tasks. Drawing on the lessons we learned from GSW, we will present the model we developed for assessing and sustaining pedagogical change and describe how it can apply to change and improvement of any size— from the institution to the classroom.

INNOVATING IN THE CLASSROOM

Modest changes to a course over time can develop into substantial innovations. Over the years we have worked with many faculty who began by making simple changes to improve student learning in their courses. Many of these changes took hold and transformed courses, and some made a substantial impact on departmental teaching practices. Regardless of their ultimate scope, however, they all drew on at least one of the six key learning principles that have served as the foundation for the GSW.

In this section we address each of these principles individually, providing examples of how they can be applied on a small scale.

Learning Deeply

- As we saw in Chapter 2, students learn deeply when they ground facts and concepts in real contexts, make connections among them, and put them together to create new knowledge. Most important, this means providing an anchor for the information presented to students so that it is not simply a collection of facts to be memorized. Students should—at least at some basic level—be able to explain *why* they are learning particular facts. What will the facts help them do in the future? Why are the facts important, not just to them passing the course but to scientists involved in solving larger problems? How were the facts derived, and what problems led to their discovery? What questions or controversies surround the facts? When students can answer these kinds of questions, the facts come to life. "Live" facts, as opposed to facts devoid of any connection to the broader context, are the ones that grow into much larger webs of knowledge that students will remember.

There are a number of simple approaches to making this happen:

- Provide a brief contextual or historical overview of a concept at the beginning of a lecture.
- Insert contextual comments throughout the lecture.
- Assign short readings on the application of concepts covered in the lecture, and ask students to comment on them either in class or through an online discussion tool.
- Ask students to make educated guesses about how particular concepts might apply to real-world problems.
- Ask students to draw connections among concepts, including those they have learned in other courses. This can happen during class through quick questions to the group, as a homework assignment, online, or in quizzes.
- Consider using a concept inventory, such as the force concepts inventory in physics,[1] or other more recently

designed concept inventories,[2] to measure students' pre- and post-course conceptual knowledge.

The experience of a young assistant chemistry professor trying to juggle her research program with her desire to teach well provides a good example of this conceptual approach. Frustrated that her students did not seem engaged in the classroom, she was searching for ways to spark their interest at the beginning of a lecture. She decided to take a few minutes at the start of the hour to introduce well-known chemists who had made important breakthroughs related to the lecture content. These mini-presentations had the intended effect—the students perked up—but they also had another important effect. Students began to ask questions about how what they were learning in class was related to what that eminent chemist had done. The professor leveraged their interest by creating an assignment out of these presentations, asking students to identify for themselves the ways in which the course's concepts related to that scientist's work. This took the form of a couple of paragraphs of written homework, which fed into a short class discussion, with students sharing their ideas with each other and the instructor. (A professor concerned about time might even hold the discussion on line.)

Engaging Problems

Many faculty hold an implicit belief that problem solving belongs mainly in upper-level courses. The idea is that beginning-level students simply are not ready to approach problems; these students need to master the facts first.

Certainly, mastering the facts is critical. But there is no reason that fact mastery cannot happen in conjunction with problem solving—in fact, it is greatly enhanced through problem solving. Students learning in problem-oriented environments, for example, score just as well on content tests as their peers who learn in more traditional environments, in particular with regard to long-term retention of knowledge. Moreover, embedding the facts to be learned within problems promotes student motivation, recall of previously learned background information, and retrieval of relevant information learned in class.[3]

To engage problems, students often need "scaffolding,"[4] or guidance on how to work through a problem, and the additional information necessary to solve the problem. Providing this scaffolding is critical; without it, students may give up prematurely.

Ideas for integrating problem solving into a course include the following:

- Model different approaches to solving problems during a lecture using simple problems related to lecture content. Later, give students similar problems to work out on their own.
- Take five to ten minutes out of lecture to present problems that incorporate key lecture concepts, and ask students to try to solve them, perhaps in pairs or small groups. Also ask students to try to persuade one another regarding the correct answer, and discuss this answer and how it can be arrived at. This method lends itself well to the personal response system technology ("clickers") that enables students to answer questions anonymously and for those responses to be immediately reflected on a summary showing on a classroom monitor.[5]

- Center an entire lecture—or even a course—around problems. Structure learning so that rather than a series of topics to be studied, the course content becomes a series of problems to be solved.
- Consider using the "problematized lecture" approach, described in Chapter 3, in which students are first presented with a problem or question, are helped to understand why it is a meaningful problem or question, are given a chance to answer or provide solutions, are presented with the teacher's answer, and finally are asked to consider a related, broader question.[6]
- Use multistage problems to span course topics so that students are returning to old problems with new material. This is a great way to help students link related concepts and retain information.

In an effort to engage his students more fully in the mathematical content of his 200-level engineering course, an engineering colleague of ours redesigned his teaching to help his students see the relevance of the material to everyday problems. He developed a group project for the course, the goal of which was to help students begin to question assumptions about chemical plant safety. Groups received a case study describing a dangerous incident at a chemical plant. They were told that their role was to respond to the local municipal authority, which was asking for information about possible hazards at the site, as well as for an explanation about why the incident had occurred. Groups worked outside of class to craft responses to the local authority. When the instructor reviewed these, he found a fair amount of variation in how well the groups understood the concepts involved, and he was able to address this lack of under-standing in class. In this case not only were students able to dive deeply into the material and gain a much stronger sense of how concepts relate to real problems, but the instructor was also able to identify student weaknesses and help correct them.

Connecting Peers

In large lecture classes students can easily make it through the term without ever talking to a classmate. In fact, many are reluctant to talk to peers about course content for fear that they may be giving away whatever edge they have in terms of a course grade. This is a shame, since learning in isolation, as we saw in Chapter 4, rarely achieves the results that learning with others offers. With a few simple techniques, however, faculty can actively encourage students to learn together, even in the largest classes, and discourage a hy-percompetitive kind of thinking at the same time.

- Allow time during lecture for students to briefly engage with one another in groups of two or three. This might be comparing homework answers and trying to resolve differences, answering questions presented during lecture, or solving short problems—always with some concrete goal (e.g., an answer to turn in), so that the exercise feels meaningful. Whatever form it takes, peer engagement should offer the opportunity for students to see other approaches to solving problems or understanding concepts and to challenge others and be challenged to rethink what they believe they know.
- Encourage students to form study groups. Some faculty even make this a requirement. Creating a sign-up sheet in

class or online can ease the process and make it more likely that students will take part. To create a stronger link between study groups and the course, faculty can ask study groups to bring in questions that have arisen during group meetings and address these questions in class.

- Hold "group office hours," described in Chapter 6. This offers multiple benefits: it reduces the time faculty devote to office hours; it enables students to engage with one another as well as the professor; it eases the reluctance that students feel about attending office hours; and it allows students to hear the answers to other students' questions as well as their own.

To get his students to think more deeply about the course material, one of the GSW chemistry professors redeveloped the way he used classroom quizzes in his large 100-level course. Having traditionally used standard quizzes (that is, giving the quizzes, having students hand them in, grading them, and returning them), he decided to modify these quizzes so that they became a springboard to peer deliberation of chemistry problems. Students took three short quizzes over the term and after each one formed a discussion group with three fellow students to present their answers and their rationale for those answers. When there were discrepancies, the groups could debate their positions. The instructor then polled the class on their answers, provided his own answers, and moved directly into a lecture on this very material.

This method accomplished several important things. First, it gave students an opportunity to think at some depth about the material they had read about before the lecture. Second, it enabled students to talk their ideas out and to hear others' ideas that may have conflicted with their own, forcing them to question those approaches as well as their own. And third, it allowed the instructor to quickly get a general sense of how accurately students were answering the questions, giving him an indication of how much the students had understood from the readings.

Mentoring Learning

Even if they sincerely want to take a personal interest in each student, faculty who teach large classes feel their hands are tied. There is just no way to have meaningful individual interaction with two or three hundred undergraduates. So mentoring needs to happen in creative ways, such as the following:

- Make use of technology to reach individuals in the crowd. One chemistry professor we know has each student in his large lecture courses post a brief bio sketch at the start of the term, listing academic or professional goals and explaining why she or he is interested in the subject. Throughout the term, the professor makes reference to these notes as appropriate topics arise—for instance, "Matthew, Jenna, and others who told me you are interested in pharmacy school should pay special attention here. . . ." (Here the faculty member is both offering mentoring and *modeling* good mentoring for the large group.)
- Offer to answer career-related questions once or twice a term. This can also be an online activity, with students submitting questions and faculty answering all or some of them, either online or "live" in class.

- Use teaching assistants as mentors for undergraduates. In addition to grading and running labs, they can offer coaching for students interested in attending graduate school themselves. For instance, teaching assistants can spend the first five minutes of a lab—or can hold office hours or offer online discussions—offering a Q&A session on graduate school.
- Encourage students to mentor one another as learners. Help them organize out-of-class study pairs or groups, and encourage them to discuss approaches to studying and share study tips.

A medical school teacher with whom we recently worked tapped the potential of mentoring in a global-health course. The course was open to undergraduate students, graduate students, medical students, and even medical school residents and fellows, who would work together on solving public health problems. All needed to apply to join the class, making for a highly motivated group. The students worked in small groups made up of people from each experience level to develop research projects on particular course topics and to make recommendations to improve public health policy. To help ensure that groups ran as smoothly as possible, the instructor used more senior-level students as group leaders. She also asked all students to comment on the process along the way so that she could make changes where necessary.

In this unorthodox structure all students were able to work directly with people increasingly more experienced, leading up to the instructor, who consulted with each group and its leader. This kind of mentoring is an experience that undergraduates in particular rarely have. Even more unusual is the opportunity for feedback that those with more experience get from the less experienced: highly engaged undergraduates with varied backgrounds will have valuable insights and perspectives that can be useful, even to medical residents.

This structure will not work for every course, but the principles can. Rather than seeing students with different talents, backgrounds, and levels of experience as barriers to smooth teaching, this professor harnessed diversity to help students extend one another's learning. This professor made her expectations explicit: students were to draw from their diverse backgrounds for the good of the project. And she provided careful guidance and feedback along the way. This kind of peer mentoring can happen on a smaller scale, within a group project, or even during a class activity, as long as students know that their goal is to help everyone learn rather than compete for the best grades.

Creating Community

In a single course it is often a struggle to get students to feel part of the class community, let alone the broader disciplinary community. But even simple invitations to engage in the community can be meaningful. The more students know about what "real-life" science looks like, the more they will begin to feel comfortable in their own novice scientist roles. For instance:

- Give students a chance to see the community in action. As we saw in the last chapter, one of the most popular events in the Science Research Workshop program was a series of faculty presentations of their own research experiences. Faculty can take a few minutes within a lecture to talk about their research, especially as it relates to topics the class is studying, and guest speakers can bring additional perspectives. They can also encourage teaching assistants to talk about their research and research interests.

- Introduce students to the research literature. Even in introductory-level courses, students can read and comment on research articles. This not only gives them a glimpse into the academic world, it also familiarizes them with the way in which research is conducted and written about in the discipline, and how to think critically about the concepts they are learning.
- Keep students abreast of broader trends and happenings in the field. Include a brief report of current research related to course topics during a lecture, for instance, to keep students engaged with the world of science. As a bonus, this also gives them a better sense of how course material is relevant to broader issues—and breaks up a lecture to keep students alert and interested.

A few years ago we collaborated with a young professor of engineering as he redesigned an upper-level nanomaterials course. He wanted to develop students' ability to evaluate research in nanotechnology,[7] a skill he felt was not being practiced in the course as it was traditionally taught. In the new design, students worked on four small-group projects that allowed them to engage with key issues in the broader community of scientists and engineers. In one of these projects, for instance, students were asked to develop a proposal, intended for university administrators, recommending the purchase of a particular nanofabrication system. To reflect the interdisciplinarity of the nanoscience and technology communities, the individual groups were composed of students from different majors and different areas of interest. For each project three of the four groups were assigned the project, and one group acted as an evaluation committee, chaired by the course teaching assistant. Groups researched and developed ideas outside of class and later presented their case in class. This committee developed specific criteria for judging the projects—guided by the National Science Foundation's two broad criteria of intellectual merit and broader impact—and evaluated them, assigning points that were incorporated into the final grades.

This course design generated a community of practice far beyond what most students experience in their individual courses. Students engaged in authentic projects that offered them real insight into the actual problems of professional academics and engineers, as well as into the decision-making processes used to carry out their work. In addition, guided by a teaching assistant mentor, the students engaged in a key community practice—peer review and evaluation—with real-world implications: the grades of their classmates.

Doing Research

Generally, research activity in undergraduate science courses is limited to lab time, and even there students often take simple "cookbook" approaches and do not engage in genuine research activity. While there is not always space for full-fledged student research in the courses themselves, students can begin to learn what it means to be a researcher. For instance:

- Ask students to "be researchers" during a lecture. Faculty can talk about a particular research project during a lecture and stop at certain points to ask students to do what the researchers have done: predict outcome, determine methods, interpret results, and so on. This not only gives students information about the research process but also engages them more actively in the class.

- Put students in the reviewer role. A biology colleague had her students read research journal articles and critique them in an online forum. Beforehand, she modeled this sort of critique in class and explained the role of peer review in research. Students were not making highly sophisticated critiques, but the assignment forced them to think critically about how research is done and enabled them to more intimately understand the steps involved in doing research.

- Take students into the lab. Faculty may not want hundreds of students wandering around their own labs, but a guided tour, followed by a discussion with the professor about his or her research, is usually feasible. Course professors can also invite a handful of especially interested students to submit their names for a more hands-on visit to the lab, perhaps led by graduate students.

"As a student myself," wrote one of our computer science professors, "I have always deeply enjoyed courses in which I have been actively challenged to solve new problems and execute cutting-edge research ideas." Wanting to generate the same excitement in his own students, this professor redesigned an Internet architecture course he was teaching to involve students in addressing a real research problem. At the beginning of the course he prompted students to think in terms of research by identifying several key problems in Internet design—for instance, how to prevent various sorts of malicious attacks. He helped students break these large problems into more specific subproblems, asked them to explore possible approaches to solving them, and then had them evaluate the efficacy of those approaches. He also required students to gather background information on the problems through the literature and coached them in reading the literature with a critical eye. In proposing solutions to the problem, students needed to identify the assumptions they were making and discuss the weaknesses that these assumptions may have created, as well as the new research questions that those weaknesses may have prompted.

IMPLEMENTING AND SUSTAINING INNOVATION

Whether large- or small-scale, implementing pedagogical innovation in science is challenging. And sustaining it after the initial pilot stage is even tougher. This is especially the case in an environment where faculty face high, and often conflicting, demands on their time, students resist new practices, and educational change does not fit neatly into existing promotion and tenure systems. Nevertheless, it is achievable. Drawing on fifteen years of lessons from the GSW experience, we developed a model for implementing and sustaining pedagogical improvement that can apply to any innovation, from making a modest change in a teaching technique to realizing a department-wide curriculum change.

The GSW innovation model comprises five stages of implementation (see Figure 8.1), from conceiving the initial idea to consolidating the innovation. The stages are iterative, so that the final stage can lead to another cycle of innovation. They are also not necessarily

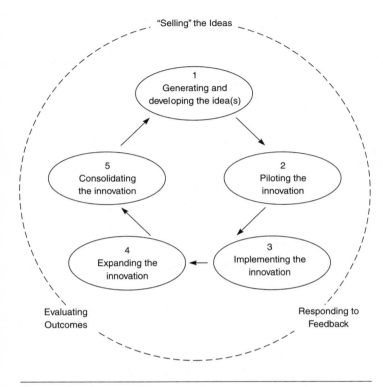

Figure 8.1   The Innovation Cycle: Implementation, Sustainability, Evaluation

linear: for instance, the pilot phase (stage 2) may lead to new ideas for implementation (stage 1), and expansion (stage 4) may involve piloting (stage 2) new twists on some of the program components. Program evaluation, responding to feedback, and "selling" the ideas are continual practices and the most important ones in ensuring the innovation's sustainability.

Stage 1: Generating and Developing the Idea

It is true in education, just as it is true in science, that good ideas emerge out of problems. As we described in Chapter 1, our initial problem was that some students in biology were not performing to the level of their capabilities.

This was a relatively modest problem but an important and widespread one. It was also a problem that a classroom professor felt important enough to warrant resources beyond his own. So he stepped outside of his everyday environment and looked for partners. As in science, faculty members often benefit from an additional perspective or outside expertise on teaching and learning. Most universities and colleges have resources such as teaching centers to assist faculty members seeking to make changes in their courses, or to connect colleagues who have a mutual interest in improving learning. (In fact, we very frequently hear from faculty that this kind of dialogue helps them better conceptualize, plan, and carry out their teaching innovations.)

The next step at this stage was to identify possible approaches to solving the problem. We went to the learning literature and talked to people who had faced similar problems and tried to solve them. We identified several possible approaches—including peer groups, but also tutoring, remedial work over the summer, and preparatory classes—and carefully worked through the pros and cons of each.

For faculty members redesigning a course, this step is no different: look to colleagues, look to the literature (both within your own discipline's teaching journals[8] and general teaching and learning journals), and talk with pedagogical experts who can help shape the innovation. A chemistry professor recently approached us about student comments that his lectures were "not useful." We collaborated with him to pinpoint the problem, which appeared to be that students were having trouble following the logic of the lectures, and so were disengaged during lectures. We talked about some possible remedies, for instance, providing an overview in advance and including short exercises throughout the class, and we helped him develop a plan for trying out and testing these ideas.

The essential activities in this stage are (1) distinctly *identifying a clear problem* and its underlying sources, (2) *finding interested colleagues* who can provide feedback or help get things started, and (3) *searching relevant literature and practices* for effective approaches to solving the problem.

Stage 2: Piloting the Idea

With its initial idea, the GSW started small. We had very limited resources in the beginning—just the volunteer time that one faculty member and one teaching and learning center staff member could squeeze out of their schedules, and no budget. The pilot consisted of a handful of biology students and a volunteer peer leader. The project goals went no further than an enjoyable quarter, increased confidence, and solid grades in the course for our few student participants.

While we hoped eventually to expand these modest goals, we knew that to sell this idea to more people (including ourselves) would require evidence that it worked. So we set up an assessment for the pilot that measured students' satisfaction and grade outcomes compared to a similar group of students who wanted to join the program but were unable to.[9]

At the classroom level a pilot can mean trying out one component of a new idea. For instance, we know an engineering professor who wanted to change her traditional lecture-style course to a project-based course in which students would work on a large project over the course of the term. She felt that this change would be too dramatic to make all at once, so she started by simply adding one small part of this project as an assignment midway through the term. That worked well, and the next time she taught the course she added on to the project assignment, with plans to continue adding slowly.

This incremental approach allowed her to evaluate the project assignments and to make adjustments as needed along the way. To evaluate the pilot projects she did not just look at student grades but also at whether the students were meeting the new goals she had set for them. For instance, one of her goals was to improve student skills in critically evaluating outside research. To measure whether she had met that goal, she included a few questions on her exam asking students to make judgments about research quality; she also included a question on her end-of-term evaluation asking whether students felt that they had improved in this respect. While she found she was generally meeting her goals, the fact that some students did poorly on the exam items told her that she needed to emphasize critical analysis skills in the future and perhaps use a quiz to check whether all students were "getting it."

With pilot data, she felt more confident talking to colleagues about what she was doing in her course, and as word spread about her new approach, fellow faculty members sought her out to learn more.

Key activities in this stage are (1) *starting small*, with realistic goals, (2) *gathering data* to show whether and how the pilot works, and (3) *gathering support* and interest from colleagues.

Stage 3: Implementing the Innovation

If the pilot is successful, implementing the innovation is not too much of a stretch. Having built support for the GSW among faculty, administrators, and students, for example, meant that asking for additional resources (time, energy, and, in some cases, money) was not as challenging as we had feared. Initial positive data also strengthened a grant application for funding to continue the project with additional staff time to expand the coordination and evaluation of the program.

Faculty colleagues in our chemistry department recently provided an interesting example of this stage at the course level. For some time they had harbored a hunch that the struggle some students were having with introductory chemistry was based on weak math skills. Verifying this was critical, because it would allow them to identify students who were at risk for doing poorly in chemistry and provide these students with academic support. So they teamed up with faculty in mathematics. In a very preliminary analysis they found a relationship between grades in math and introductory chemistry. But they wanted more evidence. They applied for and received a small grant from the university's teaching and learning center to hire a research assistant to analyze the exam data more fully. With stronger evidence that math skills are correlated with chemistry grades, the group was able to identify students at risk for struggling in chemistry and, more important, make a case for increased services to these students.

Keys to implementing the innovation are (1) *building effective support structures* for the innovation, (2) *maintaining relationships* with interested parties, (3) *continuing to collect data* to show whether the innovation is meeting its goals, and how or where it may need improvement, and (4) *seeking resources* to continue developing the project.

Stage 4: Expanding the Innovation

With funding in place the GSW program was able to expand far beyond the initial handful of groups. It went from one discipline to two, three, and eventually, with the help of a National Science Foundation grant, to five. Careful not to grow too quickly, we incrementally added courses and workshops while maintaining a central management structure so that departmental differences would not impede the program's success.

Again, the collection and analysis of data on grades, student retention, and the student experience in the course sequences was an integral part of the expansion. We shared findings with faculty, departments, and administrators through departmental meetings and with internal and external advisory boards that met annually, providing the program staff with invaluable feedback and advice.

A colleague of ours who teaches in the medical school reported similar experiences of expansion (albeit less extensive) at the classroom level. She collaborated with us some time ago to develop a problem-based learning course, drawing upon the problem-based learning literature to articulate her learning objectives, pedagogical activities, and course assessment methods. Based on her success with these changes, she then expanded her ideas by extending her new pedagogical template to a program for medical fellows, modifying the activities to allow for their more advanced knowledge.

Expansion does not need to move the innovation outside of the classroom though. In many cases faculty expand innovations by adapting an approach that has been successful in one course for another course, for instance trying out a new kind of student project in a higher-level course and then adapting it for an introductory course. Expansion is simply what happens when faculty move ideas that work in one setting into a new setting.

Critical activities for expanding an educational innovation include (1) *expanding slowly* so that management does not become unwieldy, (2) *centralizing oversight of the innovation* to help ensure consistency and smooth operation, (3) *continuing to assess the innovation regularly* to identify any "growing pains" that need to be addressed, and (4) *soliciting regular feedback,* whether from expert members of a formal advisory board or simply a fellow faculty member who shares an interest in the goals of the innovation.

Stage 5: Consolidating the Innovation

As the end of the grant funding period for the GSW loomed on the horizon, securing on-going university funding to sustain the program was critical. To do that we needed to make an even stronger case. We needed to ensure that the program was resource efficient. We also needed to convince the administration that the program had a positive impact on a large number of students, that students wanted to take part, and that faculty and departmental leaders were on board.

We achieved resource efficiency by centralizing management of the GSW program across the disciplines, and by moving from a system of paying the peer facilitators to giving them course credit for the training they received. Convincing stakeholders that the program was achieving its goals came fairly easily because of the ongoing data collection and dissemination of findings we had built into the program. With a strong case that GSW was running efficiently and was making a positive impact, we ultimately secured renewable funding. Faculty members consolidate classroom innovations when they make them a regular part of their teaching so that those innovations are, in a sense, no longer innovations. Sometimes this simply means that the changes faculty make while they are implementing and expanding the innovation become habit. Or that they extend beyond the faculty member. The simple creation of a permanent bank of materials for students and other faculty to use can help ensure continuity in the absence of the primary leader.

Consolidation can also mean that faculty embed innovations into their courses so fully that they are able to create new, additional innovations based on the first. For example, a colleague of ours in biology developed a substantial group project for advanced undergraduates. After he felt that the innovation was meeting its goal—to promote understanding of the research process—he embarked on a further innovation to help students develop critical analysis skills: a peer assessment system for the group project. The first innovation was solidly enough in place to generate a new innovation.

Critical aspects of this stage in the innovation cycle are (1) *streamlining the innovation* so that it requires the fewest resources needed to run well, (2) *gaining a commitment* from stakeholders for the ongoing provision of resources, and (3) *succession planning*—putting guidelines, materials, and any other necessary information in place for others who may be leading the innovation in the future.

SUSTAINABILITY: THREE PRACTICES OF ASSESSMENT AND EVALUATION

The common element in all five stages of implementing an innovation, described earlier, is the ongoing collection and analysis of data about how it is working. Evaluating the innovation and assessing its impact on the students' experience and learning are also critical to sustaining an innovation. An innovation cannot be meaningfully sustained without continuous improvement, and improvement cannot happen without data to guide it.

In our study of the GSW program we have identified three key practices that were critical in sustaining the project over so many years: selling the ideas (objectives and methods of the innovation), evaluating outcomes, and responding to the evaluation. These practices can be just as fruitfully applied to modest innovations: no matter how small, innovations need staying power if they are to make a real impact on student learning.

1. Selling the Ideas

Good ideas are the starting point. To push them forward requires support from everyone who will be involved in the innovation, even if only peripherally. When we began the GSW program, we sat down with students who would be attending workshops, with faculty who would be writing problems, and with department chairs who would in essence be donating resources to the developing program. We described the program objectives and methods to each of these stakeholder groups and showed them that the program would offer them more benefit than cost. Sometimes we did this by simply discussing the theories and research on which the program was based, sometimes by presenting data, and sometimes by simply letting satisfied students and faculty spread the word among their peers.

For individual faculty the key stakeholder is the student. As we have noted throughout the book, students are used to a particular approach to teaching, and to being rewarded for complying with that approach. They become uncomfortable when they are asked to deviate from what they know. The sudden appearance of in-class, ungraded quizzes in a course that always used traditional exams, for instance or of research projects in a course that strictly utilized lectures beforehand leaves many students feeling unsettled. But when instructors let students know what to expect, and provide a rationale for it, students are much more receptive to new teaching approaches.

Students grumbled the first time one of our physics professors turned a strictly lecture-oriented course into one that required a fair amount of student participation and gave her poor end-of-term evaluations. The most common remark was something like "Why didn't she just tell us what we needed to know, instead of making us do all those activities?" The next time she taught the course she took ten minutes during the first session to explain her approach. She talked about the value of learning by doing, by asking and trying to answer one's own questions. She even gave examples from her own learning to illustrate her points. While a few students still asked for more straightforward lectures, most ended the term feeling that the classroom activities had helped them learn.

Students are not the only group that needs persuading. Fellow faculty can be just as skeptical, and even more so, than students. This is partly because what one instructor does in a course may have ramifications for what another instructor experiences in her or his course. Faculty who are making real innovations in their teaching often struggle through the first year trying to convince departmental colleagues that what they are doing will improve student learning—and not make things difficult for the faculty who teach those students later. Others may worry that students will not come to their courses with the necessary background knowledge, or that they will resist more traditional styles of teaching. Many instructors find that starting slowly, providing their colleagues with a rationale for changes one is making, and keeping them abreast of developments in the course and of student feedback are excellent ways to reassure them and even generate enthusiasm for the innovation.

2. Evaluating Outcomes

As we described in Chapter 1, we have conducted a range of evaluations of the GSW. With each of these we have reviewed and discussed the feedback and data generated by the evaluation, making purposeful decisions about how to respond. As a result, we have gained a tremendous amount of information about how the program is working and have been able to make continual improvements. We have also, of course, gathered evidence for the value of the program and have been able to feed this evidence into the "selling" that was continually required early on in the program's life.

Classroom innovations are assessed in essentially the same way as large programs: identifying the goals, determining how to measure whether they have been met, and taking those measurements.[10] Sometimes the "measurement" is an exam or assignment result, and sometimes it is an additional validated measurement instrument such as a concept inventory (discussed earlier) designed to measure a student's understanding of specific science concepts. Measures can also focus on a student's subjective experience of the course.

Some years ago an engineering colleague of ours developed a classroom innovation to encourage students to get a "feel" for the concepts they were studying. In place of a fifty-minute lecture, he provided twenty minutes of lecture, put the students to work in an inquiry-oriented activity for twenty minutes, and then led ten minutes of discussion on what the students had experienced during the activity. His objectives were to (1) engage students more fully in class, (2) deepen students' understanding of core concepts, (3) prompt students to develop their own questions about those concepts, and (4) encourage general interest and enthusiasm for the course topic.

Building from those objectives, he designed the following evaluation measures for his innovation: a pre- and post-questionnaire asking students about their attitudes toward the course and the course topic; concept-oriented questions included on the two course exams; and two short assignments during the term, asking students to develop questions about the activities they had done. In addition, on his end-of-term course evaluation, this instructor added open-ended questions on overall student satisfaction with the new activities. He also talked informally with students about how they liked the activities. With this assessment structure, the goals he had set out for the innovation were aligned with the ways in which he was evaluating it, so that in the end he was able to tell how well he had met each of those goals.

Over the years we have devised the following set of simple ground rules for a good educational evaluation:

1. Clearly define the innovation's learning goals and objectives at the outset: What do you want this innovation to do for students?
2. Design the evaluation activities to align with those goals. The evaluation should tell you whether you have met each of the goals.

3. Think about evaluation up front. We have seen large numbers of faculty wait until they are midway through running an innovation to start thinking about evaluating it, by which time they have lost the opportunity to gather critical beginning-of-term data.

4. Use, when possible, existing, validated instruments to measure your variables of interest. For instance, a number of concept inventories have been developed and discussed in the literature, as have questionnaires to measure student self-efficacy in various domains.[11]

5. Use pre- and post-innovation measures to look for change in students over the term.

6. Use a control group, if one is available, to ascertain more carefully whether any gains attributed to the innovation group are absent in a group that did not take part in the innovation.

7. Include both quantitative and qualitative measures. Quantitative measures can include exam scores, course grades, or scores on numerical questionnaires; qualitative measures can include short reflection papers, open-ended questions on questionnaires, brief interviews with individual students, or focus groups. It is usually best if someone other than the course instructor conducts the interviews and focus groups. Qualitative evaluation does not need to be complex and time consuming; simply asking students to write their thoughts on a questionnaire can provide revealing information.

8. Share with colleagues and students evaluation data about how the innovation is working. This does not mean

that students need to see all of the data, but sharing some trends can help them better understand the innovation's purpose and make them feel part of the overall project. Colleagues also will feel more involved when they have seen some evaluation results, and they often have valuable insights into the innovation. Some faculty also present their results at conferences and write them up for publication in disciplinary teaching journals.

A final note: It is a common practice for the evaluators to work independently of the program developers to avoid any real or perceived bias in evaluation methods and findings. This is particularly important when collecting data in person—in focus groups or interviews, for instance—where participants may not feel comfortable speaking frankly to program staff.

3. *Responding to the Evaluation*

Sharing data, of course, is not enough. Evaluation is for controlling quality, for pinpointing what is working well and not as well, and for determining where and how to make improvements.

In the GSW we used data on grades, student retention, and student experience to help make our case, but we also used data and informal feedback to improve the program. For instance, from time to time we see a dip in enrollment in particular disciplines. When that happens, we talk with faculty in the departments to try to find out why. In some cases there has been a lack of program marketing, and we know we need to do more outreach work. We also use regular facilitator evaluations of our worksheet problems to provide feedback to faculty on problems that do not work as well in the workshops, and why. Faculty can then either replace or modify them. Students also regularly provide feedback to their facilitators, and facilitators are expected to reflect on and respond to this feedback.

In a course, evaluation feedback often does not come until late in the term, when it is too late to make many changes. For this reason, we recommend that faculty do midterm evaluations, even informal ones. In fact, just asking students for midterm feedback often increases their satisfaction with a course, because they know that the teacher cares about their experience.

Responding effectively to feedback sometimes requires a little additional digging. In the case of the professor we described earlier, for example, if assessments were to show a lack of gain on the concept-oriented tests, there could be several possible explanations. Students may not have learned the concepts, or perhaps the test failed to pick up what they had in fact learned. Some follow-up investigation, probably more in-depth and qualitative, would help illuminate the problem. Talking one-on-one or in small groups with students to find out what they know about the concepts, what kinds of problems they can solve related to those concepts, and so on would help pinpoint where things went wrong.

Following up on the data also means letting students know that the instructor is doing so. When the instructor demonstrates to students that she or he is responding to their evaluation or feedback, students feel their voices are being heard. When students see that the instructor is making an earnest attempt to help them learn, they will typically match that effort in their own approach to learning.

A Note on Costs

Not all innovations will be on the scale of the GSW program but, regardless, implementation often requires some investment of resources. We know many faculty members who have been creative in finding and using resources in their innovations. Some examples include the following:

- Join forces. As we described earlier, faculty members from chemistry and mathematics recently joined forces to develop an innovation to help students struggling in chemistry because of limited math skills. Because they represented two departments, they were able to draw support from a wider population and to draw resources from a larger pool.
- Find untapped resources within the institution. At our center we often work with faculty who are interested in developing and evaluating an innovation, and occasionally these faculty tell us, "I didn't know you were here—what a great resource!" We also know from many faculty members how easy it is to feel trapped within their own departmental walls. Getting out and talking with others around the institution who may be interested in what you are trying to do is almost always a fruitful activity. At minimum you will end up with new ideas, and at best you will find partners who can help you with components of the project.
- Look for funding, small or large. Our GSW program was initially funded by an external source, and this level of funding is a real possibility for innovations with a track

record from a pilot project. But even newer and small-scale projects can be funded. Many universities have small grants available to faculty who want to develop teaching innovations, often through the teaching and learning center, or even through the development office.

- Build time savings into the innovation. In the GSW we streamlined many of the activities to reduce faculty time considerably. For instance, "veteran" facilitators play an important leadership role in the training of peer facilitators, freeing faculty to focus on helping facilitators understand higher-level concepts. We have also developed a searchable database that faculty can use to develop problem sheets, allowing them to maintain high-quality worksheets with minimal effort.

In important ways the educational innovator is no different from the scientist. Faculty are motivated to innovate because they notice a problem, a question that needs to be answered. Why don't my students engage more actively? How can I get them to be more motivated? Why do they pass my course—or even graduate—without really understanding certain basic concepts? Just as scientists find problems in the lab, in the literature, or in the world, scientist-educators find problems in the classroom.

What they do to address those problems may not seem innovation-like at first. Innovation often results from a series of small changes, and often not until the innovator recognizes patterns and meaning in what he or she has attempted to do. For instance, say a professor is frustrated with a sleepy class and thus incorporates research problems into a lecture in an effort to awaken his students to what is inherently interesting about the material. If this seems to work, he may do it again, may expand on it, and soon this approach may become a key feature of his teaching style. That is certainly a pedagogical innovation, although at first it probably seemed to the professor nothing more than a near-desperate attempt to keep the students from drifting off.

We need innovators working at *all* levels in order to help science students become the best learners of science that they can. The best science students are not necessarily those with the best science minds, or the most comprehensive science preparation—although those things certainly help. The best science students are the ones who engage fully, who wonder and who seek to answer questions, and who want to understand for themselves, and not just to do well in the course. They learn from all sources available to them, including their peers, and they feel a personal connection to the science community. But students do not come to the university ready to do all this. In fact, many of them come prepared to do the opposite: to simply "get through," to give the teachers what they want and move on to the next level.

That is hardly a recipe for meaningful learning. It is certainly not the way we expect professionals to think about their work. To get students to begin thinking and learning more innovatively, faculty need to teach more innovatively. What the best science *students* do depends on what the best science *teachers* do.

Epilogue

What do I mean by an effective education in science? I believe a
successful science education transforms how students think, so that
they can understand and use science like scientists do.

—Carl Wieman

HALF A CENTURY AFTER Sputnik, and nearly three decades since the publication of *A Nation at Risk,* there is still much more work to be done before undergraduate science education fulfills the transformative mission that Carl Wieman articulated. In the academic literature, in the popular media, and in science departments across the country, we hear regular and urgent calls for radical improvement in the way college students learn science. The National Science Foundation,[1] the National Research Council,[2] and the Spellings Commission, along with myriad individual faculty and leaders in higher education and industry,[3] have all made post-2000 pronouncements of higher education's obligation to improve the way science is taught.

Certainly, there have been responses. We have seen scores of scholarly articles published over the past decade detailing innovative approaches to teaching college science, many with sound evaluations and evidence of their effectiveness.[4] And many universities and colleges have established comprehensive programs designed to improve science education at their institutions.[5]

As promising as all of these efforts are, they do not guarantee genuine and lasting change. For pedagogical innovation to work in science, the science community must begin to see teaching and learning as a critical part of its charge. This means that STEM faculty need to be allowed and encouraged to innovate in their classrooms and to investigate these innovations just as they investigate the merits of their science research work. For individual faculty, this means that teaching ceases to be an exercise in attempting to transfer knowledge and later puzzling over those who fail to absorb it. Wieman admitted to his own experience with this common blind spot when he quipped, "An occasional student here and there might have understood my beautifully clear and clever explanations, but the vast majority of students weren't getting them at all."[6]

The role of faculty, then, in creating genuine change is paramount. But faculty do not operate in a vacuum. Students come with their own habits and biases, and no measure of pedagogical correctness will succeed for students who, for one reason or another, fail to embrace the innovative teacher's goals and approaches. So part of the faculty members' mission must be to help students modify their attitudes, expectations, and approaches to learning. Even the most successful students—in fact, probably *mostly* the most successful students—will fall in line with what the faculty demand. If the faculty demand evidence of factual knowledge and no more, students will engage in quick, surface-oriented learning. If the faculty demand evidence of better performance than one's peers in order to succeed, students will engage in fierce competition.

But if the faculty begin to demand evidence of high-level under-standing of course concepts, students will adapt and change the way they study to accommodate this. If faculty begin to address interest-ing problems in the classroom and engage students in solving them, students will come to class and pay attention. If faculty nurture a culture of cooperation, students will cease to see their classmates as competitors and channel that competitive energy into learning.

We do not mean to suggest that these things will happen easily, or quickly. Our work with the Gateway Science Workshop program has taken a decade, and in some ways it is still developing. Unfreez-ing old habits requires change in the environment, and that takes time. For those who teach, small, local changes can provide the spark for broader environmental change. The six principles of ex-cellent science learning we have explored in this book are the cata-lyst for transformation of the learning environment.

But those six practices are more than new activities for the classroom. In fact, their real impact comes not as much through what students *do in class* as through how students, faculty, and administrators *think about learning.* Engaging problems, thinking deeply, learning with peers, belonging to a community of practice, doing research, and mentoring and being mentored all present a new paradigm for learning. This paradigm shifts away from a no-tion of student-as-laborer, the individual student amassing informa-tion in the hope of eventually emerging as a beginning professional, and toward the notion of student-as-apprentice, as a learner grad-ually taking on the habits, perspectives, and wisdom of the com-munity and contributing to its development. It is only through this process that students can become the genuine scientists-in-the-making that Wieman optimistically describes.

And what of those budding scientists? Will they all choose science majors, moving on to graduate school and professional careers in science? Some will—probably more than those who will under current university pedagogy. But surely all will not. And that is not really the point. When the study of science becomes part of what college students themselves see as essential to their intellectual development, when they try it on and find it comfortable, when they surprise themselves by enjoying the work of learning science, and when they begin to feel that in some limited sense they *are* scientists—then we will have succeeded; we will have made the best science students out of them all.

Notes
Index

Notes

INTRODUCTION

1 We wish to acknowledge the generous support of the Andrew W. Mellon Foundation and the National Science Foundation Science, Technology, Engineering, and Mathematics Talent Expansion Program (STEP) 1 Grant (No. DUE 0525550).

1. THE GATEWAY SCIENCE WORKSHOP PROGRAM

Epigraph: Sir William Henry Bragg was a British physicist, chemist, and mathematician who won the Nobel Prize in Physics in 1915. This quote is cited in Koestler, A., and Smythies, J. R., eds. (1958, 1969) *Beyond Reductionism: New Perspectives in the Life Sciences.* London: Hutchinson, 115.

1 For the purposes of the GSW program and this book, underrepresented minority students refer to African American, Hispanic American, and Native American students.

2 Light, G., Cox, R., and Calkins, S. (2009) *Learning and Teaching in Higher Education: The Reflective Professional.* Thousand Oaks, CA: Sage; Light, G. (2008) The puzzle of teaching in higher education: Implications for the structure of academic practice, in *Ideas on Teaching (Volume 6): Selected Papers from TLHE 2006—Quality in Higher Education,* 253–256. Singapore: Centre for Development of Teaching and Learning, National University of Singapore.

3 In recent years a diverse range of learning and teaching approaches with similar features to the GSW have been employed in science; see, for example, Mazur, E. (1997) *Peer Instruction: A User's Manual.* Series in Educational Innovation. Upper Saddle River, NJ: Prentice Hall; Gafney, L., and Varma-Nelson,

P. (2008) *Peer-Led Team Learning: Evaluation, Dissemination, and Institu-tionalization of a College Level Initiative.* New York: Springer; Handelsman, J., Miller, S., and Pfund, C. (2006) *Scientific Teaching.* New York: W. H. Freeman; Moog, R. S., and Spencer, J. N., eds. (2008) *Process-Oriented Guided Inquiry Learning (POGIL).* New York: Oxford University Press.

4 Entwistle, N. (1997) Contrasting perspectives on learning, in F. Marton, D. Hounsell, and N. Entwistle, eds., *The Experience of Learning,* 3–22. Edinburgh: Scottish Academic Press. For a full discussion of these distinctions, see Chapter 2 of this book.

5 The Gateway Science Workshop program includes workshops in both engineering and mathematics. As such, the term "science" in this book is used in its broad sense to include math- and science-related disciplines.

6 For a discussion of the current climate for innovations in teaching and learning in science, technology, engineering, and mathematics (STEM) disciplines, including the barriers to successful innovations, see Baldwin, R. G. (2009) The climate for undergraduate teaching and learning in STEM fields. *New Directions for Teaching & Learning* 117 (Spring): 9–17. In the final chapter of this book (Chapter 8) we discuss how successful innovation may be implemented and sustained.

7 For a more in-depth discussion of the evidence on remediation, see Attewell, P., Lavin, D., Domina, T., and Levey, T. (2006) New evidence on college remediation. *Journal of Higher Education* 77(5): 886–924. For a discussion on stereotype threat, see Steele, C. M. (1997) A threat in the air: How stereotypes shape intellectual identity and performance. *American Psychologist* 52(6): 613–629; Steele, C. M., Spencer, S. J., and Aronson, J. (2002) Contending with group image: The psychology of stereotype and social identity threat. *Advances in Experimental Social Psychology* 34: 379–440.

8 See, for example, the front-page report "10 universities cut programs for minorities" in the May 7, 2003, edition of the *Chicago Tribune.*

9 See, for example, Treisman, U. (1992) Studying students studying calculus: A look at the lives of minority mathematics students in college. *College Mathematics Journal* 23(5): 362–372; Steele et al., Contending; Tien, L. T., Roth, V., and Kampmeier, J. A. (2002) Implementation of a peer-led learning instructional approach in an undergraduate organic chemistry course. *Journal of Research in Science Teaching* 39: 606–632; Gafney, L., and Varma-Nelson, P. (2008) *Peer-Led Team Learning.* New York: Springer.

10 For a full description and discussion of the program, see Streitwieser, B., Light, G., and Pazos, P. (2010) Enabling young scientists to enter the commu-

nity of practitioners: A Science Research Workshop model. *Change Magazine* (May–June): 17–23.

11 For details on the original study, see Born, W. K., Revelle, W., and Pinto, L. (2002) Improving biology performance with workshop groups. *Journal of Science Education and Technology* 11: 347–365.

12 Drane, D., Smith, H. D., Light, G., Pinto, L., and Swarat, S. (2005) The Gateway Science Workshop program: Enhancing student performance and retention in the sciences through peer facilitated discussion. *Journal of Science Education and Technology* 14(3): 337–352.

13 See Drane, D., Micari, M., and Light, G. (working paper) Students as teachers: Effectiveness of a peer-led STEM learning program over ten years: http://www.northwestern.edu/searle/research/publications-and-presentations/working-papers.html (accessed Oct. 16, 2012).

14 Swarat, S., Drane D., Smith H. D., Light G., and Pinto L. (2004) Opening the gateway: Increasing student retention in introductory science courses. *Journal of College Science Teaching* 34(1): 18–23; Drane et al., The Gateway Science Workshop program, 347–348.

15 GPA data are unavailable for students in the first quarter of college. Therefore, we have controlled for GPA in organic chemistry and biology, but not in engineering and chemistry, which are predominantly freshman courses. (Controlling for GPA in engineering and chemistry, however, does not substantially alter the results.) In Figures 1.2 and 1.3, the data are adjusted for gender only to include as many of the minority students as possible in the data pool. For more details and additional analyses, see Drane, Micari, and Light, Students as teachers.

16 See, for example, Steele, A threat; Bowen, William G., and Derek Bok (1998) *The Shape of the River: Long Term Consequences of Considering Race in College and University Admissions.* Princeton, NJ: Princeton University Press; and Rovai, A. P., Gallien, L. B., and Stiff-Williams, H. R. (2007) *Closing the African American Achievement Gap in Higher Education.* New York: Teachers College Press.

17 Light, R. (2001) *Making the Most of College: Students Speak Their Minds.* Cambridge, MA: Harvard University Press.

18 See, for example, Boyer, E. L. (1998) *Reinventing Undergraduate Education: A Blueprint for America's Research Universities.* Commission on Educating Undergraduates in the Research University. Washington, DC: Carnegie Foundation for the Advancement of Teaching; Kuh, G. D. (2007) *Experiences that Matter: Enhancing Student Learning and Success.* Bloomington, IN: University

Center for Postsecondary Research; Kuh, G. D. (2008) *High Impact Educational Practices: What They Are, Who Has Them and Why They Matter.* Washington, DC: Association of American Colleges and Universities; Smith, M. K., Wood, W. B., et al. (2009) Why peer discussion improves student performance on in-class concept questions. *Science* 323: 122–124; Ruiz-Primo, M. A., Briggs, D., et al. (2011) Impact of undergraduate science course innovations on learning. *Science* 331: 1269–1270.

19 Barr, R., and Tagg, J. (1995) From teaching to learning: A new paradigm for undergraduate education. *Change Magazine* (November–December): 13–25.

20 Kuhn, T. (1970) *The Structure of Scientific Revolutions.* Chicago: University of Chicago Press.

21 For models of practice and activity-based theories of learning, see Lave, J., and Wenger, E. (1991) *Situated Learning: Legitimate Peripheral Participation.* Cambridge: Cambridge University Press; Engeström, Y., Miettinen, R., and Punamäki, R-L. (1999). *Perspectives on Activity Theory.* Cambridge: Cambridge University Press. For a discussion of the distinction between acquisition and participation models, see Sfard, A. (1998). On two metaphors for learning and the dangers of choosing just one. *Educational Researcher* 7(2): 4–13.

2. LEARNING DEEPLY

Epigraph: Richard Feynman won the Nobel Prize for Physics in 1965. This remark is reported to have been written on his blackboard at Caltech at the time of his death. Stephen Hawking published a picture of the quote in Hawking, S. (2001) *The Universe in a Nutshell.* New York: Bantam Books, 83.

1 Biggs, J., Tang, C., and Tang C. S-K. (2007) *Teaching for Quality Learning at University.* London: Open University Press; Pintrich, P. (2002) The role of metacognitive knowledge in learning, teaching, and assessing. *Theory into Practice* 41(4): 219–225; Richardson, J. T. E. (2005) Students' perceptions of academic quality and approaches to studying in distance education. *British Educational Research Journal* 31(1) (February): 7–27.

2 Entwistle, N. (1997) Contrasting perspectives on learning, in F. Marton, D. Hounsell, and N. Entwistle, eds., *The Experience of Learning,* 3–22. Edinburgh: Scottish Academic Press; Light, G., Cox, R., and Calkins, S. (2009) *Learning and Teaching in Higher Education: The Reflective Professional.* Thousand Oaks, CA: Sage; Marton, F., and Saljo, R. (1997) Approaches to learning, in F. Marton, D. Hounsell, and N. Entwistle, eds., *The Experience of Learning,* 39–58.

3 Transformative experiences of learning go beyond simply creating a new understanding. In some cases students regard learning as consisting of substantive changes in how they see themselves as persons. This may include, for example, constructing an identity as a scientist or an engineer. For different conceptions of learning, see Marton et al., *The Experience,* and Marton and Saljo, *Approaches.* For a discussion of identity in engineering, see Stevens, R., O'Connor, K., Garrison, L., Jocuns, A., and Amos, D. (2008) Becoming an engineer: Toward a three dimensional view of engineering learning. *Journal of Engineering Education* 97(3): 355–368.

4 Lecturing has largely remained unchanged since the mid-1800s. While the lecture can be an efficient method of communicating knowledge to students, many scientists and educators agree that the lecture format on its own is often inadequate, particularly with respect to the promotion of interest in and deeper thinking about a subject. Some commentators have even called for its total abandonment. See Barnett, R. (2000) *Realising the University.* Buckingham: SRHE/Open University Press. For research and a discussion on the lecture, see Bligh, D. (2000) *What's the Use of Lectures?* San Francisco: Jossey-Bass; Mazur, E. (2009) Farewell lecture? *Science* 323(5910): 50–51; Light et al., *Learning,* 105–126.

5 Harvard physicist Eric Mazur, for example, has developed a remarkably successful way of teaching physics to large groups of freshman that is aimed at conceptual change and understanding. See Mazur, E. (1997) *Peer Instruction: A User's Manual, Series in Educational Innovation.* Upper Saddle River, NJ: Prentice Hall.

6 Here conceptual understanding refers to learning something that one can have a conception (or, indeed, a misconception) about. It does not simply mean understanding a concept as a fact but, rather, understanding how those facts are connected to a larger concept or idea and how those concepts and ideas may be related to larger problems in the domain.

7 Micari, M., and Light, G. (2008) Reliance to independence: Approaches to learning in peer-led undergraduate science, technology, engineering, and mathematics workshops. *International Journal of Science Education* 31(13): 1713–1741.

8 For discussions of student experiences of group work versus lecture, see Bligh, *What's the Use?;* Bligh, D. (2000) *What's the Point in Discussion?* Exeter: Intellect Press; Jaques, D., and Salmon, G. (2007) *Learning in Groups: A Handbook for Face-to-Face and Online Environments.* New York: Routledge. For studies of peer-led team learning, see Tien, L. T., Roth, V., and Kampmeier,

J. A. (2002) Implementation of a peer-led learning instructional approach in an undergraduate organic chemistry course. *Journal of Research in Science Teaching* 39: 606–632; Drane, D., Smith, H. D., Light, G., Pinto, L., and Swarat, S. (2005) The Gateway Science Workshop Program: Enhancing student performance and retention in the sciences through peer facilitated discussion. *Journal of Science Education and Technology* 14(3): 337–352; Swarat, S., Drane D., Smith H. D., Light G., and Pinto L. (2004) Opening the gateway: Increasing student retention in introductory science courses. *Journal of College Science Teaching* 34(1): 18–23.

9   See Prosser, M., and Trigwell, K. (1999) *Understanding Learning and Teaching: The Experience in Higher Education.* Buckingham: SRHE and Open University Press, 58–82.

10 Comment quoted in Bain, K. (2004) *What the Best College Teachers Do.* Cambridge, MA: Harvard University Press, 144.

11 Misconceptions of key concepts in a topic are a major deterrent to meaningful learning. Students frequently take a course, diligently learn the content and facts presented to them and even do very well on their exams, but their misconceptions of the subject remain completely intact. The course failed to challenge their flawed underlying assumptions and "mental models" of essential ideas in the subject. For a discussion of the importance of challenging student misconceptions and mental models in science, see Bain, *Best College;* Handelsman, J., Miller, S., and Pfund, C. (2007) *Scientific Teaching.* New York. W. H. Freemen & Co.

12 For a discussion of metacognitive awareness and self-regulated learning and the relationship to approaches to learning, see Pintrich, P. (2004) A conceptual framework for assessing motivation and self-regulated learning in college students. *Educational Psychology Review* 16(4) (December): 385–407.

13 In fact, a learning theory known as *variation theory* is exactly this—the view that in order to change their conceptions about a particular concept or phenomenon, students need to recognize different ways of understanding it and ultimately become aware of how some understandings are richer and more valuable than others. See Marton, F., and Booth, S. (1997) *Learning and Awareness.* Mahwah, NJ: Lawrence Erlbaum Associates; Marton, F., and Tsui, A. B. M (2004) *Classroom Discourse and the Space of Learning.* Mahwah, NJ: Lawrence Erlbaum Associates. For an important example of a core science concept, see Swarat, S., Light G., Park, E.-J., and Drane D. (2011) A typology of undergraduate students' conceptions of size and scale: Identifying and characterizing conceptual variation. *Journal of Research in Science Teaching* 48(5): 512–533.

14 For further discussion of the factors relating to student approaches to learn-ing, see Kember, D., Biggs, J., and Leung, D. Y. P. (2004) Examining the multi-dimensionality of approaches to learning through the development of a re-vised version of the Learning Process Questionnaire. *British Journal of Educational Psychology* 74(2): 261–279; Light, G., and Calkins, S. (2008) The experience of faculty development: Patterns of variation in conceptions of teaching. *International Journal for Academic Development* 13(1): 17–30; Prosser and Trigwell, *Understanding;* Entwistle, N., and Smith, C. (2002) Personal understanding and target understanding: Mapping influences on the out-comes of learning. *British Journal of Educational Psychology* 72: 321–342.

15 The kinds of students called "born scientists" may not, in fact, be so born; rather, together with their early experiences, they have developed a love of science, its questions and its methods. Not much of what we do is done for purely intrinsic motivations. We require autonomy and self-determination, feelings of choice and control over our actions and environment, in order to develop. See Ryan, R. M., and Deci, E. L. (2000) Self-determination theory and the facilitation of intrinsic motivation, social development, and well-being. *American Psychologist* 55(1): 68–78. In students we see this in their per-sistence, creativity, enhanced performance, heightened self-esteem, and well-being, which are lacking when the learning environment feels more ex-ternally controlled. For a fuller discussion of these issues, also see Light et al., *Learning,* 45–72.

16 This study included faculty in disciplines from across the university, but the majority were from science and science-related disciplines and pro-fessions, including engineering and medicine. See Light and Calkins, The experience.

17 For further discussion of these and similar findings in the literature, see Kem-ber, D., and Gow, L. (1994) Orientations to teaching and their effect on the quality of student learning. *Journal of Higher Education* 65(1): 58–74; Prosser and Trigwell, *Understanding;* Ramsden, P. (2003) *Learning to Teach in Higher Education.* London: Routledge; Light, *Learning.*

18 For the remark, see www.youtube.com/watch?v=lBYrKPoVFwg (accessed September 30, 2010). For details of Eric Mazur's educational work, see Mazur, *Peer Instruction.*

19 See, for example, Prosser, *Understanding,* chap. 7, for studies and a discussion of the link between the teaching approach and the learning approach.

20 For studies of change in faculty understanding and approaches to teaching, see McKenzie, J. (2002) Variation and relevance structures for university

teachers' learning: Bringing about change in ways of experiencing teaching, research and development. *Higher Education Research and Development* 25: 234–241; Akerlind, G. S. (2003) Growing and developing as a university teacher: Variation in meaning. *Studies in Higher Education* 28(4): 375–390; Light, *Learning*. For studies of how faculty development programs might directly impact faculty understanding and approaches to teaching, see Ho, A., Watkins, D., and Kelly, M. (2001) The conceptual change approach to improving teaching and learning: An evaluation of a Hong Kong staff development programme. *Higher Education* 42: 143–169; Trigwell, K. (2003) A relational approach model for academic development, in H. Eggins and R. Macdonald, eds., *The Scholarship of Academic Development*, 23–33. Buckingham, UK: Society for Research into Higher Education; Gibbs, G., and Coffey, G. (2004) The impact of training of university teachers on their teaching skills, their approach to teaching and the approach to learning of their students. *Active Learning in Higher Education* 5(1): 87–101; Light, G., Calkins, S., Luna, M., and Drane, D. (2009) Assessing the impact of faculty development programs on faculty approaches to teaching. *International Journal of Teaching and Learning in Higher Education* 20(2): 167–179.

3. ENGAGING PROBLEMS

Epigraph: Isaac Asimov was a professor of biochemistry, widely known for his works of science fiction and for his popular science books. This quote has been widely attributed to him but, as far as we can tell, no concrete source has been identified.

1 Archimedes's famous comment reportedly arose when King Hiero II asked him to determine whether his crown was made purely of gold without damaging it. The key problem of determining the volume of an object with such an irregular shape, and the realization of its solution when Archimedes noticed that sitting in his bath raised the water level, is an archetypal example of scientific discovery. This famous story has been repeated untold times throughout history. For the original story, see Vitruvius (*De Architectura*, Book IX, paragraphs 9–12).

2 The idea of science originating in the wonder stimulated by problems and puzzles goes back to Aristotle and Plato. See, for example, "For men were first led to study philosophy, as indeed they are today, by wonder" (Aristotle, *Metaphysics*, 982b) and "the origin of philosophy is 'wonder'—however, the wonder

there spoken of is 'wonder' in the sense of 'puzzlement' or 'perplexity'" (Plato, *Theaetetus,* 155c–d, www.roangelo.net/logwitt/logwit49.html).

3   There is a widely held view that the best thing you can do for the finest college students in the country is to get out of their way. Richard Light, in *Making the Best of College,* points out, however, that the absence of teachers and their questions is not what these brilliant students want. The very best thing we can do for them is get in their way—get in their way with the most exciting problems available to challenge their talent. See Light, R. (2001) *Making the Best of College.* Cambridge, MA: Harvard University Press.

4   James Clerk Maxwell (1831–1879), Scottish physicist and discoverer of electromagnetic waves. For these comments, see Campbell, L., and Garnett, W. (1882, 1884) *The Life of James Clerk Maxwell.* London: Macmillan; Forfar, D. O. (2002) James Clerk Maxwell: His qualities of mind and personality as judged by his contemporaries. *Mathematics Today* 38(3) (June): 83.

5   Russell wrote that "at the age of eleven, I began Euclid, with my brother as tutor. This was one of the great events of my life, as dazzling as first love." He follows these comments with, "From that moment until I was thirty-eight, mathematics was my chief interest and my chief source of happiness." See Russell, B. (1969) *The Autobiography of Bertrand Russell,* 3 vols. London: George Allen and Unwin.

6   The psychologist Jerome Bruner, for example, has argued that all children have intrinsic motivations to learn and "curiosity is almost a prototype of the intrinsic motivation." See Bruner, J. S. (1966) *Toward a Theory of Instruction.* Cambridge, MA: Harvard University Press.

7   The physicist Eric Mazur, who pioneered group-based, peer-instruction approaches in science education, describes this phenomenon as reducing education to a process in which "the lecture notes of the instructor get transferred to the notebooks of the students without passing through the brains of either." See Mazur, E. (2009) Farewell lecture? *Science* 323(5910): 50–51.

8   The term PBL has been used to describe diverse educational innovations from a whole program curriculum to simple activities within one course. For a broader discussion of the history and nature of PBL in the sciences, see Boud, D., and Feletti, G. (1997) *The Challenge of Problem-Based Learning.* London: Kogan Page; Ronis, D. (2008) *Problem-Based Learning for Math and Science: Integrating Inquiry and the Internet.* Thousand Oaks, CA: Sage Publications.

9 For a discussion of new approaches to learning and teaching in the sciences, see Fox, A., and Hackerman, N. (2003) *Evaluating and Improving Undergraduate Teaching in Science.* Washington, DC: The National Academies Press; Skovsmose, O., Valero, P., and Christensen, O. R. (2009) *University Science and Mathematics Education in Transition.* New York: Springer Science; Ruiz-Primo, M. A., Briggs, D., et al. (2011) Impact of undergraduate science course innovations on learning. *Science* 331: 1269–1270.

10 Boud, D. (1985) Problem-based learning in perspective, in Boud, D., ed., *Problem-Based Learning in Education for the Professions,* 13. Sydney: Higher Education Research and Development Society for Australia.

11 For an excellent discussion of the nature and assessment of critical thinking skills in science, see Stein, B., and Haynes, A. (2011) Engaging faculty in the assessment and improvement of student critical thinking using the CAT. *Change* (March–April): 44–49.

12 For more on the relationship of workshops to lectures in the GSW program, see Born, W. K., Revelle, W., and Pinto, L. (2002) Improving biology performance with workshop groups. *Journal of Science Education and Technology* 11: 347–365; Swarat, S., Drane, D., Smith, H. D., Light, G., and Pinto, L. (2004) Opening the gateway: Increasing student retention in introductory science courses. *Journal of College Science Teaching* 34(1): 18–23; Drane, D., Smith, H. D., Light, G., Pinto, L., and Swarat, S. (2005) The Gateway Science Workshop Program: Enhancing student performance and retention in the sciences through peer facilitated discussion. *Journal of Science Education and Technology* 14(3): 337–352; Micari, M., Streitwieser, B., and Light, G. (2006) Undergraduates leading undergraduates: Peer facilitation in a science workshop program. *Innovative Higher Education* 30(4): 269–288.

13 Bain described the five key features of what he calls a natural critical learning environment in terms of questions and problems. See Bain, K. (2004) *What the Best College Teachers Do.* Cambridge, MA: Harvard University Press, 99–109.

14 The scale was a Likert type scale from 1 to 5, with 1 being low and 5 high. Comments varied in length from a few sentences to a couple of paragraphs. The analysis examined the reports of over one hundred facilitators and almost one thousand problems across all five disciplines. While different facilitators' reports sometimes disagreed on the same problem in their respective workshops, there was normally substantial agreement among them. Analyses of problems were given back to the faculty who had created them to help in future problem construction.

15 One of the reasons students have trouble distinguishing which material or concepts they need to master versus that with which they should have an acquaintance is because faculty do not make that distinction very clear in their courses. Science programs are replete with courses that tell students what the course will cover with no indication of which concepts are central and how they need to be understood. For a discussion of this, see Light, G., Cox, R. and Calkins, S. (2009) *Learning and Teaching in Higher Education: The Reflective Professional.* Thousand Oaks, CA: Sage, 86–89.

16 Teller, E., Teller, W., and Talley, W. (1991) *Conversations on the Dark Secrets of Physics.* London: Pitman, 79.

17 For a discussion of the paradoxes of learning, see Plato, (2008) *Meno.* Trans. B. Jowett. Charleston, SC: Forgotten Books; Jarvis, P. (1992) *Paradoxes of Learning.* San Francisco: Jossey-Bass.

18 This Einstein quote has been widely reproduced in scholarly papers and books, on the Internet, and even in the *Congressional Record* (June 9, 1999, 12308) but never, as far as we can tell, with a direct reference to when and where he said it.

19 For a discussion of the distinction between supportive and independent educational environments, see Light, Cox, and Calkins, *Learning*, 69–72.

20 For a discussion of the structure of problems, see Gallagher, S. A.., Stepien, W. J., Sher, B. J.; and Workman, D. (1995) Implementing problem-based learning in science classrooms. *School Science and Mathematics* 95(3): 136–146; also see www.cct.umb.edu/pblscience.html, Graduate College of Education, University of Massachusetts, Boston.

21 Mazur, for example, describes the construction of a fascinating "Fermi" type problem—which might be used as a template for the construction of conceptual problems—for helping students develop those thinking skills that the successful scientist needs to have. See Mazur, E. (1997) *Peer Instruction: A User's Manual, Series in Educational Innovation.* Upper Saddle River, NJ: Prentice Hall, 28–30.

22 A great source of problems, organized by topic, can be found in Mazur, *Peer*, 105–245. See also the University of Minnesota's physics web page, http://groups.physics.umn.edu/physed/Research/CRP/on-lineArchive/ola.html, and the Carl Weiman Science Education Initiative at the University of British Columbia, particularly the resource page on constructing problems for personal response systems ("clickers"). See www.cwsei.ubc.ca/resources/instructor_guidance.htm (accessed September 19, 2010).

23 Hinshelwood was knighted in 1948 and won the Nobel Prize for Chemistry in 1956. This comment is widely attributed to him. See www.lhup.edu/~dsimanek /sciquote.htm (accessed October 2, 2010). We have been unable to locate a concrete source for when and where it was made.

4. CONNECTING PEERS

Epigraph: Sheldon Lee Glashow won the Nobel Prize in Physics in 1979. This quote is from "Towards a Unified Theory—Threads in a Tapestry," Nobel Lecture, December 8, 1979, in Stig Lundqvist, ed. (1992), *Nobel Lectures: Physics 1971–1980.* Singapore: World Scientific Publishing (for The Nobel Foundation), 494.

1 Osborne and colleagues conducted a study among scientific experts to determine which key ideas about the nature of science should be included in school curricula. See Osborne, J., Collins, S., Ratcliffe, M., Millar, R., and Dusch, R. (2003) What 'ideas-about-science' should be taught in school science? A Delphi study of the expert community. *Journal of Research in Science Teaching* 40(7): 692–720, quotation on p. 709.

2 Finson and Sharkawy are among those who have investigated young people's beliefs about science and scientists. See Finson, K. D. (2002) Drawing a scientist: What we do and do not know after fifty years of drawings. *School Science and Mathematics* 102(7): 335–345; Sharkawy, A. (2009) Moving beyond the lone scientist: Helping 1st-grade students appreciate the social context of scientific work using stories about scientists. *Journal of Elementary Science Education* 21(1): 67–78.

3 Hildebrand, J. (1958) *Gilbert Newton Lewis 1875–1946: A Biographical Memoir.* Washington, DC: National Academy of Sciences, 212.

4 Chan, J., and Lam, S. (2008) Effects of competition on students' self-efficacy in vicarious learning. *British Journal of Educational Psychology* 78(1): 95–108; Qin, Z., Johnson, D. W., and Johnson, R. W. (1995) Cooperative versus competitive efforts and problem solving. *Review of Educational Research* 65(2): 129–143.

5 Light's 2001 book *Making the Most of College* documents the experiences of college students at Harvard, investigating what leads some to succeed and others to struggle through their undergraduate years. See Light, R. (2001) *Making the Most of College: Students Speak Their Minds.* Cambridge, MA: Harvard University Press.

6 Whitley, B. (1998) Factors associated with cheating among college students: A review. *Research in Higher Education* 39(3): 235–274.

7   Qin et al., Cooperative versus competitive.

8   Research on small-group dynamics has shown that intergroup competition, which combines competition and cooperation, can promote goal setting, co-operation, and productivity within the group; see, for example, Tauer, J., and Harackiewicz, J. (2004) The effects of cooperation and competition on intrinsic motivation and performance. *Journal of Personality and Social Psychology* 86(6): 849–861.

9   See www.pltl.org/ and http://pages.uoregon.edu/udovic/WB/index.html; www.pogil.org/ (accessed August 30, 2012).

10 For research on factors affecting the usefulness of collaborative learning, see Cohen, E. (1994) Restructuring the classroom: Condition for productive small groups. *Review of Educational Research* 64(1): 1–35; Van Boxtel, C., van der Linden, J., and Kanselaar, G. (2000) Collaborative learning tasks and the elaboration of conceptual knowledge. *Learning and Instruction* 10(4): 311–330; Webb, N. M. (1991) Task-related verbal interaction and mathematics learning in small groups. *Journal for Research in Mathematics Education* 22(5): 366–389.

11 Springer, Stanne, and Donovan performed a meta-analysis of research on the effects of small-group learning in STEM disciplines and found significant effects for achievement, persistence, and attitude. See Springer, L., Stanne, M. E., and Donovan, S. (1999) Measuring the success of small-group learning in college level SMET teaching: A meta-analysis. *Review of Educational Research* 69: 21–51.

12 See Micari, M., Pazos, P., Streitwieser, B., and Light, G. (2010) Small-group learning in undergraduate STEM disciplines: Effect of group type on student achievement. *Educational Research and Evaluation* 16(3): 269–286; Pazos, P., Micari, M., and Light, G. (2010) Developing an instrument to characterize peer-led groups in collaborative learning environments: Assessing problem-solving approach and group interaction. *Assessment and Evaluation in Higher Education* 35(2): 191–208.

13 See Pazos, P., Micari, M., and Light for a fuller description of the development of the group typology and the resulting observation instrument.

14 For details about this study, see Micari et al., Small-group learning, 269–286.

15 Among the many research studies that have examined factors contributing to the success of collaborative learning are Chinn, C. A., O'Donnell, A. M., and Jinks, T. S. (2000) The structure of discourse in collaborative learning. *Journal of Experimental Education* 69: 77–97; Cohen, E. (1994). Restructuring the classroom: Condition for productive small groups. *Review of Educational Re-*

search 64(1): 1–35; Webb, N. M., Farivar, S. H., and Mastergeorge, A. M. (2002) Productive helping in cooperative groups. *Theory into Practice* 41(1): 13–20.

16   The term *scaffolding* was introduced in education by Wood, Bruner, and Ross and draws greatly from Vygotsky. See Wood, D., Bruner, J., and Ross, G. (1976) The role of tutoring in problem solving. *Journal of Child Psychology and Psychiatry* 17: 89–100; Vygotsky, L. S. (1978) *Mind in Society: The Development of Higher Psychological Processes.* Cambridge, MA: Harvard University Press.

17   Both Vygotsky and Marton and Booth highlight the value of tutors near but slightly above the students' own levels of understanding. Bandura addresses the impact of role models on self-efficacy. See Vygotsky, *Mind in Society;* Bandura, A. (1997) *Self-Efficacy: The Exercise of Control.* New York: W. H. Freeman; Marton, F., and Booth, S. (1997) *Learning and Awareness.* Mahwah, NJ: Lawrence Erlbaum Associates.

18   For a description of the original stereotype-threat research and theory, see Steele, C. M. (1997) A threat in the air: How stereotypes shape intellectual identity and performance. *American Psychologist* 52(6): 613–629; for a review of the stereotype-threat literature, see Steele, C. M., Spencer, S. J., and Aronson, J. (2002) Contending with group image: The psychology of stereotype and social identity threat. *Advances in Experimental Social Psychology* 34: 379–440.

19   For details of the study, see Micari, M., and Drane, D. (2007) Promoting success: Possible factors behind achievement of underrepresented students in a peer-led small-group STEM workshop program. *Journal of Women and Minorities in Science and Engineering* 13(3): 279–293.

20   See, for example, Eimers, M. T., and Pike, G. R. (1997) Minority and non-minority adjustment to college: Differences or similarities? *Research in Higher Education* 38(1): 77–97; Loo, C. M., and Rollison, G., (1986) Alienation of ethnic minority students at a predominantly white university. *Journal of Higher Education* 57(1): 58–77; Seymour, E., and Hewitt, N. (1997) *Talking about Leaving: Why Undergraduates Leave the Sciences.* Boulder, CO: Westview; Terenzini, P. T. Rendon, L. I., Upcraft, M. L., Millar, S. B., Allison, K. W., Gregg, P. L., and Jalomo, R. (1994) The transition to college: Diverse students, diverse stories. *Research in Higher Education* 35: 57–73.

21   Marx, D., and Roman, J. (2002) Female role models: Protecting women's math test performance. *Personality and Social Psychology Bulletin* 28: 1183–1193; McIntyre, R. B., Paulson, R. M., and Lord, C. G. (2003) Alleviating women's mathematics stereotype threat through positive group achievements. *Journal*

of Experimental Social Psychology 39: 83–90; Steele, Spencer, and Aronson, Contending.

22 Jaques, D. (2000) *Learning in Groups*. Boston: RoutledgeFalmer, 16.

23 Born, W., Revelle, W., and Pinto, L. (2002) Improving biology performance with workshop groups. *Journal of Science Education and Technology* 11: 347–365.

24 See, for example, Saleh, M., Lazonder, A., and de Jong, T. (2005) Effects of within-class ability grouping on social interaction, achievement and motivation. *Instructional Science* 33(2): 105–119; Lou, P., Abrami, J., Spence, B., Chambers, C., Poulsen, C., and D'apollonia, S. (1996) Within-class grouping: A meta-analysis. *Review of Educational Research* 66(4): 423–458.

25 See, for example, O'Reilly, C., Caldwell, D. F., and Barnett, W. P. (1989) Workplace group demography, social integration, and turnover. *Administrative Sciences Quarterly* 34: 21–37; Jackson, S. E., Brett, J. F., Sessa, V. I., Cooper, D. M., Julin, J. A., and Peyronnin, K. (1991) Some differences make a difference: Individual dissimilarity and group heterogeneity as correlates of recruitment, promotion, and turnover. *Journal of Applied Psychology* 76(5): 675–689.

26 Wilkinson, I., and Fung, Y. (2002) Small-group composition and peer effects. *International Journal of Educational Research* 37(5): 425–447.

27 Some research (e.g., Saine et al.) has found that a size smaller than the conventional five to seven is ideal, although there is evidence (e.g., Carnes, Lindbeck, and Griffin) that groups of fewer than three are less effective. See Saine, T. J., Schulman, L. S., and Emerson, L. C. (1974) The effects of group size on the structure of interaction in problem-solving groups. *Southern Speech Communication Journal* 39(4): 333–345; Carnes, E., Lindbeck, J., and Griffin, F., Effects of group size and advance organizers on learning parameters when using microcomputer tutorials in kinematics. *Journal of Research in Science Teaching* 24[9]: 781–789).

28 Barrows and Pfeiffer have written on the ideal size for peer-learning groups. See Barrows, H. S. (1994) *Practice-Based Learning: Problem-Based Learning Applied to Medical Education*. Springfield: Southern Illinois University School of Medicine; Pfeiffer, J. W. (1991) Problem solving. In J. W. Pfeiffer, ed., *Theories and Models in Applied Behavioral Science*, vol. 3, 3–111. San Diego, CA: Pfeiffer & Co.; for a discussion of the experience of high-ability students in mixed-ability groups, see Webb, Task-related verbal interaction.

29 Birmingham, C., and McCord, M. (2004) Group process research: Implications for using learning groups, in L. K. Michaelsen, A. B. Knight, and L. D. Fink, eds., *Team-Based Learning: A Transformative Use of Small Groups in College Teaching*, 73–93. Sterling, VA: Stylus.

30 See Micari, M., and Drane, D. (2011) Intimidation in small learning groups: The roles of social-comparison concern, comfort, and individual characteristics in student academic outcomes. *Active Learning in Higher Education,* 12, 175–187.

31 This quotation is frequently attributed to Edison in the *World Book Encyclopedia,* although there are many variants widely quoted. See the *World Book Encyclopedia,* vol. E (1993). Chicago: World Book, 78.

32 Committee on Science, Engineering, and Public Policy, National Academy of Sciences, National Academy of Engineering, and Institute of Medicine. (1995) *On Being a Scientist: Responsible Conduct in Research.* Washington, DC: National Academy Press, 3.

5. MENTORING LEARNING

Epigraph: Tosteson, D. C. (1979) Learning in medicine. *New England Journal of Medicine* 301(13): 690–694, quotation on p. 693.

1 While mentoring has always been a critical part of the development of scientists, its importance has recently received greater attention (see Crisp and Cruz for a discussion of the recent prominence of mentoring at the undergraduate level). Dozens of scholarly articles on the value and practice of mentoring in the sciences have been published over the past decade, and in 2009 the National Science Foundation began to require that mentoring for postgraduates be a key component of any grant proposal involving postdoctoral research. See Crisp, G., and Cruz, I. (2009) Mentoring college students: A critical review of the literature between 1990 and 2007. *Research in Higher Education* 50: 525–545.

2 There is a growing body of research on the impact of student mentoring, with mentoring shown to be linked to higher grades, persistence, and satisfaction in college. See, e.g., Mangold, W. D., Bean, L. G., Adams, D. J., Schwab, W. A., and Lynch, S. M. (2003) Who goes who stays: An assessment of the effect of a freshman mentoring and unit registration program on college persistence. *Journal of College Student Retention* 4(2): 95–122; Strayhorn, T. L., and Terrell, M. C. (2007) Mentoring and satisfaction with college for black students. *Negro Educational Review* 58(1–2): 69–83.

3 Crisp and Cruz, Mentoring college students.

4 These interviews were conducted between 2003 and 2005 and lasted about forty-five minutes each.

5   Vygotsky defined the "zone of proximal development" as the difference be-
    tween a young person's actual developmental level and her or his potential
    level, which could be reached with guidance by teachers or "in collaboration
    with more capable peers." See Vygotsky, L. S. (1978) *Mind in Society: The De-*
    velopment of Higher Psychological Processes. Cambridge, MA: Harvard Uni-
    versity Press, 86.

6   Chew discusses the research showing students' tendency to hold on to mis-
    taken conceptions. Misconceptions are often developed over years, and it can
    be extremely challenging to dislodge them. Chew, S. L. (2005) Seldom in
    doubt but often wrong: Addressing tenacious student misconceptions, in D. S.
    Dunn, and S. L. Chew, eds., *Best Practices in Teaching General Psychology*, 211–
    223. Mahwah, NJ: Lawrence Erlbaum Associates.

7   Research on student motivation has shown that the degree to which students
    believe that the teacher cares about them influences their motivation to learn
    and their attitudes about learning. See, e.g., Comadena, M., Hunt, S., and Si-
    monds, C. (2007) The effects of teacher clarity, nonverbal immediacy, and
    caring on student motivation, affective and cognitive learning. *Communication*
    Research Reports 24(3): 241–248.

8   See Micari, M., and Drane, D. (2011) Intimidation in small learning groups:
    The roles of social-comparison concern, comfort, and individual characteris-
    tics in student academic outcomes. *Active Learning in Higher Education* 12:
    175–187.

9   For a full description of the training course and associated facilitator learning
    gains, see Micari, M., Knife Gould, A., and Lainez, L. (2010) Becoming a leader
    along the way: Embedding leadership training into a large-scale peer-learning
    program in the STEM disciplines. *Journal of College Student Development*
    51(2): 218–230.

10 Shulman first used the term *pedagogical content knowledge* to refer to a teach-
    er's knowledge of how to teach his or her subject effectively. See Shulman,
    L. S. (1986) Those who understand: Knowledge growth in teaching. *Educa-*
    tional Researcher 15(2): 4–14.

11 Webb, Farivar, and Mastergeorge and Good, Halpin, and Halpin discuss the
    benefit of peer learning and mentoring programs for the mentors, most likely
    because they must first make sense for themselves the material they are teach-
    ing. See Webb, N. M., Farivar, S. H., and Mastergeorge, A. M. (2002) Produc-
    tive helping in cooperative groups. *Theory into Practice* 41(1): 13–20; Good,
    J., Halpin, Glennelle, and Halpin, Gerald (2000) A promising prospect for

minority retention: Students becoming peer mentors. *Journal of Negro Education* 69: 375–383.

12 For a full description of this study, see Micari, M., Streitwieser, B., and Light, G. (2006) Undergraduates leading undergraduates: Peer facilitation in a science workshop program. *Innovative Higher Education* 30(4): 269–288.

13 See Micari, Gould, and Lainez, Becoming a leader, for details.

14 See Streitwieser, B., and Light, G. (2011) When undergraduates teach undergraduates: Conceptions of and approaches to teaching in a peer-led team learning intervention in the STEM disciplines—Results of a two year study. *International Journal of Teaching and Learning in Higher Education* 22(3): 346–356.

15 Smith, Sheppard, Johnson, and Johnson review the research on engaged approaches to teaching and learning, with a wealth of evidence for the cognitive, social, and affective benefits of approaches that encourage them to play an active role in the classroom. See Smith, K. A., Sheppard, S. D., Johnson, D. W., and Johnson, R. T. (2005) Pedagogies of engagement: Classroom-based practices. *Journal of Engineering Education,* Special Issue on the State of the Art and Practice of Engineering Education Research 94(1): 87–102.

16 Much has been written about engendering cognitive conflict in learners, most stemming from Piaget's original writings on the concept. Posner et al., in a seminal paper on the process of conceptual change through cognitive conflict in science learners, give as conditions for such change initial dissatisfaction with one's existing conceptions and a new, alternative model that makes sense to the learner and that seems a realistic alternative to the currently held model. See Piaget, J. (1985) *The Equilibration of Cognitive Structure: The Central Problem of Intellectual Development.* Chicago: University of Chicago Press; Posner, G. J., Strike, K. A., Hewson, P. W., and Gertzog, W. A. (1982) Accommodation of a scientific conception: Toward a theory of conceptual change. *Science Education* 66(2): 211–227.

17 The survey was sent to 538 former facilitators via e-mail; 135 (25 percent) responded.

18 Johnson, W. B. (2007) *On Being a Mentor: A Guide for Higher Education Faculty.* Mahwah, NJ: Lawrence Erlbaum Associates.

19 Calkins and Kelly found that preparation for faculty mentoring graduate students was practically nonexistent, and that many faculty members simply relied on the mentoring models they had experienced as students, which in a number of cases they viewed as deficient. See Calkins, S., and Kelley, M. R. (2005) Mentoring and the faculty-TA relationship: Faculty perceptions and practices. *Mentoring & Tutoring* 13(2): 259–280.

20 See Johnson, *On Being a Mentor*, 119–120, on the level of mentoring in U.S. higher education.

6. CREATING COMMUNITY

Epigraph: Chubin, D. E., and Hackett, E. J. (1990) *Peer Review and U.S. Science Policy*. Albany: State University of New York Press, 8. Reprinted by permission from Peerless Science.

1 For a comment on the impact of the weed-out mentality on student retention, see Epstein, D. (2006) So that's why they're leaving. *Inside Higher Ed,* www.insidehighered.com/news/2006/07/26/scipipeline (accessed July 26, 2010).

2 McMillan, D., and Chavis, D. (1986) Sense of community: A definition and theory. *Journal of Community Psychology* 14(1): 6–23.

3 See, for example, Brickhouse, N. W., and Potter, J. T. (2001) Young women's scientific identity formation in an urban context. *Journal of Research in Science Teaching* 38: 965–980.

4 Committee on the Conduct of Science and National Academy of Sciences. (1989) *On Being a Scientist*. Washington, DC: National Academy Press, 10.

5 Lave, J., and Wenger, E. (1991 [2007]) *Situated Learning: Legitimate Peripheral Participation*. Cambridge: Cambridge University Press.

6 Wenger, E. (1998) *Communities of Practice: Learning, Meaning, and Identity*. Cambridge: Cambridge University Press, 45.

7 Lave and Wenger, *Situated Learning*.

8 Hunter, A. B., Laursen, S., and Seymour, E. (2006) Becoming a scientist: The role of undergraduate research in students' cognitive, personal, and professional development. *Science Education* 91(1): 36–74.

9 Light, G., Cox., R., and Calkins, S. (2009). *Learning and Teaching in Higher Education: The Reflective Professional*. 2nd ed. Thousand Oaks, CA: Sage Publications.

10 The 2009 National Survey of Student Engagement found that 40 percent of first-year students reported never talking with faculty about academic work outside of the classroom.

11 Astin, A. W. (1977) *Four Critical Years*. San Francisco: Jossey-Bass; Terenzini, P., and Pascarella, E. (1980) Student-faculty relationships and freshman year educational outcomes: A further investigation. *Journal of College Student Personnel* 21 (6): 521–528; Tinto, V. (1987) *Leaving College: Rethinking the Causes and Cures of Student Attrition*. Chicago: University of Chicago Press.

12 Bodner, G. (2007) Strengthening conceptual connections in introductory
    chemistry courses. *Chemistry Education Research and Practice* 8(1): 93–100;
    Jensen, E. (2008) *Brain-Based Learning: The New Paradigm of Teaching.* Thou-
    sand Oaks, CA: Corwin Press.

13 Bradley, J., Paul, R., and Seeman, E. (2006) Analyzing the structure of expert
    knowledge. *Information & Management* 43(1): 77–91; Feltovich, P. J., Prietula,
    M. J., and Ericsson, K. A. (2006) Studies of expertise from psychological
    perspectives, in K. A. Ericsson, N. Charness, P. Feltovich, and R. R. Hoffman,
    eds., *Cambridge Handbook of Expertise and Expert Performance,* 39–68. Cam-
    bridge: Cambridge University Press.

14 Wenger, E., McDermott, R., and Snyder, W. (2002) *Cultivating Communities of
    Practice: A Guide to Managing Knowledge.* Boston: Harvard Business School
    Publishing.

15 Polanyi, M. (1966 [2009]) *The Tacit Dimension.* Chicago: University of Chicago
    Press, 4.

16 See, for instance, Berg, G. (2010) *Low-Income Students and the Perpetuation of
    Inequality: Higher Education in America.* Burlington, VT: Ashgate Press.

17 Marton, F., Dall'Alba, G., and Beaty, E. (1993) Conceptions of learning. *Inter-
    national Journal of Educational Research* 19(3): 277–299.

18 Kuh, G., Kinzie, J., Schuh, J., and Whitt, E. (2005) *Student Success in College:
    Creating Conditions That Matter.* San Francisco: Jossey-Bass.

19 National Science Foundation. (2009) *Science and Engineering Degrees, by
    Race/Ethnicity: 1997–2006. Detailed Statistical Tables (NSF 10–300),* www.nsf
    .gov/statistics/nsf10300/pdf/nsf10300.pdf (accessed September 3, 2012).

20 National Science Foundation. (2009) *S&E Degrees 1966–2006: Detailed Statis-
    tical Tables (NSF 08–321),* www.nsf.gov/statistics/nsf08321/pdf/tab11.pdf (ac-
    cessed September 3, 2012).

21 For a lengthy discussion of the impact of socioeconomic status on college stu-
    dent experience and outcomes, see Terenzini, P. T., Cabrera, A. F., and Bernal,
    E. M. (2001) *Swimming against the Tide: The Poor in American Higher Educa-
    tion. The College Board Research Report No. 2001-1.* New York: College Entrance
    Examination Board; Walpole, M. B. (2008) Emerging from the pipeline: Afri-
    can American students, socioeconomic status, and college experiences and
    outcomes. *Research in Higher Education* 49(3): 237–255.

22 Walpole, Emerging.

23 Lent, R. E., Brown, S. D., Schmidt, J., Brenner, B., Lyons, H., and Treistman, D.
    (2003) Relation of contextual supports and barriers to choice behavior in en-
    gineering majors: Test of alternative social cognitive models. *Journal of Coun-
    seling Psychology* 50: 458–465; Lindley, L. D. (2005) Perceived barriers to ca-

reer development in the context of social cognitive career theory. *Journal of Career Assessment* 13: 271–287.

24 Tinto, V. (2006–2007) Research and practice of student retention: What next? *Journal of College Student Retention* 8(1): 1–19.

25 Hurtado, S., Han, J., Saenz, V., Espinosa, L., Cabrera, N., and Cerna, O. (2007) Predicting transition and adjustment to college: Biomedical and behavioral science aspirants' and minority students' first year of college. *Research in Higher Education* 48(7): 841–887; Hurtado, S., Eagan, K., Cabrera, N., Lin, M., Park, J., and Lopez, M. (2008) Training future scientists: Predicting first-year minority student participation in health science research. *Research in Higher Education* 49: 126–152.

26 Johnson, A. (2007) Unintended consequences: How science professors discourage women of color. *Science Education* 91(5): 805–821; Goodman, I. F., Cunningham, C. M., Lachapelle, C., Thompson, M., Bittinger, K., Brennan, R. T., and Delci, M. (2002) *Final Report of the Women's Experiences in College Engineering (WECE) Project.* Cambridge, MA: Goodman Research Group, www.grginc.com/WECE_FINAL_REPORT.pdf (accessed September 3, 2012)); Seymour, E., and Hewitt, N. (1997) *Talking about Leaving: Why Undergraduates Leave the Sciences.* Boulder, CO: Westview.

27 Sax, L. (2000) Undergraduate science majors: Gender differences in who goes to graduate school. *Review of Higher Education* 24(2): 153–172.

28 Anderson-Rowland, M. (1996) *A First-Year Engineering Student Survey to Assist Recruitment and Retention. Proceedings of the 1996 Conference of the Institute of Electrical and Electronics Engineers,* http://fie-conference.org/fie96/(accessed September 3, 2012); Grandy, J. (1998) Persistence in science of high-ability minority students: Results of a longitudinal study. *Journal of Higher Education* 69(6): 589–620.

29 Good, C., Dweck, C., and Aronson, J. (2007) Social identity, stereotype threat, and self theories, in A. Fuligni, ed., *Contesting Stereotypes and Creating Identities: Social Categories, Social Identities, and Educational Participation,* 115–135. New York: Russell Sage Foundation.

30 See www.northwestern.edu/residentialcolleges/index.html for the Northwestern Residential Colleges program, www.lsa.umich.edu/mlc for information on the Michigan communities, and www.columbia.edu/cu/vpas/finance-ops-it/faculty_dinners.html for the Columbia faculty dinners program (accessed September 6, 2012).

31 Karabenick, S. A. (2003) Help seeking in large college classes: A person-centered approach. *Contemporary Educational Psychology* 28: 37–58; Ryan, A. M., and Pintrich, P. R. (1997) Should I ask for help? The role of motivation

and attitudes in adolescents' help seeking in math class. *Journal of Educational Psychology* 89: 329–341.

32 Kulick and Wright's grading simulation demonstrates weaknesses in the curve system, particularly at elite institutions. See Kulick, G., and Wright, G. (2008) The impact of grading on the curve: A simulation analysis. *International Journal for the Scholarship of Teaching and Learning* 2(2), http://academics .georgiasouthern.edu/ijsotl/v2n2/articles/_Kulick/index.htm (accessed September 3, 2012).

33 See Loebbaka, C. (2007) Clicker technology can dramatically alter the atmosphere in large lecture classes, transforming students into engaged learners, Northwestern University analysis shows, www.northwestern.edu/newscenter /stories/2007/05/clickers.html (accessed September 3, 2012).

7. DOING RESEARCH

Epigraph: Paul Erdos was a Hungarian mathematician, famous for his eccentric personality and for the brilliance and volume of his research output. For this quote—his greeting to fellow mathematicians with whom he traveled all over the world to work—see Hoffman, P. (1987) The man who loved only numbers. *Atlantic Monthly* (November): 60.

1 Since the publication of the Boyer report in 1998, undergraduate research experiences have flourished. Most universities and colleges in the United States now report providing some opportunities for student research participation. See Boyer, E. L. (1998) *Reinventing Undergraduate Education: A Blueprint for America's Research Universities.* Commission on Educating Undergraduates in the Research University. Washington, DC: Carnegie Foundation for the Advancement of Teaching; Katkin, W. (2003) The Boyer Commission report and its impact on undergraduate research. *New Directions for Teaching and Learning* 93: 19–38. For a study of the different kinds of research experiences provided to students, see Jenkins, A., and Healey, M. (2009) *Developing Undergraduate Research and Inquiry.* York, UK: Higher Education Academy.

2 Streitwieser, B., Light, G., and Pazos, P. (2010) Enabling young scientists to enter the community of practitioners: A Science Research Workshop Model. *Change Magazine* (May–June): 17–23.

3 See, for example, Seymour, E., and Hewitt, N. (1997) *Talking about Leaving: Why Undergraduates Leave the Sciences.* Boulder, CO: Westview.

4 See the National Science Foundation (NSF) (2010) descriptions of the merit criteria by which "all NSF proposals are evaluated": The intellectual merit of

the proposed activity and the broader impacts of the proposed activity. NSF's *Proposal and Award Policies and Procedures Guide* (October): III-1.

5 This comment has been attributed to John Alejandro King, aka the "Covert Comic"; see www.covertcomic.com.

6 The "original" quality of the research is defined here in terms of its role as part of the original research being conducted in the lab. It does not mean that the student has come up with an entirely original research project but, rather, has been guided in this effort as part of the overall work of the lab. This is not to downplay its originality, its ownership, and (if funded) its original contribution by the student. Rather, it recognizes that, along with the ability and persistence of the student, "originality" is a function, as in most scientific research, of the opportunity, the resources, the colleagues, and the associated work that is prior to and concurrent with the student's work.

7 We wish to acknowledge the generous support for this program by the National Science Foundation Science, Technology, Engineering, and Mathematics Talent Expansion Program (STEP) 1 Grant (No. DUE 0525550).

8 The structure of the program has been extremely popular with science faculty. As they generally like to talk about their work, they have been extremely forthcoming in volunteering to lead a science café. In the first three years of the program, over forty faculty have participated. Even more gratifying is the number of labs that have been willing to host freshman students. In the period 2009–2010, for example, fifty-five lab places were made available to students, over twice the number of participating students.

9 As the students have rarely had instruction or experience in writing science proposals, annotated examples of successful proposals and other resources to help students with their writing are also made available. For examples and a discussion of this kind of support, see Yalvac, B., Smith, H. D., Troy, J. B., and Hirsch, P. (2007) Promoting advanced writing skills in an upper-level engineering class. *Journal of Engineering Education* 96(2): 117–128.

10 Undergraduate research proposals submitted for funding need to include an Introduction, Background, Literature Review, Methodology, Preparation, and Conclusion and are assessed on three main criteria: (1) completeness and clarity of the description of what will be done and how it will be done; (2) originality, merit, and student ownership (i.e., not the professor's project); and (3) how people outside the field can understand and appreciate the work proposed. For further details, see "Crafting a Research Proposal," http://undergrad research.northwestern.edu/crafting-research-proposal.

11 For full details of the SRW study, see Streitwieser et al., Enabling. For a more comprehensive discussion of the impact and benefits of undergraduate research, see Laursen, S., Hunter, A-B., Seymour, E., Thiry, H., and Melton, G. (2010) *Undergraduate Research in the Sciences: Engaging Students in Real Science.* San Francisco: Jossey-Bass; Brownell, J., and Swayner, L. (2010) *The Impact of Engaged Educational Practices: What Research Shows about Learning Outcomes, Completion and Quality,* Association of American Colleges and Universities (AAC&U) Report. Washington, DC: Liberal Education and America's Promise (LEAP); Lopatto, D. (2004) Survey of undergraduate research experiences (SURE): First findings. *Cell Biology Education* 3: 270–277.

12 While we were unable to randomize students into the SRW and control groups, the control group was drawn from the same pool of students—those who expressed strong interest in the program and attended orientation meetings about the program but whose schedules prevented them from coming to the workshops. In addition, an analysis of pretest data showed no significant differences in the confidence levels between the control group and the SRW group, which allayed our concerns that SRW students may have come into the program with higher levels of confidence. See Streitwieser et al., Enabling, 21.

13 Hurtado, S., and Carter, D. F. (1997) Effects of college transition and perceptions of the campus racial climate on Latino college students' sense of belonging. *Sociology of Education* 70: 324–345.

14 The Nobel Prize–winning professor of chemistry Dudley Herschbach describes this aspect of the scientific mind-set very well: "In real science you're not too worried about the right answer. . . . Real science recognizes that you have an advantage over practically any other human enterprise because what you are after—call it truth or understanding—waits patiently for you while you screw up." Cited in Bain, K. (2004) *What the Best College Teachers Do.* Cambridge, MA: Harvard University Press, 144.

15 Micari, M., Knife Gould, A., and Lainez, L. (2010) Becoming a leader along the way: Embedding leadership training into a large-scale peer-learning program in the STEM disciplines. *Journal of College Student Development* 51(2): 218–230.

16 See, for example, the work of Eric Mazur (Harvard), in Mazur, E. (1997) *Peer Instruction: A User's Manual.* Upper Saddle River, NJ: Prentice Hall; John Belcher (MIT), in Belcher, J. W. (2001) Studio physics at MIT. *MIT Physics Annual,* 58–64; Carl Wieman (UBC), in Wieman, C. (2007) Why not try a scientific approach to science education? *Change* 39(5): 9–15; Bill Wood (Colo-

rado, Boulder), in Wood, W. (2009) Innovations in undergraduate biology teaching and why we need them. *Annual Review of Cell and Developmental Biology* 2: 93–112; Jo Handelsman (Princeton), in Handelsman, J., Miller, S., and Pfund, C. (2006) *Scientific Teaching*. New York: W. H. Freeman & Co.

17 See the National Science Foundation, particularly the research grants available through the Division of Undergraduate Education, www.nsf.gov/div/index .jsp?div=DUE.

18 For a comprehensive discussion on designing and evaluating these experiences, and for resources for implementing them, see Laursen, S., Hunter A-B., Seymour, E., Thiry, H., and Melton, G. (2010) *Undergraduate Research in the Sciences: Engaging Students in Real Science*. San Francisco: Jossey-Bass. See also Boyd, M. K., and Wesemann, J. L., eds. (2008) *Broadening Participation in Undergraduate Research: Fostering Excellence and Enhancing the Impact*. Washington, DC: Council on Undergraduate Research.

19 See, for example, Colby, A., Erlich, T., Beaumont, E., and Stephens, J. (2003) *Educating Citizens: Preparing America's Undergraduates for Lives of Moral and Civic Responsibility*. San Francisco: Carnegie Foundation for the Advancement of Teaching / Jossey-Bass; Streitwieser, B. (2009), Undergraduate research during study abroad: Scope, meaning, and potential, in R. Lewin, ed., *The Handbook of Practice and Research in Study Abroad: Higher Education and the Quest for Global Citizenship*, 399–419. New York: Routledge.

20 See, for example, Lopatto's comment that "the signature distinction is that in high research-like courses, undergraduate students conduct research in which the outcome is not known (even to the course instructor) and have at least some input into the research topic and design of the methodological approach," in Lopatto, D. (2010) Undergraduate research as a high-impact student experience. *Peer Review,* Association of American Colleges and Universities 12(2) (Spring): 27–30.

21 Lopatto, D. (2004) Survey of undergraduate research experiences (SURE): First findings. *Cell Biology Education* 3: 270–277; Lopatto, D. (2010) *Science in Solution: The Impact of Undergraduate Research on Student Learning*. Washington, DC: Council on Undergraduate Research, www.cur.org; Jenkins and Healey, *Developing*.

22 A new SRW-like course in biology has been developed for freshmen: http:// www.novibe.northwestern.edu/bioscientist/overview (accessed Oct. 14, 2012).

23 Many researchers have reported low or declining student interest in science. See Anderman, E. M., and Maehr, M. L. (1994) Motivation and schooling in

the middle grades. *Review of Educational Research* 64(2): 287–309; Hidi, S., and Harackiewicz, J. M. (2000) Motivating the academically unmotivated: A critical issue for the 21st century. *Review of Educational Research* 70(2): 151–179. See also research of students who start out "liking science" but change their minds during their college years, in Osguthorpe, R. T., and Osguthorpe, L. S. (2009) *Choose to Learn: Teaching for Success Every Day.* Thousand Oaks, CA: Corwin Press; Stewart, K. K., and Lagowski, J. J. (2003) Cognitive apprenticeship theory and graduate chemistry education. *Journal of Chemical Education* 80(12): 1362–1366.

24 See, for example, research on students who persist in research, in McGee, R., and Keller, J. L. (2007) Identifying future scientists: Predicting persistence into research training. *CBE Life Sciences Education* 6(4): 316–331. Five major themes were reported to be indicative of these students: curiosity to discover the unknown, enjoyment of problem solving, a high level of independence, a desire to help others through research, and a flexible, minimally structured approach to the future.

8. CREATING LASTING CHANGE IN THE STEM CLASSROOM

Epigraph: Quotation commonly attributed to Kay in his address at the 1971 meeting of the Xerox Palo Alto Research Center.

1 Hestenes, Wells, and Swackhamer first developed the force concepts inventory; see Hestenes, D., Wells, M., and Swackhamer, G. (1992) Force concept inventory. *The Physics Teacher* 30(3): 141–151; also see Savinainen and Scott, who review its development and provide comments on its usefulness, in Savinainen, A., and Scott, P. (2002) The force concept inventory: A tool for monitoring student learning. *Physics Education* 37(1): 45–52.

2 A number of concept inventories in STEM disciplines have recently been developed; many are still being validated: see http://cihub.org (accessed Oct. 15, 2012).

3 Hung, W., Jonassen, D. H., and Liu, R. (2008) Problem-based learning, in J. M. Spector, J. G. van Merriënboer, M. D. Merrill, and M. Driscoll, eds., *Handbook of Research on Educational Communications and Technology,* 3rd ed., 485–506. Mahwah, NJ: Lawrence Erlbaum Associates; Karpicke, J. D., and Roediger, H. L. (2008) The critical importance of retrieval for learning. *Science* 319: 966–968.

4 As noted in Chapter 4, the term *scaffolding* was introduced in education by Wood, Bruner, and Ross and parallels Vygotsky's ideas related to the zone of

proximal development. In scaffolding, the teacher provides support to help the student work slightly beyond her or his capabilities, and to help the student begin to share the teacher's understanding of the ideas at play. Vygotsky, L. S. (1978) *Mind in Society: The Development of Higher Psychological Processes,* ed. M. Cole, V. John-Steiner, S. Scribner, and E. Souberman. Cambridge, MA: Harvard University Press; Wood, D. J., Bruner, J. S., and Ross, G. (1976) The role of tutoring in problem solving. *Journal of Child Psychiatry and Psychology* 17(2): 89–100.

5   Eric Mazur has written extensively on the use of clickers in the physics classroom, and Martina Bode, one of our GSW mathematics faculty members, has written on clickers in the math classroom. See Mazur, E. (2009) Farewell lecture? *Science* 323(5910): 50–51; Bode, M., Drane, D., Ben-David Kolikant, Y., and Schuller, M. (2009) A clicker approach to teaching calculus. *Notices of the AMS* (February): 253–256.

6   See Bain, K. (2004) *What the Best College Teachers Do.* Cambridge, MA: Harvard University Press, 100–104, on creating a natural critical learning environment. Light, Cox, and Calkins describe this approach as "problematizing" the lecture, in Light, G., Cox., R., and Calkins, S. (2009) *Learning and Teaching in Higher Education: The Reflective Professional,* 2nd ed. Thousand Oaks, CA: Sage Publications, 120–121.

7   See Hersam, M., Luna, M., and Light, G. (2004) Implementation of interdisciplinary group learning and peer assessment in a nanotechnology engineering course. *Journal of Engineering Education* 93: 49–57.

8   Journals that publish research on teaching and learning in the STEM disciplines include the *Journal of Engineering Education, Journal of Chemical Education, Journal of Research in Science Teaching, International Journal of Science Education,* and *Journal of Science Education and Technology,* among many others.

9   For details on the study of the initial group of GSW students, see Born, W. K., Revelle, W., and Pinto, L. (2002) Improving biology performance with workshop groups. *Journal of Science Education and Technology* 11: 347–365.

10   In recent years increasing numbers of faculty have engaged in the rigorous study of the effectiveness of their classroom teaching approaches and have used this study to inform their teaching and that of others. This practice is known as the scholarship of teaching and learning (SoTL), and there is evidence that faculty who engage in SoTL are better teachers, based on a variety of student experience measures; see Brew, A., and Ginns, P. (2008) The relationship

between engagement in the scholarship of teaching and learning and students' course experiences. *Assessment & Evaluation in Higher Education* 33(5): 535–545.

11 Examples include the Sources of Mathematics Self-Efficacy Scale in Lent, R. W., Lopez, F. G., Brown, S. D., and Gore, P. A. (1996) Latent structure of the sources of mathematics self-efficacy. *Journal of Vocational Behavior* 49: 292–308; and the sources of science self-efficacy scale, which was adapted from the former, in Britner, S., and Pajares, F. (2006) Sources of science self-efficacy beliefs of middle school students. *Journal of Research in Science Teaching* 43(5): 485–499.

EPILOGUE

Epigraph: Nobel laureate 2001. From Wieman, C. (2007) Why not try a scientific approach to science education? *Change* (September–October): 9–15.

1 See, for example, the National Science Foundation (2004) An emerging and critical problem of the science and engineering labor force: A companion to science and engineering indicators. NSB 04–07.

2 See, for example, National Research Council (2003) *Improving Undergraduate Instruction in Science, Technology, Engineering, and Mathematics: Report of a Workshop.* Washington, DC: National Academies Press.

3 See, for example, Henderson, C., Finkelstein, N., and Beach, A., Henderson, C., Finkelstein, N., and Beach A. (2010) Beyond dissemination in college science teaching: An introduction to four core change strategies. *Journal of College Science Teaching* 39(5): 18–25; Wood, W. B. (2009) Innovations in undergraduate biology teaching and why we need them. *Annual Review of Cell and Developmental Biology* 2: 93–112.

4 Just a few of the numerous articles detailing and providing evidence for the effectiveness of innovative science teaching methods include Gess-Newsome, J., Southerland, S. A., Johnston, A., and Woodbury, S. (2003) Educational reform, personal practical theories, and dissatisfaction: The Anatomy of change in college science teaching. *American Educational Research Journal* 40(3): 731–767; Mazur, E. (2009) Farewell lecture? *Science* 323(5910): 50–51; Tessier, J. (2007) Small-group peer teaching in an introductory biology classroom. *Journal of College Science Teaching* 36(4): 64–69.

5 Apart from the GSW program, the peer-led team learning (PLTL) consortium, headquartered at City College of New York, which uses a model very similar to that of GSW, is an excellent example of a broad, multi-institutional

innovation; see www.pltl.org/; MIT's TEAL (Technology-Enabled Active Learning) initiative is likewise an excellent example of a large-scale single institution innovation; see http://web.mit.edu/8.02t/www/; POGIL (Process-Oriented Guided Inquiry Learning), www.pogil.org/, and Workshop Biology, http://pages.uoregon.edu/udovic/WB/index.html, are excellent examples of classroom-based, multi-institutional innovation.

6 Wieman, Why not try, 10.

Index